W9-CPE-706

Exploring the
Black Hills & Badlands

Revised & Updated

EXPLORING THE
BLACK HILLS &
BADLANDS

A Guide for Hikers, Cross-country Skiers, & Mountain Bikers

HIRAM ROGERS

Johnson Books

BOULDER

Copyright © 1993 and 1999 by Hiram Rogers

All rights reserved. No part of this publication may be reproduced or transmitted in any form or by any means, electronic or mechanical, including photocopy, recording, or any information storage and retrieval system, without permission in writing from the publisher.

Published in the United States by Johnson Books, a division of Johnson Publishing Company, 1880 South 57th Court, Boulder, Colorado 80301.
E-mail: books@jpcolorado.com

9 8 7 6 5 4 3 2 1

Cover design by Debra B. Topping
Cover Photo: © Paul Horsted/Dakota Photographic
Composition and Maps by Trish Wilkinson

Library of Congress Cataloging-in-Publication Data
Rogers, Hiram
    Exploring the Black Hills & Badlands / Hiram Rogers.
        p.   cm.
    ISBN 1-55566-240-4 (pbk. : alk. paper)
    1. Outdoor recreation—Black Hills Region (S.D. and Wyoming)—
Guidebooks. 2. Outdoor recreation—North Dakota—Badlands Region—
Guidebooks. 3. Outdoor recreation—Badlands Region (S.D. and
Neb.)—Guidebooks. 4. Black Hills Region (S.D. and Wyoming)—
Guidebooks. 5. Badlands Region (N.D.)—Guidebooks. 6. Badlands
Region (S.D. and Neb.)—Guidebooks. I. Title. II. Title:
Exploring the Black Hills and Badlands.
GV191.42.B53R64   1999
796.5'09783'9—dc21   98-56035
                                                                   CIP

Printed in the United States by
Johnson Printing
1880 South 57th Court
Boulder, Colorado 80301

 Printed on recycled paper with soy ink

Contents

Abbreviations
Badlands National Park (BNP)
Bear Butte State Park (BBSP)
Black Hills National Forest (BHNF)
Centennial Trail (CT)
Custer State Park (CSP)
Devils Tower National Monument (DTNM)
Jewel Cave National Monument (JCNM)
Little Missouri National Grassland (LMNG)
Theodore Roosevelt National Park (TRNP)
Wind Cave National Park (WCNP)

Tables & Maps

Acknowledgments

This guide would not have been possible without the help of many people. Galen Roessler and Paul Bosworth of the Black Hills National Forest kindly reviewed substantial portions of the manuscript. Marianne Mills of Badlands National Park, Ron Terry of Wind Cave National Park, Steve Baldwin of the Black Hills Parks and Forests Association, Craig Pugsley of Custer State Park, Loren Poppert of the Custer Ranger District, Scott Spleiss of the Harney Ranger District, Jerry Hagen of the Bearlodge Ranger District, Rusty Wilder of the Black Hills National Forest, Riley Mitchell of Devils Tower National Monument, Curtis Glasoe and Russ Walsh of the Medora Ranger District, and Bruce Kaye of Theodore Roosevelt National Park all generously reviewed manuscripts concerning their areas of responsibility.

On my own trips in the Black Hills and Badlands I've enjoyed the company of various hikers, mountain bikers and skiers. Craig and Stacey Hall, Bob Nutsch, Eric and Laura Caddey, Tod Leferve, Karl Marlowe, Kathy and Leroy Hart, Doug Thompson, Don Gifford, Brad Young, Sandy Snyder, and Mike Besso have all patiently endured long trips filled with mapping and photography stops. Without their companionship and enthusiasm, this guide would never have been finished, nor would any of the trips have been as fun.

My wife, Jean, read most of the manuscript, scouted many of the changes for the second edition and endured many evenings filled with muttering, scrawling and thrashing through trail maps. Without her love, humor, and patience, this project would never have been completed.

A Note of Caution

Hiking, skiiing, or biking in mountainous terrain can be a high-risk activity. This guidebook is not a substitute for your experience and common sense. The users of this guidebook assume full responsibility for their own safety. Weather, terrain conditions, and individual abilities must be considered before undertaking any of the activities in this guide.

Introduction

This guide describes hiking, cross-country skiing, and mountain biking trips in the Black Hills and Badlands region of South Dakota, North Dakota and Wyoming. The Black Hills region includes the Black Hills National Forest, Jewel Cave National Monument, Wind Cave National Park, Custer State Park, Mount Rushmore National Memorial, Bear Butte State Park, and Devils Tower National Monument. To the north and east of the Black Hills are some of North America's best examples of badlands topography, well represented by Badlands National Park, Little Missouri National Grassland and Theodore Roosevelt National Park.

The area contains three long trails. South Dakota's Centennial Trail traverses the rugged eastern side of the Black Hills for 120 miles, from Wind Cave National Park to Bear Butte State Park. The George S. Mickelson Trail is a 107-mile rails-to-trails conversion in the Black Hills between Edgemont and Deadwood. The Maah Daah Hey Trail provides a 100-mile connection between the South and North units of Theodore Roosevelt National Park in North Dakota. Both the Mickelson and Maah Daah Hey Trails were completed in 1998.

The Black Hills and Badlands form a distinct geographic subunit of the northern Great Plains. Both regions are characterized by extremes of weather and by a lack of water. The limit of Pleistocene glaciers helps to define the boundaries of this guide. The Black Hills were never covered by alpine glaciers, while the higher ranges to the west in the Rocky Mountains were heavily glaciated. The Missouri River in the Dakotas roughly marks the limit of continental glaciation. The water-rich terrain left behind by the glaciers east of the Missouri River is much different from the dry prairie west of the river.

This second edition has been expanded to include every hiking trail in the region. Most trails receive detailed coverage, except for Badlands National Park, Wind Cave National Park, Custer State Park, the Norbeck Wildlife Preserve, Eagle Cliff, Sundance Trails and Theodore Roosevelt National Park, where extensive trail networks exist, some trails are described only briefly. A dozen unofficial off-trail routes are also described. These are collections of active and abandoned roads, paths and cross-country routes where there are no trail markers and no maintenance. Over 500 miles of maintained trails are described in detail. Two hundred and forty miles of trails, mostly in Theodore Roosevelt National Park, the Sundance Trail system and the Maah Daah Hey Trail, are described more generally. The dozen off-trail routes give you another one hundred miles to explore.

The trips described range from short, self-guided interpretive trails, such as Rankin Ridge in Wind Cave National Park, to multiday expeditions, such as the Sage Creek Wilderness in Badlands National Park. While each trip may not be suitable for everyone, there are trips for families with children and trips for experienced backpackers looking for off-trail excitement. Trips are included for hikers, skiers, mountain bike riders and equestrians.

Each chapter begins with a brief trip description indicating which user groups are allowed. The General Location will help you find the area. Trip Highlights help the reader select trails that will most interest them. Detailed information on how to reach each trailhead is provided. Distances are given for each trip, and often for optional variations. In most cases, trail distances were measured with an odometer on a mountain bike, but some distances were measured solely from maps or estimated. These are given in fractions of a mile.

Good maps are critical for exploring any new area. Most trip descriptions in this guide include a topographic-based map of the route. Please note that most of the trails described here are newer than the current U.S. Geological Survey quadrangles. In addition to the maps included here, a few others may be useful. The Trails Illustrated map of Badlands National Park is the best resource available for exploring the Sage Creek/Badlands Wilderness. In the Black Hills, most visitors will find the Black Hills National Forest map essential both for navigating the Hills' seemingly endless network of back roads, and for locating trailheads. The BHNF map is sufficient for following the Mickelson Trail. Trails Illustrated also publishes a frequently-updated map of Wind Cave National Park, Custer State Park and the Norbeck Wildlife Preserve that is extremely useful. The Black Hills Group of the Sierra Club also publishes a topographic-based map of the Norbeck Wildlife Preserve. If you're exploring the Black Hills by mountain bike, the Black Hills Snowmobile Trail map is surprisingly helpful. The snowmobile trails are marked year-round, and they are often better marked than the Black Hills National Forest roads. For Theodore Roosevelt National Park, the U.S. Geological Survey provides topographic maps of both the North and South units of the park. The Medora

Ranger District sells a generalized map of the Maah Daah Hey Trail and a map of the Little Missouri National Grassland.

The detail of each route description corresponds to the difficulty of finding your way. Descriptions for well-marked trails are brief, while descriptions of obscure trails are very detailed. The directions for some sections of the Centennial Trail are lengthy, due to the distance covered and the number of potential trouble spots.

Road networks in the Black Hills National Forest are constantly evolving. In the Black Hills, and to a lesser extent in the badlands, there are many more roads than are shown on U.S. Geological Survey or Black Hills National Forest maps. Avoid the temptation to navigate solely by watching road intersections. I have simplified the BHNF road classification system by calling all roads by number. These roads are generally permanent, are signed and have numbers such as BHNF Road 607-1D. The degree of upkeep and signing varies greatly between district offices. Roads lacking numbers or signs should not be considered permanent.

Trail systems throughout the Black Hills and Badlands are being expanded and improved. For example, major relocations are planned for the Centennial Trail between Nemo and Elk Creek. Be aware that a trail guide cannot remain current forever, and that the conditions of trail markers can deteriorate over time. If you find an error in a trail description, or discover a relocation of one of the trails, let us know about it so we can include the change in the next edition of this book. Write me in care of the publisher at: Johnson Books, 1880 South 57th Court, Boulder, Colorado 80301.

To keep yourself on track, it is always a good idea to check your map each time you stop on an unfamiliar trail or route, and to check with the appropriate management agency (see Appendix D) before starting on an unfamiliar trail.

Ride, Stride or Glide? Hints for Multiple Use

Many outdoorspeople own hiking boots, skis and a mountain bike and use them all as the seasons change. Many trails and routes in the Black Hills National Forest are open to all three uses. Unless otherwise noted, trails in National Park Service units are closed to mountain bikes. All National Park Service units in this guide rarely receive enough snow for skiing.

This guide is intended to be used year-round. Winter is the season to explore the cross-country ski trails in the northern Black Hills. Cool temperatures, without lingering snow, make spring hiking ideal in the southern Black Hills or in the Badlands. In summer, escape from the heat of the prairie lowlands into higher areas of the Black Hills, such as the Norbeck Trails around Harney Peak. In fall, dry soil and mild weather combine to make superb hiking and mountain bike riding anywhere in the region.

Hiking

Day hikes in the Black Hills and Badlands require only a little advance planning. You need to know the length of the route, and whether or not the trip requires a car shuttle. In summer, your main worries are water, plus sun and wind protection. Handy items to carry, include food, water, first aid kit, sunscreen, lip balm and a hat for shade. Few trailheads provide drinking water and you should never drink untreated water in the Black Hills or Badlands. Snakes, bison and other wildlife can pose hazards for hikers. Do not disturb any wildlife you encounter. Poison ivy grows in many moist areas.

Hikers are allowed on all the trails described in this guide. A few trips, such as Burno Gulch, Ward Draw and Bear Mountain use gravel roads, and only sections of such routes will be of interest to hikers. Hikers should note that nearly all of the cross-country ski trails established by the Black Hills National Forest follow abandoned roads.

Backpacking in the Black Hills differs little from that in other areas. Badlands backpacking, on the other hand, can be quite different. The major difference is that some areas have no water and you must pack in all of your own. The weight and bulk of a large water supply can be a major burden on a long trip, so many parties elect to hike in a short distance and set up a basecamp. The intricacies of the Badlands landscape make competent map and compass use essential. Getting lost in Sage Creek is a real possibility. Careful attention to your map in any badlands area will allow you to plan a more efficient and enjoyable route.

Skiing

Skiing in the Black Hills is limited in most winters to a poorly defined snowbelt that includes the Limestone Plateau and the northern Black Hills around Lead. Bear Mountain is the southern limit, and there is rarely skiable snow south or east of Galena. The snowbelt is crisscrossed by the Black Hills Snowmobile Trail system, so get a copy of the snowmobile trails map and check it before trying out any new routes. Use this map to learn where not to go. Many routes that look good in the summer will be covered with snowmobile tracks come winter. You should also note that in some winters the "snowbelt" does not extend beyond the range of the snowmaking equipment at the downhill ski area on Terry Peak.

Preparation for cross-country skiers should include dressing in layers. Drink plenty of water since dehydration can reduce your resistance to the cold. Wind protection is essential, and it is always a good idea to carry an extra hat and gloves.

Skiers will learn to adapt to the pattern of Black Hills winters. Often snowfalls are followed by rapid warming, so it is important to try to ski soon after a storm, before the snow melts. Even during the harshest cold spells, midday temperatures may be moderate enough for pleasant outings. By late winter, mid-day temperatures often climb well above freezing. This creates wet, soft snow that can stick to ski bottoms like glue. To avoid this "snowball snow" start your trip early and avoid the mid-day melt.

By late spring the repeated freeze and thaw of the snowpack builds a hard, thick crust on the snow surface. Ideally, skiers can glide on, and often skate across, this crust without breaking through. Unfortunately, this hardpack only forms over small areas and seldom lasts long.

Mountain Biking

The Black Hills are paradise for mountain bike riders. Literally thousands of miles of dirt roads and paths await exploration. The routes described here are only a small fraction of a seemingly limitless number of rides. Mountain bike riders should also prepare for their trips. Special equipment includes tools, tire pump, patch kit and money to call for a ride if things go wrong. Riders should wear a helmet and gloves for those inevitable crashes. Only a few hiking trails in the Black Hills National Forest are too rough for mountain bikes. Crow Peak and the Centennial Trail around Samelias Peak are probably the most difficult. You may be able to ride these trails, but for mere mortals, walking is easier and more enjoyable. Cross-country hikes are usually too rough for mountain bikes. Bikes are not allowed on the Flume Trail or in the Black Elk Wilderness. Mountain bikers should also note that it is illegal to ride trails in the National Parks, Devils Tower, or in Custer State Park north of U.S. 16A, except the Centennial Trail.

To help mountain bikers in selecting their trips, the footway for each is described as either a trail, two-track dirt road, maintained dirt road or gravel road. Skiers and mountain bikers should note that terrain that is exciting on a bike is often equally exciting on skis. All the cross-country ski areas in the northern Black Hills are fun to ride in summer.

Recommended Trips

The trips listed below are mostly my personal favorites, although some were chosen with the help of other Black Hills experts. Most have at least one or two special features such as tremendous views, wilderness solitude, a remote summit or intricate granite pinnacles to recommend them. If you don't have a lot of time to explore the area, these are the trips to take.

I've arranged each list subjectively from the easiest (1) to most difficult (5). Trail difficulty can be hard to gauge. Distance, elevation changes and roughness of footing are the most important factors. But the weather on any particular day can make a bike trail slippery, a ski trail slushy or a hiker cold and wet. Since there is such a range between the strongest hikers seeking challenging trips and casual hikers seeking shorter diversions, I've refrained from rating each of the seventy-six trips described in this book. However, under "General Descriptions," many trails are described as short, easy or suitable for families. Trails at the other end of the spectrum are labelled long, rugged or difficult. If you're not sure of your abilities, be conservative. I can tell you that it is better to have some energy left when you get back to the car than to struggle through a long afternoon simply hoping for the end of the trail.

RECOMMENDED TRIPS
A subjective list from easiest (1) to hardest (5).

BEST HIKES FOR KIDS
1. Door, Window and Notch trails, BNP
2. Tower Trail, DTNM
3. Roughlock and Spearfish Canyon Floor trails, BHNF
4. Bear Butte Summit and Ceremonial trails, BBSP
5. Little Devils Tower Trail, CSP

BEST HIKES WITH VIEWS
1. Tower Trail, DTNM
2. Bear Butte Summit and Ceremonial trails, BBSP

3. Little Devils Tower Trail, CSP
4. Harney Peak via Sylvan Lake and Cathedral Spires, BHNF
5. Sage Creek Area in the Badlands Wilderness, BNP

BEST DAY HIKES
1. Red Beds Trail, DTNM
2. Medicine Root and Castle trails, BNP
3. Crow Peak Trail, BHNF
4. Harney Peak via Sylvan Lake and Cathedral Spires, BHNF
5. French Creek, Custer State Park
Honorable Mention: Flume Trail, BHNF; Caprock Coulee, TRNP
  North Unit; Centennial Trail Boxelder Canyon loop, BHNF

BEST BACKPACK TRIPS
1. Centennial and Highland Creek trails, WCNP
2. Petrified Forest Loop, TRNP, South Unit
3. Achenbach Loop, TRNP, North Unit
4. Harney Peak via Willow Creek and Lost Cabin trails, BHNF
5. Sage Creek Area in the Badlands Wilderness, BNP

BEST MOUNTAIN BIKE RIDES
1. Mickelson Trail, Englewood to Deadwood
2. Little Spearfish and Rimrock trails, BHNF
3. Centennial Trail, Legion Lake to Iron Creek, CSP
4. Deerfield Trail, BHNF
5. Centennial Trail, Dalton Lake to Alkali Creek, BHNF

BEST ROAD BIKE RIDES
1. Needles Highway, Sylvan Lake to Center Lake, South Dakota 87
2. Rochford Road, U.S. 85 to Rochford
3. Spearfish Canyon, Cheyenne Crossing to Spearfish
4. Nemo Road, Brownsville to Nemo
5. Wildlife Loop Road, CSP

BEST CROSS-COUNTRY SKI TOURS
1. Loop A at Big Hill, BHNF
2. Carson Draw, BHNF
3. Dead Ox and Roller Coaster trails loop at Eagle Cliff, BHNF
4. Loop D at Big Hill, BHNF
5. Holey Rock and Clifftop trails loop at Eagle Cliff, BHNF

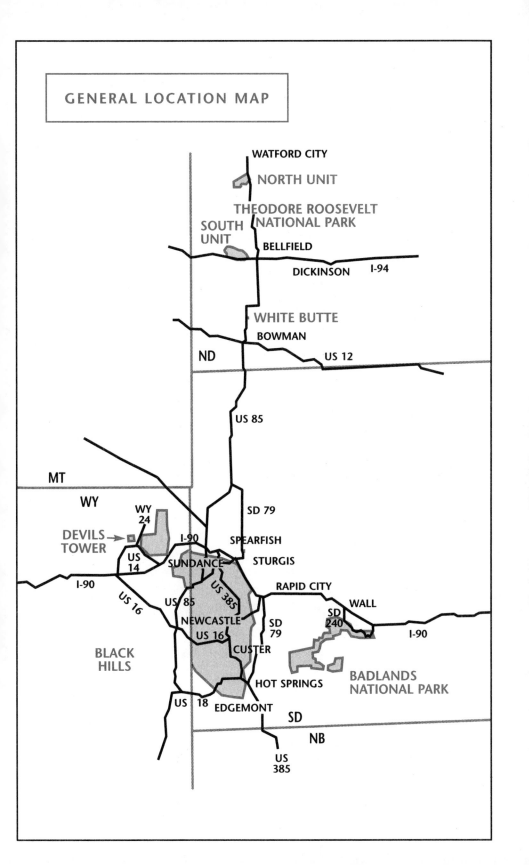

GENERAL LOCATION MAP

WATFORD CITY

NORTH UNIT

THEODORE ROOSEVELT
NATIONAL PARK

SOUTH
UNIT

BELLFIELD

DICKINSON   I-94

WHITE BUTTE

BOWMAN

ND

US 12

US 85

MT

WY

WY
24

DEVILS
TOWER →

SD 79

I-90

SPEARFISH

US
14

SUNDANCE

STURGIS

I-90

US 16

US 85

US 385

RAPID CITY

WALL

SD
240

NEWCASTLE

SD
79

I-90

BLACK
HILLS

US 16

CUSTER

HOT SPRINGS

BADLANDS
NATIONAL PARK

US 18

EDGEMONT

SD

NB

US
385

Exploring the
Black Hills & Badlands

Badlands National Park

Door, Notch, and Window Trails

Description: Three short, easy trails that leave from the Windows parking area.

General Location: Five miles northeast of Interior, South Dakota.

Highlight: A perfect introduction to the Badlands landscape.

Access: From Interior, drive two miles northeast on South Dakota 377 to the park loop road (South Dakota 240). Turn right onto the loop road and drive about 2.5 miles to the Windows parking area. The parking area can also be reached by taking Exit 131 from Interstate 90 onto South Dakota 240 and driving south past the Badlands National Park Northeast Entrance Station.

Distance: The Door Trail is .66-mile round trip, the Notch Trail is a 1.5-mile round trip and the Window Trail is .25 mile round trip.

Maps: Trails Illustrated Badlands National Park Trails and page 2.

All of the established trails in Badlands National Park are located on the east side, near the Ben Reifel Visitor Center. Four trails leave from the Windows parking area. The Castle Trail leads west, while the Door, Window, and Notch trails explore the Badlands to the east. These three trails can be combined for a leisurely half day of hiking.

The *Door Trail* leaves from the north end of the parking area. This is an interpretive trail that focuses on the geologic history of the park. Stops along the way illustrate the formation of the ash beds, fossil soils and claystones that are exposed along the route. The role of water in depositing, cementing, coloring and finally sculpting these rocks is also explained. The trail is handicapped-accessible to the spectacular views from the "door" in the Badlands Wall.

The *Notch Trail* leaves from the south end of the parking area. The trail wanders south in a small draw before climbing steeply on a ladder, then traverses the west side of a small canyon. The trail ends at a

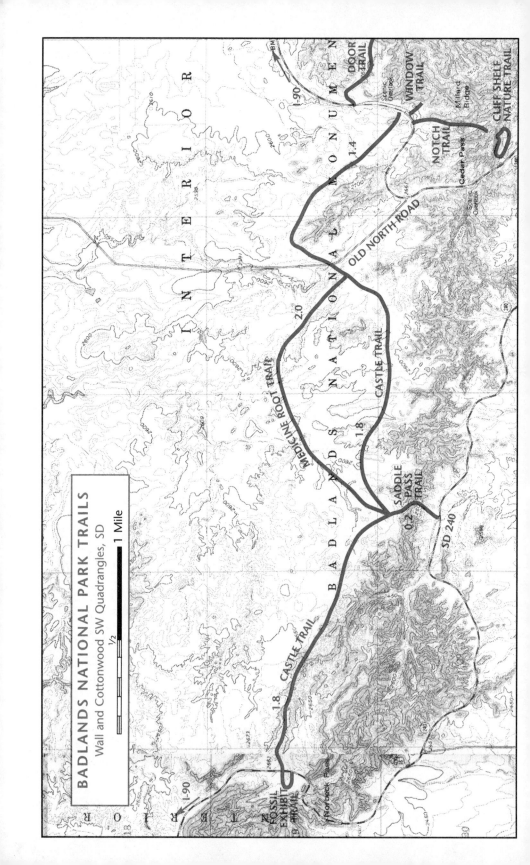

BADLANDS NATIONAL PARK TRAILS
Wall and Cottonwood SW Quadrangles, SD

½   1 Mile

dramatic "window" in the Badlands Wall that overlooks the Cliff Shelf Nature Trail.

The *Window Trail* is a short walk from the parking area to an overlook. The badlands below form the head of the Rake Creek Drainage. Millard Ridge forms the west and south sides of the upper basin. The trail is handicapped accessible. The Window is one of the park's most spectacular overlooks.

The rocks exposed higher on Millard Ridge above the Notch Trail are part of the Oligocene-age Sharps formation. The Sharps is mostly pinkish-tan siltstone, but the lowest layer, called the Rockyford Member, is a thick ash bed. Below the Sharps is the Oligocene-age Brule formation. Brule formation rocks form most of the Badlands Wall and contain abundant oreodont (a sheep-like mammal) and turtle fossils. Brule formation rocks are diverse and include clay, silt, sand, volcanic ash and fossil soil beds.

All three trails are well-marked and easy to follow. Hikers in any badlands should protect themselves from heat, wind and sun. Use these trails to familiarize yourself with the badlands landscape, then try the Castle Trail or visit the Sage Creek Wilderness on your next hike.

Medicine Root & Castle Trails Loop

Description: An easy day hike along the northern edge of the Badlands Wall.

General Location: Two miles west of the Badlands National Park Ben Reifel Visitor Center near Interior, South Dakota.

Highlight: Spectacular badlands formations and mixed-grass prairie.

Access: Drive 2.0 miles west of the Visitor Center on South Dakota 240 to the Saddle Pass Trailhead. The trailhead can also be reached by driving 28 miles east from Wall, South Dakota, on South Dakota 240.

Distance: About a 4.2-mile loop.

Maps: Trails Illustrated Badlands National Park and page 2.

Hiking in Badlands National Park is a much different experience than hiking in the Black Hills. Besides the obvious differences in topography and elevation, the contrast between lush prairie and stark, barren badlands makes hiking in the Badlands unique. The Medicine Root

Loop, Saddle Pass and Castle trails can be combined into a loop hike that serves as an excellent introduction to hiking in the park.

The *Saddle Pass Trail* is a short, steep climb, but provides a relatively easy route from the base of the Badlands Wall to the grasslands above. One-quarter mile from the parking area the trail ends at a four-way intersection with the Medicine Root Loop and Castle Trail. From this junction the Castle Trail also leads west to the Fossil Exhibit parking area, but our route follows the *Castle Trail* for 1.8 miles to the east as it skirts the top of the wall. Along the way the trail passes through the sod tables, massive pinnacles and steeply eroded gullies characteristic of the Badlands.

Just before the Castle Trail reaches the gravel Old Northeast Road, turn left onto the *Medicine Root Trail*. The loop then swings north away from the wall into the grasslands. Follow the loop back to the junction with the Saddle Pass Trail and descend Saddle Pass to return to the trailhead.

Hikers who can arrange a car shuttle, or are willing to hike 12 miles round trip, can try the entire Castle Trail. The eastern 1.4 miles between the Windows Trailhead and the Old Northeast Road winds through an endless array of sharp pinnacles and gullies.

In addition to its famous fossil heritage, the park is known for bizarre badlands landforms. The combination of soft, easily eroded sediments, dry climate and sudden torrential rains produce extremely high rates of erosion. The most prominent topographic feature in the park is the Badlands Wall, which is an erosional boundary between lower grasslands in the plain of the White River and an upper plain of grasslands. The wall is a succession of pinnacles and vertical knife-edge ridges carved into the soft sedimentary rocks. It is composed of poorly consolidated clay and ash beds. Steep canyons and gullies cut the wall intermittently, providing access between the two levels of grasslands. Learning to follow gullies and ridge systems over the crumbling sediment and to be able to climb the wall are the essential tools to exploring off trail in the most rugged parts of the park.

The grasslands support a variety of wildlife. Deer, pronghorn antelope, coyotes, and bighorn sheep are found within the park. The park also supports a herd of approximately 500 bison, which are commonly found around prairie dog towns. Magpies, meadowlarks and turkey vultures are some of the most commonly seen birds. Hikers in the grasslands grow accustomed to the constant soft chirping of the ever-present meadowlarks. Cliff swallows and grouse are also found.

Buffalograss, western wheatgrass, needle and thread grass and blue gramma are some of the most common prairie grasses in the park.

Few trees can grow in the arid climate. Hardy junipers are restricted to small slump blocks where the broken sediments can hold enough shallow groundwater.

Hikers should prepare differently for a hike in the Badlands than for a hike in the Black Hills. Heat, lack of water and absence of shade are the most important factors. Warning: This hike can be hot. This hike can be very hot. Carry water. Carry at least one gallon per person per day. Hot sun and persistent dry winds can cause dehydration and severe sunburn. Use sunscreen liberally and wear a hat for protection from the blazing sun.

Sage Creek Area
BADLANDS WILDERNESS

Description: Off-trail hiking through the heart of the Badlands Wilderness.

General Location: Eight miles south of Wall, South Dakota.

Highlight: Find unmatched tranquility in the region's largest wilderness.

Access: From Interstate 90 in Wall, drive eight miles south on South Dakota 240 to the junction with the Sage Creek Rim Road, which leads west. There is easy access at the Sage Creek Campground, but it is possible to enter the Wilderness from almost anywhere along this road. The Conata Picnic area is a convenient starting point for trips on the east side of the wilderness.

Distance: There are no marked trails.

Maps: Trails Illustrated Badlands National Park.

The 64,250 acres preserved in the Badlands Wilderness make it easily the largest wilderness in the northern Great Plains. The heart of the wilderness is the west side of the north unit of Badlands National Park, and is commonly known as Sage Creek. This is a land of profound solitude and quiet. It is also a place that will change your idea of what wilderness really is. To most Americans wilderness is rugged, alpine mountains too steep and too rocky to have been altered by man. Sage Creek meets none of these expectations, yet is far more wild than most alpine ranges.

There are no maintained trails in the Sage Creek Wilderness. A trail is shown on the topographic map leading south in a loop from the Sage Creek Campground, but it is not maintained and indistinguishable from the hundreds of bison trails that cross the Badlands. Based on my experience, I can recommend no particular route over any other, but must rely on the advice of a friend who said, "Just tell them to go there, they'll have fun."

The north boundary of the wilderness is roughly defined by the Badlands Wall, which divides the upper grasslands from lower grasslands in the White River watershed. The "baddest" badlands in the park lie along the wall and in a basin south of Pinnacles Overlook. To reach the roughest places you will need to learn to climb the Badlands Wall. The wall is not high, but the steep, crumbling slopes can be dangerous. A rule of the thumb is to not climb anything you would not want to slide down. Sage Creek and McGinty passes cross the wall, and there is another easy pass in section 25 between Hay Butte and Deer Haven.

If you enjoy scrambling on the Badlands Wall, you will definitely enjoy the rest of Sage Creek Wilderness. Perhaps the best way to explore is to follow a drainage to its head as far as you can. Often the draws are so steep, and the meanders in them so tight, that you must walk almost sideways to follow the channel that the runoff has carved. The more resistant rock layers form shelves that can be used to connect adjacent drainages. Throughout the wilderness the hiker sees a constantly changing array of the towers, pinnacles and tables characteristic of badlands.

Remember that it is illegal to disturb any fossils that you may find. Westward in Sage Creek elevation increases and the rocks become older. Most of the bedrock around the main forks of Sage Creek is sandstone and clay of the Eocene-age Chadron formation. To the east, the flat areas are covered with the eroded remains of Chadron and Brule formation rocks. The Badlands Wall itself is composed of Brule formation, and landslide deposits shed from it.

Deer Haven is the most prominent landslide in the wilderness. Landslides shed from the wall's steep slopes break up the impermeable clay and ash-rich sediments. Water from subsequent rainfalls can be trapped in the broken sediments. Juniper trees tap this groundwater and their roots help to stabilize the wildly jumbled surface. Deer and other animals use the juniper groves for shelter. The landslides have thus created small oases in the Badlands. Park rangers consider Deer Haven excellent for both hiking and camping. You can stop at the visitor center for directions before beginning your trip.

Wildlife watching is spectacular in the wilderness. Bring binoculars and a telephoto lens for your camera. Bison can often be found grazing in the main forks of Sage Creek. Give these giants plenty of space, since there is nowhere to hide if they become annoyed. Bison show aggravation by pawing the ground, rolling on the ground or raising their tails. The park supports a small herd of bighorn sheep that may be found near the Pinnacles, Deer Haven and the Cliff Shelf, and the Door and Notch trails near Cedar Pass. The wilderness also contains several prairie dog towns.

The Conata and Sage Creek Wilderness areas inside Badlands National Park are now home to a small colony of endangered black-footed ferrets. The elusive ferrets depend on prairie dogs for 95 percent of their food supply. With the elimination of prairie dogs from 98 percent of their historic range, ferret populations had declined to the point where biologists feared them extinct. However, in 1981 a small colony was discovered in Wyoming and by 1994 the population was stable enough to justify an experimental release into Badlands National Park. The reintroduction has been largely successful, with the population of 55–65 animals now, including three generations of wild-born kits.

If you must have a goal for your hike, there are three obvious trips to try. Deer Haven is easy to reach from Conata Picnic area, or you can try to follow the old loop trail south of the Sage Creek Campground. A longer trip circles Hay Butte via Sage Creek Pass. However, it is easier to go wherever the terrain leads you. Once in rugged badlands it can be difficult to pinpoint your location, and it is possible to spend all day exploring a very small area.

To fully appreciate Sage Creek Wilderness you should camp overnight. For as long as you stay, there will be no interruption from the modern world. You will probably not see another person, and may not see a footprint but your own. There are almost none of the relics of mining or ranching that you might see in other wildernesses. The remains of a few homesteads can be found, but the badlands are too wild, and too formidable to have been settled for long.

No permits are necessary to camp overnight in the backcountry of Badlands National Park, but you must camp at least one-half mile from a road and be out of sight of the road. Be prepared to be baked and dried by the sun and buffeted and dehydrated by the wind. At all costs avoid the badlands after one of the rare heavy rains, as the water turns the clay and ash into an impenetrable sea of sticky mud called gumbo. This is a stark landscape subject to extremes of temperatures. For milder conditions, it is best to visit in the spring or fall.

Other Badlands National Park Trails

The *Fossil Exhibit Trail* is a .25-mile loop which starts at the west end of the Castle Trail on South Dakota 240. It passes covered replicas of many of the badlands most famous fossils. See map on page 2.

The *Cliff Shelf Nature Trail* is a 0.5-mile interpretive loop that begins just north of the Visitor Center. Here a landslide block, called a slump, is covered with juniper trees and has created a rare haven for plants and animals from the harsh sun and wind of the Badlands. See map on page 2.

George S. Mickelson Trail

Few hiking areas in this country are blessed with a single one hundred-mile trail, let alone a pair of them. The 107-mile George S. Mickelson Trail was fully opened in October, 1998, offering a gentler long distance alternative to the often rugged Centennial Trail that runs across the Black Hills of South Dakota. The gentle grades and open terrain of the Mickelson Trail make it ideally suited to easy hiking, biking, bird watching and where possible, cross-country skiing.

The Mickelson Trail will probably see most of its use by hikers locally in Custer, Hill City, Lead and Deadwood. But it is a trail ideal for mountain bikes—perhaps the best way to explore the Black Hills. Though some sections closely follow major roads, others offer solitude, scenery, and sometimes excitement, as the trail passes through rehabilitated railroad tunnels and over bridges.

The Mickelson Trail began as a rails to trails conversion project in 1991. Extensive legal battles over the right of the state to use the abandoned railway as a trail ended with a 1992 decision by the South Dakota Supreme Court in favor of the project. Two demonstration sections were built around Lead and Custer in 1992 under the administration of South Dakota Governor George S. Mickelson, who was a strong advocate of the project. Mickelson realized that the trail offered South Dakotans a unique opportunity for public recreation at a time when access to public and private lands was becoming restricted. He considered the recreation benefit of the trail to be as important as the arrival of railroads was to the Black Hills one hundred years ago. After Governor Mickelson's death in a 1993 plane crash, the project timetable was accelerated, and the trail was renamed in his honor. Reinstalling old bridges and reopening tunnels has consumed much of the work, along with the process of working with landowners along the route to ensure that their properties will not be harmed by the trail.

The Mickelson Trail is administered by the South Dakota Department of Game, Fish and Parks. It has a $2 daily, or $10 annual, user fee for bikers, horseback riders or cross-country skiers sixteen and older. The fee does not apply to runners or hikers, or to anyone within the city limits of Edgemont, Pringle, Custer, Hill City, Rochford, Lead or Deadwood.

MICKELSON & CENTENNIAL TRAILS
Black Hills National Forest

US 85

I-90 — SPEARFISH

SD 79

BEAR BUTTE
STATE PARK

US
14A

17

STURGIS

SD 34

23

16

18

US
85

DEADWOOD

US 14A

15

13

21

CENTENNIAL TRAIL

I-90

14

11

LEAD

12

20

19

8

US 385

10

9

SD 44

7

RAPID
CITY
I-90

22

6

US
85

5

4

US
16

HILL
CITY

MOUNT
RUSHMORE
NATIONAL
MONUMENT

BLACK ELK
WILDERNESS

3

US
16

2

NEWCASTLE

SD 89

CUSTER

CUSTER
STATE
PARK

US
16

1

JEWEL CAVE
NATIONAL
MONUMENT

US
385

SD
87

US
85

WIND CAVE
NATIONAL
PARK

MICKELSON TRAIL

US
385

SD
79

US
385

SD
79

US 18

HOT
SPRINGS

| TRAIL |
| BHNF |
| ROAD |

EDGEMONT

US 18

Key to map on facing page:
Other Trails and Routes in the
Black Hills National Forest

Number	*Trip*
1	Hell Canyon Trails
2	Sylvan Peak Route
3	Bear Mountain Trails
4	Flume Trail
5	Lake Loop Trail
6	Deerfield Trail
7	Swede Gulch Route
8	Custer Peak Route
9	Ward Draw Route
10	Eagle Cliff Trails
11	Roughlock & Spearfish Canyon Floor Trails
12	Little Spearfish & Rimrock Trails
13	Old Baldy Trail
14	Red Lake Route
15	Iron Creek Route
16	Big Hill Trails
17	Crow Peak Trail
18	Burno Gulch Route
19	North Hanna Route
20	Dutch Flats Route
21	Pillar Peak Route
22	Beaver Creek Trails
23	Sand Creek Route

Mickelson Trail Mileage Table

0 = Edgemont Trailhead

7.9 = Fall River County Road 185

16.0 = Minnekahta Trailhead, U.S. 18

32.1 = Pringle Trailhead, junction of South Dakota 89 and U.S. 385

35.7 = White Elephant Trailhead, U.S. 385 and South Dakota 89

44.5 = Harbach Park Trailhead, Custer, U.S. 16 and South Dakota 89

49.6 = The Mountain Trailhead, U.S. 16

54.7 = Oreville Campground, BHNF, U.S. 16

60.1 = Tracey Park Trailhead, Hill City, U.S. 16

64.2 = Newton Lake Picnic Ground, Pennington County Road 308

72.5 = Deerfield Trailhead, junction with BHNF Deerfield Trail, Pennington County Road 318

74.8 = Mystic Townsite, Pennington County Road 318

78.5 = Junction of BHNF roads 231 and 237

82.6 = Rochford, BHNF Road 17

88.4 = Cross Swede Gulch

92.8 = Dumont Trailhead, BHNF Road 17

98.5 = Englewood Trailhead, BHNF Road 277

100.7 = Start of Sugarloaf Spur

   2.7 mi. to Sugarloaf Trailhead

   4.9 mi. to Kirk Trailhead

103.7 = Kirk Trailhead

107.4 = Deadwood Trailhead, U.S. 385, northern end of Mickelson Trail

108.9 = Deadwood Rodeo Grounds (on Deadwood Recreation Trail), U.S. 385

Edgemont to Pringle

Description: This long ride through Elk Mountain, across the Race Track Valley and into the Black Hills opened in October, 1998.

General Location: Edgemont is at the intersection of U.S. 18 and South Dakota 471.

Highlight: Isolated terrain in the southern Black Hills.

Access: From the junction at the north end of town follow South Dakota 471 through downtown Edgemont for 1.1 miles to the signed trailhead that is on the east side of the road. The Minnekahta Trailhead is located on U.S. 18, just one half mile east of the junction with South Dakota 89. There is a small parking area on the south side of the highway. The Pringle Trailhead is located at the junction of U.S. 385 and South Dakota 89, just behind the Pringle fire station.

Distance: 32.1 miles, almost all uphill.

Maps: Black Hills National Forest and page 10.

The Mickelson Trail begins its journey northward from just outside the Black Hills proper. Around the main mass of the Black Hills is the Race Track Valley, which marks a zone of easily eroded sedimentary rocks. The Valley is in turn surrounded by a ridge formed of harder sandstones, locally called the Elk Mountains. Edgemont lies just outside this outer ring, more a part of the prairie than part of the Black Hills.

Finding your way out of Edgemont can be the most complicated part of this ride. Begin by heading north from the trailhead behind the city park and between a small pond and the active Burlington Northern rail line. Cross the tracks onto A street, then cross the Cheyenne River on a paved bridge. At 1.3 miles reach the abandoned rail line where it crosses paved Fall River County Road 185. The Mickelson Trail next follows a gravel service road along a narrow strip between U.S. 18 and a section of abandoned track where the rails are still in place.

At 3.1 miles the trail joins the abandoned grade by a small wooden bridge. As you begin to turn away from U.S. 18 look for a small prairie dog town wedged between a rail line and the highway. Climb to a broad ridge that features your last views of Edgemont before entering Sheep Canyon. This shallow, narrow canyon with its steep sandstone walls looks like Hollywood's image of western ranching country with scattered ponderosa pines and sagebrush blooming in the short grass prairie. You'll cross the canyon on an earthen dam, which was built on top of an abandoned railroad trestle. Across the dam on the east wall of the canyon are two small tunnels, probably dug by uranium prospectors.

At 7.9 miles cross under a bridge below paved Fall River County Road 185. A side trail leads up to the road, but there is no room to park near the bridge. Next enter broad, open Chilson Canyon, with its healthy cattle population. Cross three wooden bridges before exiting the Elk Mountains next to 4,848-foot Parker Peak. You'll ride parallel to U.S. 18 for two miles before reaching the Minnekahta Trailhead at 16.0 miles.

From Minnekahta, the Mickelson Trail follows South Dakota 89 north, making side trips around a gravel pit and around the Argyle

Loop Road. At Carrol Creek the trail leaves South Dakota 89 to follow County roads 510 and 315 into the small town of Pringle.

Edgemont, now just a quiet railroad town, was once the center of an energy boom spurred by the search for uranium ore. Sandstone formations nearby contain low grade deposits of uranium that were the target of extensive drilling programs in the 1960s and 1970s. The ore proved too low grade for profitable mining, and by 1980, in the aftermath of the nuclear accident at the Three Mile Island Plant, the bottom had dropped out of the uranium market and quiet returned to Edgemont.

Pringle to Custer

Description: A pretty ride through the Beaver Creek Valley alongside U.S. 385.

General Location: Eleven miles south of Custer, South Dakota.

Highlight: Pegmatite mines and granite spires.

Access: The Pringle Trailhead is located at the junction of U.S. 385 and South Dakota 89, just behind the Pringle fire station. The White Elephant Trailhead, along U.S. 385 south of Custer, has parking only. From the junction of U.S. highways 16 and 16A in Custer drive one block south, nearly to the railroad grade, and then one block east to the parking area at Harbach Centennial Park.

Distance: 12.4 miles.

Maps: Black Hills National Forest and page 10.

From Pringle to Custer, the Mickelson Trail stays close by U.S. 385 until reaching the White Elephant Trailhead at 35.7 miles, where it veers west through private land. This is the heart of the Precambrian-age core of the Black Hills. The granite of Harney Peak forms the high country to the east. Along the granite's margin, the last of its molten magma became solidified. These latest-forming rocks form large crystals and contain rare elements not found in the main body of granite. Called pegmatites, these rocks are still mined for mica, feldspar and lithium around Custer.

At 40.8 miles the trail crosses U.S. 385 and enters the town of Custer at 44.0. At 44.5 miles reach the Harbach Park Trailhead and headquarters for the Friends of the Mickelson Trail.

Driving through Custer one sees only its present, a town dependent on the motels, gift shops and restaurants of the tourist trade. The Mickelson Trail allows you to see remnants of Custer's past as you pass the plants that processed and shipped pegmatite minerals from the many mines around town.

~

Custer to Hill City

Description: A scenic ride past the Crazy Horse Monument.
General Location: Custer and Hill City are connected by U.S. 16.
Highlight: Views of Crazy Horse Mountain, Harney Peak and the Black Elk Wilderness.
Access: From the junction of U.S. highways 16 and 16A in Custer drive one block south, nearly to the railroad grade, and then one block east to the parking area at Harbach Centennial Park. The turnoff for The Mountain Trailhead is 3.0 miles north of the intersection of U.S. 16A and 385 in Custer. Follow a dirt road 0.1 miles east to the trailhead. The Tracey Park Trailhead in Hill City is located at the south end of the U.S. 385 truck bypass on Newton Road.
Distance: 15.6 miles.
Maps: Black Hills National Forest and page 10.

Between Custer and Hill City are two distinct sections of the Mickelson Trail. After leaving Harbach Park, the trail crosses U.S. 16A, turns north and reaches the Custer High School athletic fields at 45.4 miles. Beyond the fields, the trail becomes surprisingly isolated as it winds along Laughing Water Creek. To the east lies rugged Buckhorn Mountain, the southern-most of a chain of peaks that divides Crazy Horse Mountain from Sylvan Lake. Buckhorn Mountain and the granite spires around it make this area a local favorite. The geologically inclined should look for a beautiful exposure of south-plunging folds in phyllite in a railroad cut just west of a powerline crossing.

Beyond The Mountain Trailhead at 49.6 miles, the Mickelson Trail hugs the U.S. 16/385 right-of-way. Pass Crazy Horse Mountain at 52.0 miles. In 1948, Korczak Ziolkowski began carving a colossal figure of the mounted warrior as the Native American counterpart to Mount Rushmore. Since the sculptor's death in 1982, work on the project has continued on the planned 500-foot high by 600-foot long sculpture.

If you desire a closer view of the carving, remember that Crazy Horse is a fee area.

Near 54.7 miles, the Black Hills National Forest Oreville Campground is on the east side of the highway. At 57.6 miles cross above U.S. 16 on a metal bridge. The Tracey Park Trailhead in Hill City is reached at 60.1 miles.

Hill City to Mystic

Description: A scenic ride through the heart of the Black Hills on trail opened in October, 1998.
General Location: Hill City is in the central Black Hills on U.S.16.
Highlight: The historic town of Mystic and a ride along Crooked Creek.
Access: The Tracey Park Trailhead in Hill City is located at the south end of the U.S. 385 truck bypass on Newton Road. The Deerfield Trailhead is located 3.1 miles south of Mystic on Pennington County Road 318. To find Mystic, drive 4.7 miles east from Rochford on BHNF Road 231, or 7 miles west on BHNF Road 237 from U.S. 385 to Pennington County 318. Mystic lies another two miles south.
Distance: 14.7 miles.
Maps: Black Hills National Forest and page 10.

From Tracey Park in Hill City, the Mickelson Trail leads north through town to Major Lake after crossing U.S. highway 16/385. The next few miles follow the Deerfield Lake Road (Pennington County 308) past Newton Picnic Ground. At 69.8 miles the trail turns north again to follow County Road 318 along Crooked Creek toward Mystic.

At 72.1 miles enter a short wood-framed tunnel that was reopened by the Black Hills National Forest in 1997. Here the Deerfield Trail enters from the right from the trailhead along the road below. The Deerfield Trail leaves to the east at Lind Gulch at 72.5 miles. Reach a second tunnel at 73.0 miles, and continue north to the tiny townsite of Mystic at 74.8 miles.

From Hill City to Mystic the Mickelson Trail regains the rural character that it lost in the previous sections along U.S. 16/385. Between Hill City and Lead the Black Hills can seem very empty, the ponderosa pine forests broken only by scattered ranches and tiny communities like Mystic and Rochford. Here the riding is quiet and soothing, a perfect reward for a small effort of travel.

Mystic to Dumont

Description: A scenic ride on one of the most remote sections of the Mickelson Trail.

General Location: Mystic is located on BHNF Road 238, about 8 miles southeast of Rochford.

Highlight: The small community of Rochford.

Access: To reach Rochford drive south from Lead on U.S. 85 to paved BHNF Road 17. Drive south 15 miles to gravel BHNF Road 231 and the town site of Rochford. The Dumont Trailhead is located 6.2 miles south of U.S. 85 on the Rochford Road.

Distance: 17.8 miles.

Maps: Black Hills National Forest and page 10.

One of the highlights of the Mickelson Trail is the isolated section north of Mystic. From the townsite, the trail follows Castle Creek to a bridge, and the confluence with Rapid Creek at 76.2 miles. Then it turns north and passes through another tunnel before rejoining BHNF Road 231 at its junction with BHNF Road 237 at 78.5 miles. The trail then turns west to follow Rapid Creek and Road 231 to the historic mining town of Rochford at 82.7 miles. With two bars, and little else, Rochford is a welcome sight for thirsty riders.

Rochford was once a booming mining town boasting gold deposits similar to its northern neighbor, the mighty Homestake. But the ore bodies proved much smaller and only the Standby Mine, one-half mile east of town, was very productive. Homestake Mining Company, and other firms, explored the area extensively in the 1980s, but found no minable ore, so it is likely that the Rochford mines will remain inactive.

From Rochford, the Mickelson Trail leaves BHNF Road 231 to follow the North Fork of Rapid Creek. It passes through a small tunnel at 85.4 miles, then rejoins the road at 88.4 miles at the mouth of Swede Gulch. The *Swede Gulch Route* heads west from this point. From Swede Gulch, the Mickelson Trail parallels the Rochford Road reaching the Dumont Trailhead at 92.8 miles. The Dumont Trailhead is a major snowmobile trailhead in winter. The network of marked snowmobile trails here mostly follows dirt roads, and can be fun to explore on a mountain bike.

Road bikers should note that the paved road between Rochford and U.S. 85 is one of the Black Hills' best road rides. There is little traffic and lots of small hills, but few long, steep grades. The terrain and scenery will be similar to the Mickelson Trail between Rochford and Englewood.

Dumont to Deadwood

Description: A pleasant ride on one of the first trail sections to be completed. Parts of the trail can be skied in winter.

General Location: The abandoned townsite of Dumont is on the Rochford Road, (BHNF 17) about eight miles south of Lead.

Highlight: A diverse ride featuring narrow canyons, views of the Homestake Gold Mine and the historic town of Deadwood.

Access: The Dumont Trailhead is located 6.2 miles south of U.S. 85 on the Rochford Road (BHNF Road 17). The Englewood Trailhead is one mile east of the Rochford Road on BHNF Road 277. The Sugarloaf Trailhead is located about 1.5 miles south of Lead on U.S. 85. To reach the Kirk Trailhead, drive 1.5 miles east of Lead on the unpaved Kirk Road. Turn south on the unpaved Yellow Creek Road and turn immediately right. Follow a gravel road to the trailhead located on the east bank of Whitewood Creek. The Deadwood Railroad Trailhead, and northern end of the Mickelson Trail, is located in Deadwood on U.S. 85.

Distance: 14.6 miles with a spur to the town of Lead and a loop south of the Sugarloaf Trailhead.

Maps: Black Hills National Forest and page 10.

From the Dumont Trailhead, go north on the Mickelson Trail, which follows Snowmobile Trail 7A. At 94.7 miles, cross BHNF Road 205 where the trail begins following Snowmobile Trail 5A. Enjoy a fast downhill ride, mostly out of sight of the Rochford Road, before reaching the Englewood Trailhead at 98.5 miles.

North of Englewood, the original railroad track split at 98.9 miles. The main branch descends along Whitewood Creek and an upper branch leads to Whitetail Summit. The Mickelson Trail follows the upper branch above a Homestake Mining Company pump house to reach a junction with the *Sugarloaf Spur* of the Mickelson Trail at 100.7 miles.

From the junction with the Sugarloaf Spur, the main Mickelson Trail turns sharply right and descends the steepest and most difficult hill on its entire length. If you can keep your bike under control, look for a flume pipe suspended above the trail on your descent. At 101.2 miles the trail rejoins Whitewood Creek and the main branch of the railroad grade. Reach the site of the long-abandoned Wasp Mine sand tailings disposal area and the road leading north from Englewood at 101.8 miles. You'll cross four bridges over Whitewood Creek before reaching the Kirk Trailhead at 103.7 miles.

The Sugarloaf Spur follows a level grade north away from the Mickelson Trail for 1.9 miles to Whitetail Summit. The spur then turns sharply left and descends steeply to the Sugarloaf Trailhead at 2.7 miles on U.S. 85 just south of Lead. To ride into Lead from this point, continue on the spur trail for 0.4 mile before crossing the highway near the Terry Peak Road and following Snowmobile Trail 7 along yet another railroad grade to Walter Green Park at 1.3 miles, and Lead High School at 1.5 miles. The Sugarloaf Spur continues to follow Whitetail Creek past the Kirk Power Plant to reach the Kirk Trailhead at 4.9 miles.

From the Kirk Trailhead, the Mickelson Trail next passes behind and below the Homestake Gold Mine. Gold was first discovered in the northern Black Hills in Deadwood in 1876. Miners followed gold in stream beds uphill to the present townsite of Lead where they soon discovered the Homestake Lode and began mining underground. With a total production of over 35 million ounces of gold (with a current value of over 10 billion dollars), Homestake is a world-class gold deposit. Today miners labor at depths down to 8,000 feet, where rock temperatures reach 135 degrees. The Mickelson Trail passes two large fans which are used to ventilate the mine. The large metal head frames of the 5,000-foot deep Ross and Yates shafts are visible on the skyline.

The Mickelson Trail crosses U.S. 385 at 105.6 miles near the abandoned Pluma School. It then follows U.S. 85 through the heart of Deadwood, reaching its northern limit at 107.4 miles at the historic Deadwood Railroad Station and Museum.

By continuing along Whitewood Creek, riders can reach the Deadwood History and Information Center. From here turn right onto

Sherman Street to find the start of the *Deadwood Recreation Trail*. Riding to the end of the trail at the Deadwood Days of '76 Rodeo Grounds will extend your trip by 1.5 miles for a total distance of 108.9 miles from Edgemont.

The Mickelson Trail around Lead and Deadwood is one of the most popular trails in the Black Hills. It is used in midweek by local residents, and is starting to attract mountain bikers from farther away on the weekends. Despite this use, expect to see deer along the trail, and to see wild turkeys along Whitetail Summit in the spring and fall.

Parts of the trail have already proven to be some of the best cross-country ski trail in the Black Hills for beginning skiers. From Kirk to Englewood, the trail is in a deep valley which collects snow and is protected from afternoon snowmelt. The flat railroad bed is broken only by three crossings of Whitewood Creek. Reconstruction of the trail resulted in a very smooth surface, so the trail can be skied even with minimal snow cover.

From Englewood to U.S. 85, the ski trail is part of the Black Hills snowmobile trail system. Snowmobiles are allowed on this part of the trail from December 1 to March 31. Competition from snowmobiles, and the steady climb to Whitetail Summit from either Whitetail Creek or U.S. 85, make this segment less attractive. However, experienced skiers may find this section ideal for practicing their skating technique on the groomed trail. Skiing is permitted elsewhere on the Black Hills snowmobile trail system, but is not recommended due to heavy snow machine traffic.

South Dakota Centennial Trail

Because of its length, scenery and diversity the Centennial Trail is the premiere hiking trail in the Black Hills and Badlands region. Mountain bikers and backpackers are attracted to the trail by the rare chance to spend a long trip on a single route. Likewise, hikers see the one-hundred-and-twenty-mile journey as both a challenge and a chance to experience the diversity of the Black Hills up close. The Centennial Trail became part of the National Recreation Trail system in 1997.

As it traverses the length of the hills, the Centennial Trail becomes the responsibility of a variety of government agencies. The regulations that apply to the trail vary according to the administrative agency, and are summarized in the Black Hills National Forest's Centennial Trail User's Guide. The allowed uses of the trail will be of the most concern to readers. Mountain bikes are prohibited on the trail in Wind Cave National Park, Black Elk Wilderness and the northern part of Bear Butte State Park. Conversely, motorized vehicles are allowed on the trail between Pilot Knob and Dalton Lake.

As regulations vary between agencies, so do standards of trail marking and maintenance. Much of the original Centennial Trail has been rebuilt and removed from roads. Other sections are scheduled for improvement in the next few years. Since the first addition of this guide was published, major relocations have been completed between Pilot Knob and Boxelder Creek, and between Elk Creek Trailhead and the Fort Meade Recreation Area.

If you have hiked substantial parts of the trail, let someone know about your experience. Government agencies can be surprisingly responsive to comments about trail use. If you see a problem, don't hesitate to report it. Be specific, note exactly where an unmarked trail junction is located, or report exactly where motorized vehicles access a trail that they are not permitted on. Just be sure to be equally diligent about reporting the positive aspects of your trip.

You can also help by doing some routine maintenance on your trip. Simple things, such as cleaning out water bars, replacing fallen signs, picking up litter or throwing a few rocks out of the trail help to make the trail a lot nicer for those who follow you.

~

Centennial Trail Mileage Table
SOUTH TO NORTH

	CUMULATIVE MILEAGE	DISTANCE BETWEEN POINTS
Norbeck Dam Trailhead, South Dakota 87	0.0	0.0
Leave Beaver Creek	2.0	2.0
WCNP Trail 5	4.5	2.5
NPS Road 5	6.0	1.5
CSP Road 7	9.5	3.5
Wildlife Loop Road	13.5	4.0
CSP Road 4	15.0	1.5
French Creek Trailhead, CSP Road 4	15.5	0.5
South End Bypass 1	17.0	1.5
North End Bypass 1	19.5	2.5
South End Bypass 2	20.7	1.2
Badger Hole Trailhead, CSP Road 9	21.1	0.4
U.S. 16A	21.7	0.6
North End Bypass 2	22.8	1.1
South Dakota 87	28.8	6.0
Iron Creek Trailhead, BHNF Road 345.2A	29.8	1.0
Grizzly Creek Trail	31.1	1.3
Mountain Bike Bypass	31.8	0.7
Enter Black Elk Wilderness	32.9	1.1
Norbeck Trail	33.9	1.0
Horsethief Lake Trail	35.6	1.7
Leave Wilderness	37.1	1.5
Willow Creek–Rushmore Trail	37.4	0.3
Big Pine Trailhead, South Dakota 244	38.0	0.6
BHNF Road 353	38.5	0.5
Samelias Trailhead, U.S. 16	41.5	3.0
BHNF Road 531	42.1	0.6
Mount Warner	44.8	2.7
BHNF Road 392	48.0	3.2
Flume Trailhead	48.7	0.7

Sheridan Dam	49.7	1.0
North End Dam Bypass	50.7	1.0
Dakota Point Trailhead, BHNF Road 434	51.0	0.3
Sheridan Lake Road	50.7	0.7
BHNF Road 551	53.0	1.3
BHNF Road 160	54.5	1.5
North End Bald Hills	55.8	1.3
Brush Creek Trailhead, BHNF Road 772	57.4	1.6
Exit Gold Standard Gulch	60.6	3.2
Tamarack Trailhead	61.9	1.3
Rapid Creek Trailhead	62.5	0.6
U.S. 385	63.8	1.3
BHNF Road 264	64.3	0.5
Smoker Gulch	66.3	2.0
Deerfield Trail	67.0	0.7
Deer Creek Trailhead, Silver City Road	67.3	0.3
U.S. 385	69.2	1.9
Pilot Knob Trailhead, BHNF Road 208	70.6	1.4
BHNF Road 152	72.3	1.7
BHNF Road 140	76.8	4.5
BHNF Road 678	77.8	1.0
Nemo Road	78.6	0.8
Contour Road—East	81.3	2.7
Dalton Lake Campground	83.4	2.1
BHNF Road 704—South	84.4	1.0
BHNF Road 704—North	86.0	1.6
BHNF Road 702	88.1	2.1
BHNF Road 137	89.6	1.5
Elk Creek	93.0	3.4
Elk Creek Trailhead, BHNF Road 108	94.8	1.8
BHNF Road 169	95.5	0.7
BHNF Road 139—South	97.6	2.1
BHNF Road 139—North	101.6	4.0
BLM/BHNF Boundary	105.6	4.0
Interstate 90	106.2	0.6
Alkali Creek Trailhead	106.7	0.5
Fort Meade Road	109.1	2.4
Fort Meade Trailhead	111.6	2.5
BLM/BBSP Boundary	115.8	4.2
Bear Butte Lake Trailhead	117.0	1.2
Bear Butte Trailhead	118.4	1.4
Bear Butte Summit	120.0	1.6

Hikers will require at least one week to hike the entire Centennial Trail. Their greatest obstacle will be getting water. Few trailheads have drinking water supplies and there are only a few streams along the trail that flow year-round. Water from streams and lakes should be treated before drinking. In addition to the Black Hills National Forest campgrounds, there are several private campgrounds with small stores located along U.S. 385. Supplies are also available in Custer, Hill City, Lead and Deadwood.

For mountain bike riders or horseback riders water problems are less serious, since they can travel farther per day than hikers. Most mountain bikers can ride the trail in 3 or 4 long days. They often use a sag wagon to carry gear and can easily travel between campgrounds. One possible ten-day itinerary for the entire Centennial Trail is listed below. Keep in mind that the campgrounds at Sheridan and Pactola lakes are often full during summer weekends. Mileages shown for these two campgrounds do not include the extra distance between the Centennial Trail and the campground. At some of these sites you may want to do your cooking and fill up with water before moving on to a quieter campsite.

Possible Ten-Day Itinerary

	Daily Miles	Total Miles	
Day 1	15.0	15.0	French Creek Horse Camp (first water)
Day 2	14.8	29.8	Iron Creek Horse Camp
Day 3	8.2	38.0	Horsethief Lake (longer via Harney Peak)
Day 4	10.8	48.8	Calumet Trailhead (Sheridan Southside Campground)
Day 5	13.7	62.5	Rapid Creek Trailhead (Pactola Campground)
Day 6	14.1	76.6	Boxelder Campground (add 1.0 mile to campground)
Day 7	6.8	83.4	Dalton Lake Campground (add 1.0 mile from campground)
Day 8	9.6	106.7	Elk Creek (camp along creek)
Day 9	13.7	106.7	Alkali Creek Campground
Day 10	13.3	120.0	Finish (add 1.5 miles to descend Bear Butte)

Norbeck Dam to NPS Road 5

WIND CAVE NATIONAL PARK

Description: A scenic hike along the south end of the Centennial Trail through mixed prairie and forest.

General Location: Eleven miles southeast of Custer, South Dakota.

Highlight: Wildlife watching and solitude.

Access: The *Norbeck Dam Trailhead* is the southern terminus of the Centennial Trail. A small parking area on the east side of South Dakota 87 is located 0.6 mile north of the junction of South Dakota 87 and U.S. 385. This is also the start of the Lookout Point Trail (NPS 4). The trailhead can also be reached by driving south 6.4 miles on South Dakota 87 from the boundary of Wind Cave National Park and Custer State Park. The *Highland Creek Trailhead* is located 1.4 miles east of South Dakota 87 on NPS Road 5.

Distance: This section is 6.0 miles one way.

Maps: Trails Illustrated Black Hills Southeast and page 26.

The Centennial Trail begins in mixed prairie and woodland along the southern flank of the Black Hills in Wind Cave National Park. The meeting of forest and prairie provides excellent opportunities to view bison, elk, deer and other wildlife where they utilize both habitats for forage and shelter.

From the trailhead at Norbeck Dam, drop north into the valley of Beaver Creek and then meander downstream to the east. The route passes Reaves Gulch and Curley Canyon before turning north at the head of a large meadow, where the trail leaves the Beaver Creek valley at 2.0 miles. A 0.5 mile spur to *Highland Creek Trail* continues east from here along Beaver Creek. Long-distance hikers now have a tough job ahead, for this is the low point on the Centennial Trail until it leaves the Black Hills near the Black Hills National Cemetery almost 100 miles to the north.

Ascend from Beaver Creek, first steeply and then steadily. Continue hiking north through an open area to an intersection at 4.5 miles with the *Sanctuary Trail*, which leads northwest 2.1 miles to South Dakota 87 and southeast 1.5 miles to the Highland Creek Trail. Stay on the Centennial Trail, which heads northeast, crossing two small gullies. After passing the pens used for holding bison during the park's annual fall roundup, you reach the Highland Creek Trailhead on NPS Road 5 at 6.0 miles.

Much of the Centennial Trail in Wind Cave National Park originally

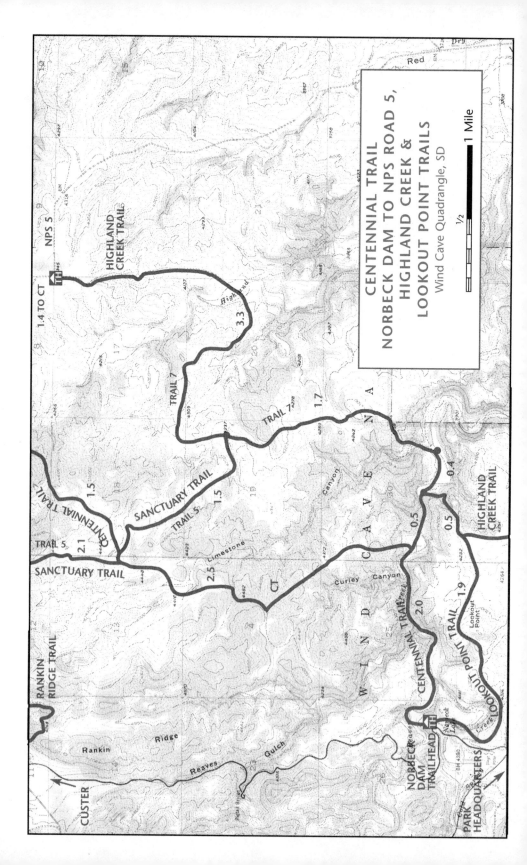

CENTENNIAL TRAIL
NORBECK DAM TO NPS ROAD 5,
HIGHLAND CREEK &
LOOKOUT POINT TRAILS
Wind Cave Quadrangle, SD

½   1 Mile

followed faint, overgrown jeep trails. The Park Service is now in the process of rehabilitating the old roads into single track trails. The trails are marked with brown carsonite posts (similar to fiberglass) and blazes. Trail intersections are marked with bison-proof posts. Throughout its length, the Centennial Trail is marked by carsonite posts with the number 89 and the symbol of the appropriate managing agency. In some places mileage posts are placed along the trail, but both types of trail markers are used as scratching posts by bison and can be easily flattened.

Travel across open prairie is hot, dry work in summer. Hikers unfamiliar with this terrain should be careful not to underestimate the full effects of powerful sun and limited shade. Mountain bikes are not allowed on any of the hiking trails in the park, but bikers can ride the park's gravel roads.

NPS Road 5 to French Creek Horse Camp
CUSTER STATE PARK

Description: A trip through the south half of Custer State Park for hikers and mountain bikers.

General Location: Eleven miles southeast of Custer, South Dakota.

Highlight: The Centennial Trail enters the ponderosa pine forests typical of the Black Hills.

Access: The *Highland Creek Trailhead* is 1.4 miles east of South Dakota 87 on NPS Road 5. To reach the *French Creek Trailhead* drive 2.6 miles east of South Dakota 87 on CSP Road 4. Blue Bell Lodge, general store, and campground are located at the junction of CSP Road 4 and South Dakota 87.

Distance: This section is 9.5 miles one way.

Maps: Trails Illustrated Black Hills Southeast and pages 28 and 30.

The Custer State Park portion of the Centennial Trail leads from mixed prairie and woodlands into terrain more typical of the eastern Black Hills. The land is heavily forested and deeply dissected by meandering streams. The topography is rolling with numerous small ridges and divides. Since the Black Hills were not covered by ice during the Pleistocene glaciation, streams draining off the uplifted core of

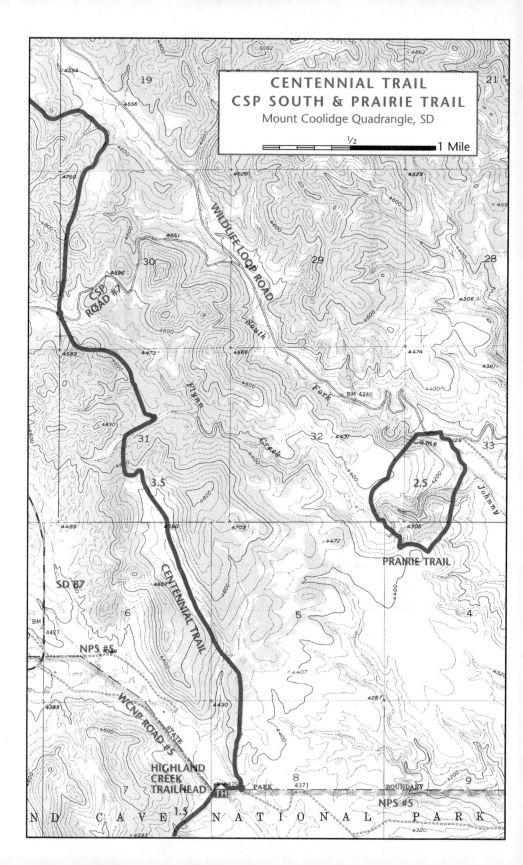

CENTENNIAL TRAIL
CSP SOUTH & PRAIRIE TRAIL
Mount Coolidge Quadrangle, SD

½   1 Mile

the hills have been free to cut their own channels, rather than being confined to straight, U-shaped valleys left by glaciers. French Creek Gorge is a wonderful example of the valleys cut by these streams.

From the Highland Creek Trailhead, enter Custer State Park by crossing through a gate in the bison fence. The route follows an old road along a broad, open ridge. Pass a faint trail to the west that may be signed "Coe Pocket" and continue northwest along an unnamed drainage. Near Coe Pocket is a line of foundations and overgrown furrows that are all that remain from a farm once located nearby. Cross another gate through a bison fence that runs along the section 6/31 boundary. This southern part of Custer State Park is excellent for seeing bison; just be sure to give these giants a wide berth. The Centennial Trail is now a faint path as it crosses a small divide into the Flynn Creek drainage and then follows an old, faint road along the south fork. Cross two dry forks of Flynn Creek and hike gradually upstream along the southwest side of the bed of the main fork. Turn west away from Flynn Creek, then follow a small gully north to reach gravel CSP Road 7 at 3.5 miles.

Cross CSP Road 7 and continue north as the route follows an old road to ascend a small ridge, then turn east down a small draw. The trail next turns north to skirt the west edge of a meadow. After passing another small draw, enter another meadow regaining sight of the Wildlife Loop Road. Beyond this meadow, cross the Parker Canyon Horse Trail, pass by one gully and turn up the second, still following a faint road. The trail then skirts the edge of a larger meadow before turning sharply east down a prominent draw to reach the Wildlife Loop Road (CSP Road 1) at 7.5 miles.

To stay on the Centennial Trail, cross the Wildlife Loop Road and follow an old dirt road up a small draw before exiting east and climbing a small divide. Continue on this road northeast into the broad, open valley of French Creek, reaching CSP Road 4 at 9.0 miles. Blue Bell Lodge and Resort are located 2.1 miles west at the junction of CSP Road 4 and South Dakota 87. Continue east on CSP Road 4 to reach the French Creek Horse Camp Trailhead at 9.5 miles.

Prospectors with Lieutenant Colonel George Armstrong Custer's 1874 Black Hills expedition first found gold in the Black Hills along French Creek, confirming decades of rumors. Their discovery triggered one of the largest, and wildest, gold rushes in the history of the West, culminating in the discovery of the rich Deadwood placers in the northern Black Hills. However, geologists with Custer's party were skeptical about the French Creek discovery. There has been speculation that one of the goals of Custer's expedition was to find gold.

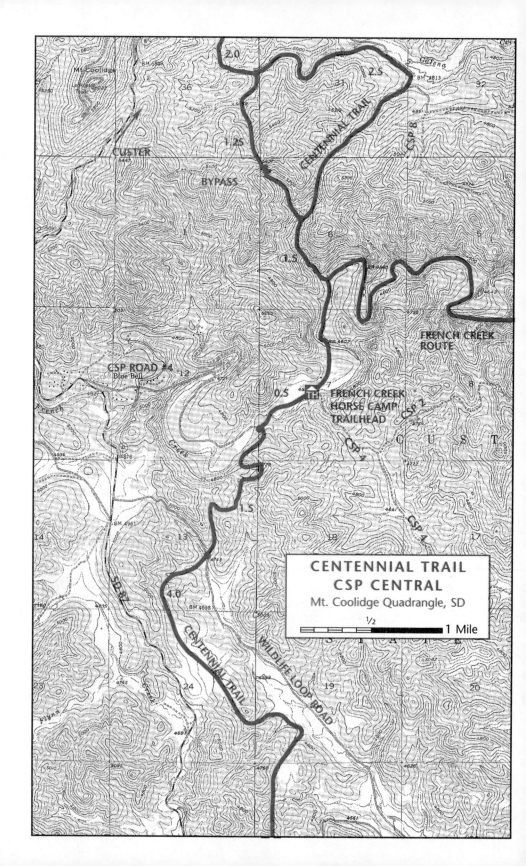

**CENTENNIAL TRAIL
CSP CENTRAL**

Mt. Coolidge Quadrangle, SD

½

1 Mile

There has been only minor placer gold mining along French Creek, and today the area is the major natural area in Custer State Park. Perhaps the doubts of the geologists were well-founded.

The Custer State Park section of the Centennial Trail is open to mountain bikes and horses. Custer State Park marks the Centennial Trail with plenty of blazes and carsonite posts. No drinking water is found along the trail. The French Creek Horse Camp has the first water available to northbound hikers. Supplies can be purchased at Blue Bell Lodge and Resort.

~

French Creek Horse Camp to
Iron Creek Horse Camp
CUSTER STATE PARK

Description: A trip through northern Custer State Park for hikers and mountain bikers.

General Location: Five miles east of Custer, South Dakota.

Highlight: An exciting mountain bike ride through the park's remote northern end.

Access: To reach the *French Creek Trailhead*, drive 2.6 miles east of South Dakota 87 on CSP Road 4. Blue Bell Lodge, general store, and campground are located at the junction of CSP Road 4 and South Dakota 87. From the intersection of U.S. 16A and South Dakota 87 in Custer State Park drive 1.6 miles east on U.S. 16A to CSP Road 9. Drive 0.9 mile south on CSP Road 9 to the *Badger Clark Trailhead*. To reach *Iron Creek Horse Camp* take South Dakota 87 to gravel BHNF Road 345, which is the Camp Remington Road. Turn left onto BHNF Road 345.2A and drive about 0.5 mile to the trailhead.

Distance: This section is 12.0 miles long one way.

Maps: Trails Illustrated Black Hills Southeast and pages 30 and 32.

The northern part of Custer State Park is wilder and has fewer roads than the southern part. The Centennial Trail here offers more solitude, though the forest setting offers fewer vistas. Mountain bike riders will especially enjoy the rolling section of trail north of Legion Lake.

From the French Creek Horse Camp Trailhead, cross a gate onto a dirt road. Follow this dirt road beside French Creek, passing a cabin

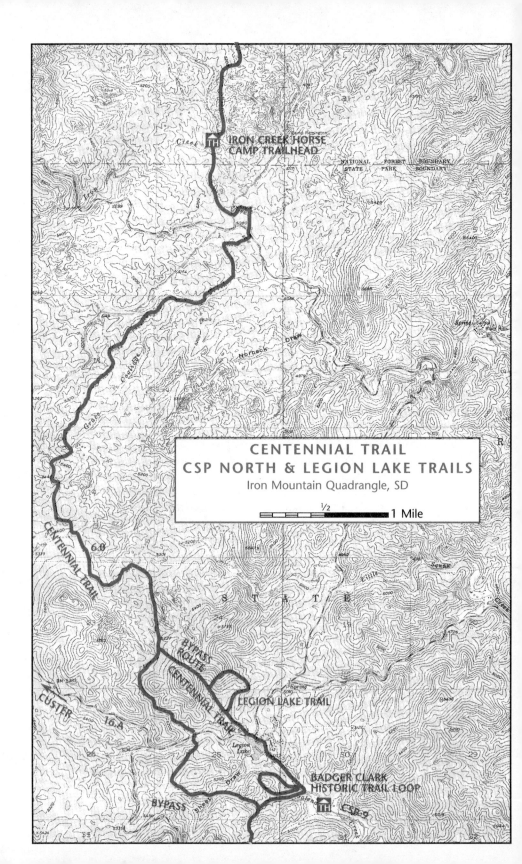

CENTENNIAL TRAIL
CSP NORTH & LEGION LAKE TRAILS
Iron Mountain Quadrangle, SD

½ 1 Mile

and a side road to the west. Leave the road to follow a tributary of French Creek to the north. From this point the road continues east along French Creek, and leads to a campsite in the *French Creek Natural Area*.

The Centennial Trail meanwhile makes up for the gentle grade of the last mile and a half by climbing steadily out of the valley of French Creek. The climb may in fact be too steep for horses or mountain bikes. Soon the south end of *Bypass Trail 1* is reached at 1.5 miles. The main Centennial Trail follows an old road to the northeast along Switchback Draw, turns northwest toward CSP Road 9 and climbs Heddy Draw to rejoin the bypass at 4.0 miles.

From the south junction, Bypass Trail 1 ascends three switchbacks to reach a new high point at 5,437 feet. From the ridge, descend to the southern limit of the 1988 Galena Fire. South Dakota's version of the 1988 Yellowstone fires was also caused by extended drought, but was not caused by long term accumulation of forest fuels. This lightning-caused fire burned 16,000 acres. Custer State Park uses both selective logging and controlled burns to manage its forests. Like the Yellowstone fires, the Galena fire totally devastated some areas, but regrowth has also been rapid.

The Bypass Trail crosses several roads and fire lines built during the fire which may obscure the trail before reaching the north end of Centennial Trail 1 in Heddy Draw, 2.75 miles from its beginning. The Centennial Trail then climbs over a small ridge crossed by a powerline. At the bottom of the next descent, reach a junction with *Bypass Trail 2* for horses at 5.2 miles.

Bypass Trail 2 goes left, crossing Sheep Draw and U.S. 16A/South Dakota 87 along the original route of the Centennial Trail before rejoining the current route north of Legion Lake in 2.0 miles. From the junction, the main Centennial Trail turns east to reach the Badger Hole Trailhead and CSP Road 9 at 5.6 miles. From the Badger Hole, follow Galena Creek to Legion Lake and U.S. 16A/South Dakota 87 at 6.2 miles. Go through the Legion Lake Campground on the west side, passing both the south and north ends of the *Legion Lake Trail* before rejoining the Bypass Trail 2 at 7.3 miles.

The Centennial Trail continues along an old dirt road past a ridge lined with spectacular granite pinnacles. Then climb to a junction with a dirt road near a powerline and follow this road, crossing under the powerline to another road junction. The roller coaster descent from this point to the Needles Highway (South Dakota 87) offers perhaps the best section of mountain biking along the entire Centennial Trail. Keep an eye peeled for euphoria-crazed bikers as the trail winds past a

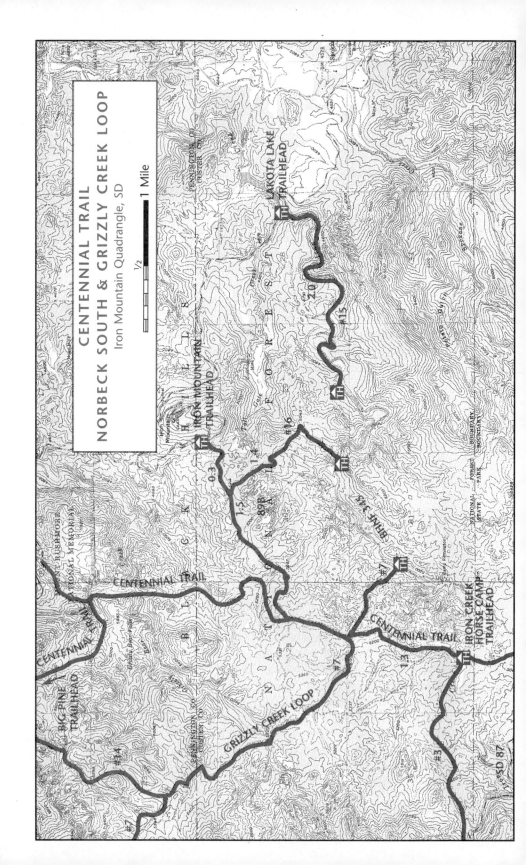

CENTENNIAL TRAIL
NORBECK SOUTH & GRIZZLY CREEK LOOP
Iron Mountain Quadrangle, SD

½   1 Mile

junction with a side road leading east. Then drop alongside Grace Coolidge Creek and climb a ridge northwest of the creek. President Calvin Coolidge and his wife established their summer White House in Custer State Park in 1927. Many of the park's features, including Mount Coolidge, the highest point in the main body of Custer State Park, still visible to the south, were named for the Coolidges. Pass several old roads left from logging operations, then reach a sign explaining the park's Big Squaw logging unit. The open, park-like appearance of this area is a typical result of logging operations in the park.

At the north end of the ridge, drop east again beside Grace Coolidge Creek and follow it to a grassy ridge where the trail turns north into a side drainage. The trail then climbs over a small divide, to descend again to the Needles Highway (South Dakota 87) at 13.3 miles, just west of a junction with BHNF Road 345 to Camp Remington.

To continue north on the Centennial Trail, cross the Needles Highway. The trail crosses the boundary between Custer State Park and the Black Hills National Forest before reaching BHNF Road 345.2A and the Iron Creek Horse Camp Trailhead at 14.3 miles.

Water, supplies and camping are available at Legion Lake. No other drinking water is found along the route.

Iron Creek Horse Camp to Big Pine Trailhead
CUSTER RANGER DISTRICT, BLACK HILLS NATIONAL FOREST

Description: A moderate hike through the Norbeck Wildlife Preserve and Black Elk Wilderness.

General Location: Five miles southwest of Keystone, South Dakota.

Highlight: Granite formations and wilderness solitude.

Access: To reach *Iron Creek Horse Camp*, take South Dakota 87 to gravel BHNF Road 345, which is the Camp Remington Road. Turn left onto BHNF Road 345.2A and drive about 0.5 mile to the trailhead. *Big Pine Trailhead* is located on the north side of South Dakota 244, 2.9 miles west of Mount Rushmore.

Distance: This hike is 8.2 miles long.

Maps: Sierra Club Hiking Map of the Norbeck Wildlife Preserve, Trails Illustrated Black Hills Southeast and pages 34 and 36.

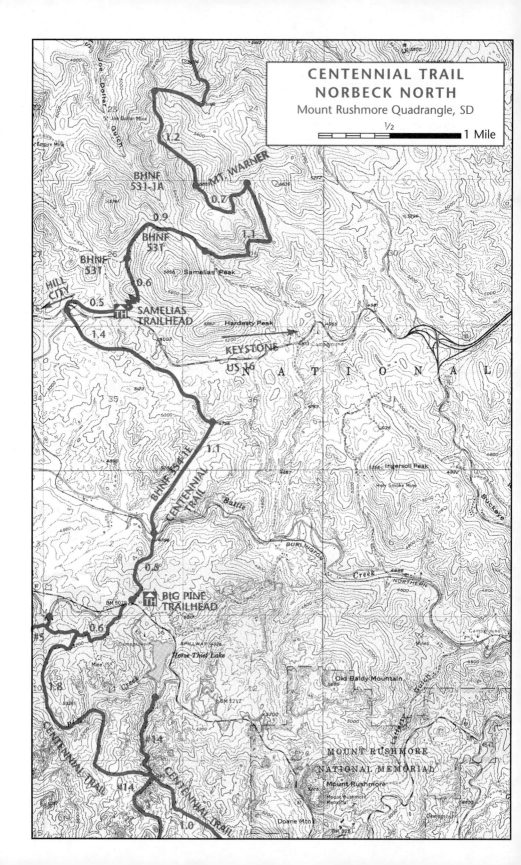

CENTENNIAL TRAIL
NORBECK NORTH

Mount Rushmore Quadrangle, SD

½   1 Mile

This section of the Centennial Trail crosses the only designated wilderness area in the Black Hills. Wilderness designation prohibits the use of motorized vehicles and mountain bikes, so the Black Hills National Forest has developed a bypass (Trail 89B) for mountain bikes around the wilderness. The Centennial Trail crosses the little-travelled east side of the Norbeck Trail system through an area of profound solitude and true wilderness experience.

From the trailhead at Iron Creek Horse Camp, hike north on trail constructed in 1992. Climb over a small ridge, then cross Iron Creek via a bridge. Hike along the west side of a group of spires, then climb to a ridge with views to the west of Harney Peak. Descend to cross an intermittent creek. Climb up and over one more granite ridge to reach a junction with the east side of *Grizzly Creek Trail* at 1.3 miles.

Turn left on former BHNF Road 346 for 0.2 mile to an intersection with the west part of *Grizzly Creek Trail*. At the junction is a group of rugged spires from which Harney Peak can be seen. Follow the Centennial Trail north up a dry side draw to a four-way junction at 2.0 miles. Former BHNF Road 347 leads west from the junction and *Trail 89B*, the beginning of the bypass route for mountain bikers, leads east to the Iron Mountain Trailhead on U.S. 16A. Continue to follow the Centennial Trail north, immediately passing an abandoned gravel pit.

Descend to reach a small draw and old logging road leading east at 2.5 miles. Go up and over a small divide to reach another old logging road leading east at 2.6 miles. Pass one more side road east before reaching the Black Elk Wilderness boundary in a small draw at 3.1 miles.

Once in the wilderness, hike north to Grizzly Bear Creek, then up a side draw to a junction with a side trail to Mount Rushmore National Memorial at 4.1 miles. The Centennial Trail crosses a small corner of the memorial then passes over the divide between Grizzly Bear and Pine Creeks. Cross through a spectacular line of spires just before reaching the junction with the *Horsethief Lake Trail* at 5.8 miles. To reach the BHNF Horsethief Lake Campground, turn north on the Horsethief Lake Trail and hike to the lake, which is located just off South Dakota 244.

Continue west to a branch of Pine Creek. Follow the branch north to the main stem, then head upstream to another small draw. Follow the draw north to a divide that forms the Black Elk Wilderness boundary at 7.3 miles. Descend on an old road, to a trail junction at 7.6 miles.

Turn right onto the Centennial Trail where the *Willow Creek–Rushmore Trail* continues west. Hike northeast, crossing a network of old logging roads to reach South Dakota 244 at 8.2 miles. The Big Pine Trailhead is across the highway.

If you're hiking the entire Centennial Trail, but want to climb Harney Peak, try an alternate route along the Grizzly Creek, Sylvan Lake–Harney and Willow Creek–Rushmore trails. Though longer, this route includes a beautiful hike along Grizzly Creek as well as the top of Harney Peak.

~

Big Pine Trailhead to Dakota Point Trailhead

HARNEY AND PACTOLA DISTRICTS, BLACK HILLS NATIONAL FOREST

Description: A rugged hike from South Dakota 244 to Sheridan Lake.
Highlight: Sheridan Lake and the view from Mount Warner.
General Location: Seven miles northwest of Keystone, South Dakota.
Access: The *Big Pine Trailhead* is on the north side of South Dakota 244, 2.9 miles west of Mount Rushmore. To reach the *Samelias Trailhead*, drive 3.0 miles west on U.S. 16 from the junction of U.S. 16 and 16A. Or drive 2.6 miles east on U.S. 16 from the 16/385 junction. The trailhead is on the north side of the road. To reach the *Flume Trailhead*, drive 1.7 miles north on U.S. 385 from the junction with U.S. 16. Turn east on paved BHNF Road 192 for 0.7 mile. Then turn left onto a paved road toward the South Marina and reach the Flume, or Calumet, Trailhead at 1.5 miles. The *Dakota Point Trailhead* is located 1.6 miles east of U.S. 385 on the Sheridan Lake Road (Pennington County C228) and 0.3 mile south on dirt BHNF Road 434.
Distance: 13.0 miles one way.
Maps: Trails Illustrated Black Hills Southeast and Black Hills Northeast, pages 36 and 39.

One of the roughest sections of the Centennial Trail lies between the northern limit of the Harney Peak trail system and Sheridan Lake. Unsuspecting mountain bikers accustomed to relatively easy riding elsewhere on the Centennial Trail are easily lured onto this section, then mangled by steep grades, tight turns and a boulder-strewn trail. Determined bikers can make it through this section, but it is much easier to walk.

Badlands National Park. Jean Gauger.

Badlands National Park. Tim Schoon.

Sage Creek Area, Badlands Wilderness. Hiram Rogers.

Trail up Bear Butte, Centennial Trail, South Dakota. Edward Raventon.

Cathedral Spires, Black Hills. Edward Raventon.

Aspen Grove, Black Hills. Edward Raventon.

Mountain Goats near Harney Peak, Black Hills. Hiram Rogers.

Cross-country Skier, Eagle Cliff, Black Hills. Hiram Rogers.

Triplet Fawns, Black Hills. Edward Raventon.

Prairie Rattlesnake, Black Hills.
Edward Raventon.

Bison, Black Hills. Edward Raventon.

Devils Tower, Wyoming. Eric Caddey.

Belle Fourche River and red beds, near Devils Tower. Tim Schoon.

Painted Canyon, Theodore Roosevelt National Park. Bruce M. Kaye, NPS.

Badlands, Theodore Roosevelt National Park. North Dakota Tourism.

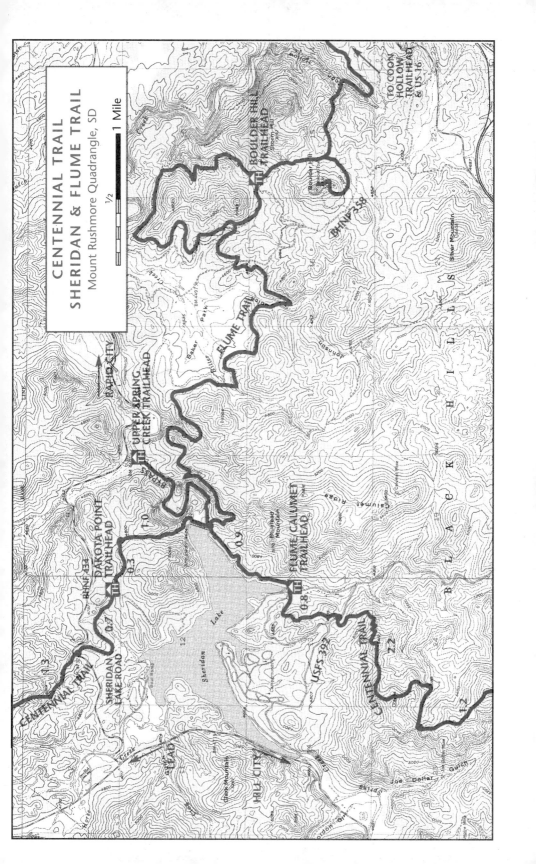

CENTENNIAL TRAIL
SHERIDAN & FLUME TRAIL
Mount Rushmore Quadrangle, SD

½   1 Mile

Hikers will have the opposite experience, and enjoy the trail because of the solitude it offers. The roughest section, between Samelias Peak and BHNF Road 392 at Sheridan Lake, is a rough single track, but no more difficult to hike than any other well-travelled, but poorly maintained, hiking trail in the Rocky Mountains.

Hike north from the Big Pine Trailhead, ignoring three forks that lead right, to reach a single track at 0.1 mile. Descend to reach paved BHNF Road 353 in the valley of Battle Creek at 0.5 mile. Cross the road, and a set of railroad tracks, then follow dirt BHNF Road 354-1E along a small draw that leads northeast. Crest a small divide and turn right, then left at a junction at 1.6 miles. The left turn leads onto a single track through a narrow draw.

At 1.9 miles the Centennial Trail enters a meadow, then follows a series of old dirt roads leading northwest. At 3.0 miles, turn onto a single track and then cross under U.S. 16 via a highway underpass. Head east above the highway embankment to reach the Samelias Trailhead at 3.5 miles.

From the Samelias Trailhead, switchback up to a prominent saddle on the west side of Samelias Peak. At 4.1 miles turn right onto dirt BHNF Road 531. Follow Road 531 past a junction with Road 531-1A, and over a small saddle. Then turn onto an overgrown logging road at 5.0 miles. This is the point where the difficult mountain biking begins. The road quickly becomes a trail that contours east, then north. At 6.1 miles reach another saddle and begin the climb up Mount Warner. At 6.8 miles the summit of Mt. Warner is just a short bushwhack to the west. From the top of the 5,889-foot summit, Harney Peak looms over Elkhorn Ridge. Mount Rushmore, Samelias Peak, and Hill City are also visible.

Beyond Mount Warner, the Centennial Trail follows a rough ridge to the north. At 7.8 miles, turn east off of the ridge to briefly follow a grassy logging road. The trail turns north, then east and follows a rugged set of ridges over boulders of Precambrian age quartzite. Descend the ridges to reach BHNF Road 392 at 10.0 miles.

North of BHNF Road 392 the trail becomes much easier to ride on a mountain bike. Traverse a ridge north to reach the Flume (or Calumet) Trailhead on the shore of Sheridan Lake at 10.7 miles. The Centennial Trail follows the *Flume Trail* for the next one mile along the bed of the historic flume. At 11.7 miles leave the Flume Trail. Just beyond, a bypass trail for horses leaves to the right to go around Sheridan Dam.

The Centennial Trail crosses the dam and ascends a stairway made of slabs of slate. The trail crosses Spring Creek on a large bridge. At

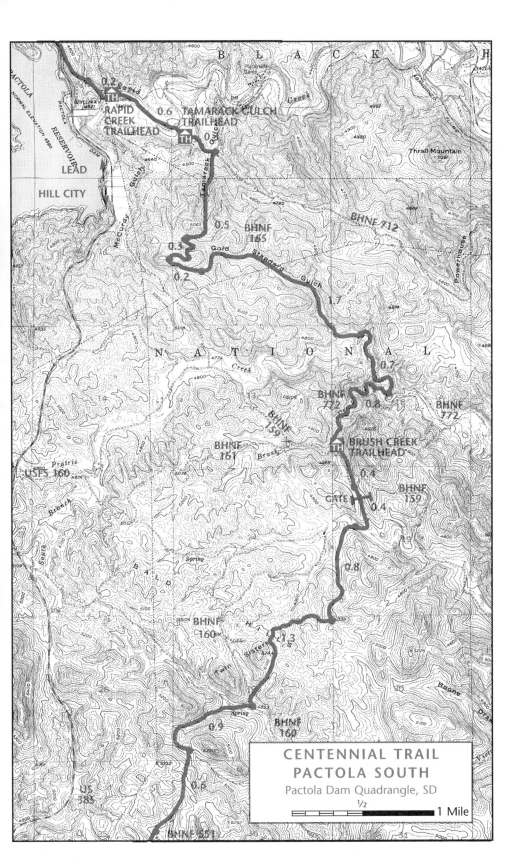

CENTENNIAL TRAIL
PACTOLA SOUTH
Pactola Dam Quadrangle, SD

12.7 miles the horse bypass trail reenters the main trail from the right. The trail then follows BHNF Road 381 west to reach a locked gate and the Dakota Point Trailhead at 13.0 miles.

The town of Sheridan was founded in 1875 soon after A. J. Williams discovered gold along Spring Creek. The town was initially named Golden City, a name which proved too optimistic. Placer mining in Spring Creek was short-lived and none of the hardrock mines around Sheridan proved productive. The town was briefly deserted in 1876 when its miners joined the stampede to Deadwood, but recovered briefly to become the first seat of Pennington County. The town then dwindled to a few small ranches that were covered when the waters of Spring Creek became impounded behind Sheridan Dam.

With the exception of a short section between Dakota Point and Sheridan Dam, the Centennial Trail here is well marked by blazes, carsonite posts, and the occasional Silver Arrow. This entire section is closed to motorized vehicles, although few signs indicate this closure.

Dakota Point Trailhead to
Pilot Knob Trailhead
PACTOLA RANGER DISTRICT,
BLACK HILLS NATIONAL FOREST

Description: A long hike or mountain bike ride from Sheridan Lake to Pactola Reservoir.

General Location: Ten miles northeast of Hill City, South Dakota.

Highlight: Gold Standard Gulch and views of Pactola Lake.

Access: The *Dakota Point Trailhead* is located 1.6 miles east of U.S. 385 on the Sheridan Lake Road (Pennington County C228) and 0.3 miles south on dirt BHNF Road 434. To reach the *Brush Creek Trailhead* drive 8.6 mile north of U.S. 16 on U.S. 385. Then turn east and drive 2.9 miles on BHNF Road 159. Turn left onto BHNF Road 772 and drive 0.3 mile to the trailhead. To reach the *Rapid Creek* and *Tamarack* trailheads, drive 2.0 miles south past South Dakota 44 on U.S. 385 to Pactola Dam. Switchback for 0.5 mile down a gravel road to an offset four-way junction. From the junction, the Rapid Creek Trailhead is 0.1 mile to the left and the Tamarack Trailhead is 0.7 mile straight ahead on the main gravel road. To reach the Deer Creek Trailhead, drive 1.4 miles north of South Dakota 44 on U.S. 385 to the paved

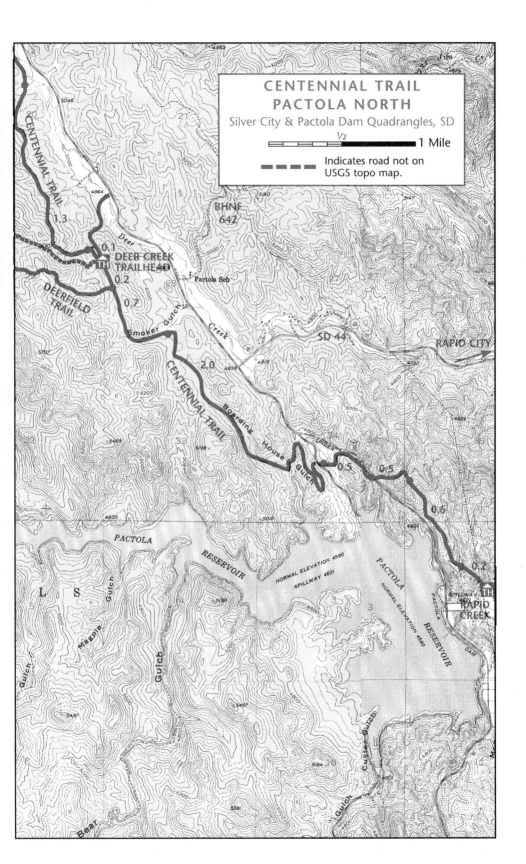

CENTENNIAL TRAIL
PACTOLA NORTH
Silver City & Pactola Dam Quadrangles, SD

½   1 Mile

Indicates road not on
USGS topo map.

Silver City Road (Pennington County 321). Drive 0.3 mile west on the Silver City Road, then 0.1 mile west on a dirt road. The *Pilot Knob Trailhead* is 2.9 miles north of the Silver City Road (Pennington County 321) on U.S. 385 and 1.0 mile east on BHNF Road 208.

Distance: 19.6 miles one way.

Maps: Trails Illustrated Black Hills Northeast and pages 39, 41, 43, and 46.

If any section of the Centennial Trail is ideal for a mountain bike ride, it is the section from Dakota Point to Pilot Knob. Close access to U.S. 385 makes it easy to shuttle cars and ease the burden of this long haul. While the entire section is hilly, none of the hills are long or difficult. If you feel up to the challenge of a long trip on the Centennial Trail, this is the section to try.

From the Dakota Point Trailhead, go west for 0.2 mile to a power-line, then turn north onto a trail. At 0.7 mile, cross the Sheridan Lake Road and continue north. Go right at the next fork, which leaves the main draw, then turn left onto a dirt road at 1.4 miles. At 2.0 miles cross unmarked BHNF Road 551 and then turn left in an aspen grove onto another dirt road.

At 2.6 miles, turn left at a junction in a small saddle, then left again onto a dirt road. Watch carefully as the trail gradually diverges from this road. The trail crosses a gate and passes two cattle-fouled springs on the next descent. BHNF Road 160 is crossed at a three-way junction at 3.5 miles.

At the triple junction take the northwest fork and follow it for 0.1 mile before turning off onto a trail that leads into the Bald Hills. Many travelers have lost the trail at this junction. The Bald Hills are heavily grazed, and following the Centennial Trail through an assortment of trails and old roads requires a sharp eye. Exit the Bald Hills at 4.8 miles on a ridge top that offers a view west of the Seth Bullock Fire Tower on Scruton Mountain.

Follow the ridge to the east, drop off the north side, cross a gate and then reach a fork of Victoria Creek at 5.6 miles. Cross another gate near the divide with Brush Creek. Then cross BHNF Road 159 before reaching the Brush Creek Trailhead and BHNF Road 772 at 6.4 miles.

Follow Road 772 northeast before turning north into Gold Standard Gulch at 7.2 miles. The next 0.7 mile in the tight, winding canyon is easily the prettiest part of this trail section. Exit the canyon at 7.9 miles and continue up the main stem of Gold Standard Gulch following and criss-crossing a dirt road. At 9.6 miles leave Gold Standard Gulch to the north.

Climb to a saddle on the divide between Gold Standard and Tamarack Creek at 9.8 miles. A side trail from here leads west a short distance to an overlook above Pactola Reservoir. The descent from the divide is confused by many intersections with old roads, but the Centennial Trail eventually follows the main stem of Tamarack Creek to reach the Tamarack Trailhead at 10.9 miles.

From Tamarack Creek, the Centennial Trail winds through a wide plain below Pactola Dam to reach the Rapid Creek Trailhead at 11.5 miles. From the trailhead, cross Rapid Creek, then turn right off the gravel road onto a dirt road at 11.7 miles. Pass a side road to the east, then turn right, then left at road junctions to reach a ridge crest at 12.3 miles. The trail climbs over one more ridge before crossing U.S. 385 at 12.8 miles.

The Centennial Trail next crosses paved BHNF Road 264 at 13.3 miles. At 13.5 miles the trail reaches a ridge top on the east side of Boardinghouse Gulch and a rusted sign indicating that an overlook above Pactola Reservoir is one-quarter mile south. Follow the ridge top for one-half mile to a four-way junction and go straight through the junction on a two-track dirt road. The trail follows this road for a mile, then is a single track briefly before descending to the bottom of Smoker Gulch, and its scenic trailer park, at 15.3 miles.

Beyond Smoker Gulch, follow dirt roads north to a junction with the *Deerfield Trail* at 16.0. Silver City is three miles west on the Deerfield Trail. Cross the paved Silver City Road at 16.2 miles. Just past the road a short side trail leads right 75 yards to the Deer Creek Trailhead at 16.3 miles.

From the Deer Creek Trailhead follow a single track north for 0.6 mile before turning left onto a dirt road. Stay right at the next two forks. At 17.6 miles turn right onto a well-travelled dirt road behind a house and a trailer. Follow this road to U.S. 385 at 18.2 miles, then turn right onto gravel BHNF Road 202. At 18.7 miles turn left onto a dirt road by a powerline, then climb over a small divide. At 19.6 miles cross BHNF Road 208 and reach the Pilot Knob Trailhead.

The Centennial Trail from Dakota Point to Pilot Knob traverses a sea of ponderosa pine and slate. Deer, which adapt easily to an environment altered by man, are the most common wild animals. Cattle graze along many parts of this trail.

The name Pactola is derived from Pactolus, the mythical Lydian river of golden sands. The name reflects the lofty, but unfulfilled, hopes of the miners who prospected Rapid Creek during the 1875 gold rush.

It should be obvious from the route description that route finding on this section of the Centennial Trail is made difficult by many inter-

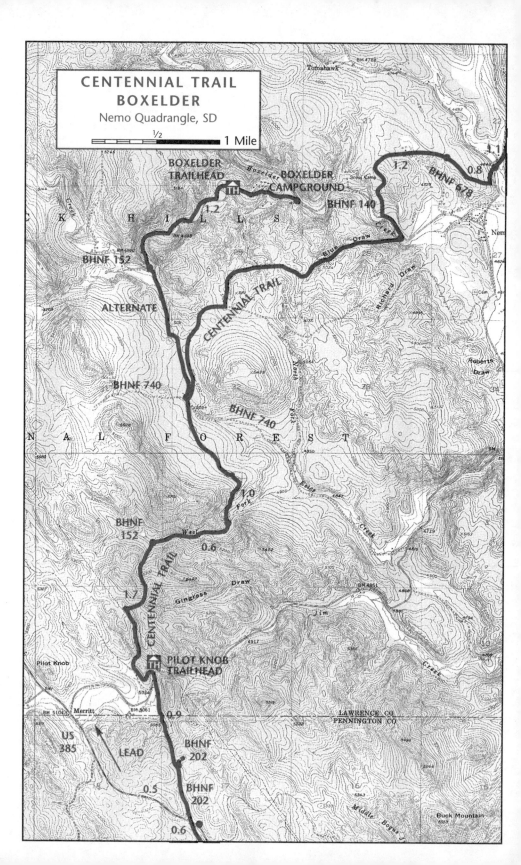

sections with two-track dirt roads. But the route is not as complicated as it may sound and most travellers should be able to follow the blazes and carsonite posts. Most of this section also follows the route of the old Silver Arrow Trail and many of those old markers are still in place.

Pilot Knob Trailhead to Boxelder Creek

SPEARFISH RANGER DISTRICT, BLACK HILLS NATIONAL FOREST

Description: A moderate hike or mountain bike ride through the central Black Hills.

General Location: Between the towns of Silver City and Nemo, South Dakota.

Highlight: An optional side trip through Boxelder Canyon.

Access: The *Pilot Knob Trailhead* is 2.9 miles north of the Silver City Road (Pennington County 321) on U.S. 385 and 1.0 mile east on BHNF Road 208. *Boxelder Forks Campground* is located 2.1 miles west of Nemo on BHNF Road 140. It is possible to shuttle cars via the Nemo Road and BHNF Road 208.

Distance: This hike is 6.2 miles long one way. The loop via Boxelder Canyon is also 6.2 miles long.

Maps: Trails Illustrated Black Hills Northeast and page 46.

The central Black Hills have a look and feel all their own. This is an area dominated more by pine and slate than any other in the hills. Dense coats of ponderosa pine have crowded out almost all other vegetation—even along streams there are few woody shrubs or grasses. The slate bedrock is broken only sporadically by quartz veins. Slate weathers to form thin nutrient-poor soils further reducing diversity in vegetation. Still, the area has rugged topography suitable for challenging trips.

From Pilot Knob, the Centennial Trail follows a rough jeep road for 1.7 miles over a divide to reach unmarked BHNF Road 152 in the valley of the West Fork of Estes Creek. Follow the jeep road east before turning north on newly constructed trail at 2.3 miles. On the crest of a small divide, begin following a 1996 relocation designed to move the

Centennial Trail off travelled roads. Follow the relocation west, then north along a faint jeep road to a sign at a junction at 3.6 miles indicating that Nemo lies 4.5 miles north, Pilot Knob lies 3.5 miles south and the South Boxelder Trailhead is 2.0 miles north on the spur trail.

From this junction a new section of Centennial Trail leads northeast to Boxelder Creek, while the older, and more scenic, route reaches the same point via Boxelder Forks Canyon and gravel BHNF Road 140.

To stay on the main trail keep right at the junction, pass Caryl Springs and a sign indicating the junction of Richards and Blue Draws. Continue on a two-track dirt road down Blue Draw to reach a gate and bridge over Boxelder Creek at 6.1 miles. There is limited parking here. Turn left onto BHNF Road 140 before turning right again to exit Boxelder Forks Canyon at 6.2 miles.

Hikers seeking a refreshing hike through Boxelder Forks Canyon or backpackers planning to stay at Boxelder Campground can follow the *Boxelder Canyon Route*. To follow the older route from the south, turn left at the junction 3.6 miles north of Pilot Knob and follow an old dirt road for 1.1 miles to a junction with a gravel road. At the gravel road turn right to pass through a gate. The 1.2 miles of trail beyond the gate are the highlight of this section as the trail passes through the spectacular upper canyon of Boxelder Creek. Fall is the best time to hike Boxelder Canyon as you are more likely to stay dry on the eight crossings of Boxelder Creek in low water.

At 2.3 miles reach the former Boxelder Forks Trailhead. Then follow gravel BHNF Road 140 east to reach Boxelder Campground at 2.6 miles. Another 1.0 mile of walking on BHNF Road 140 leads to the point where the main Centennial Trail leaves Boxelder Canyon via BHNF Road 140-1B. Though BHNF Road 140 has moderate traffic and can be a bit dusty, the views of the creek and the sheer cliffs above it make for pleasant walking. You can combine the Boxelder Canyon Route and the main Centennial Trail in a beautiful 6.2-mile loop.

Many people think of the Centennial Trail as being the first long-distance hiking trail in the Black Hills. In fact, the Centennial Trail uses much of the route of an earlier hiking trail. From U.S. 16 to Boxelder Campground, the Centennial Trail follows the route of the former Silver Arrow Trail. The Silver Arrow Trail was a 55-mile trail developed by Black Hills area Boy Scouts as a place where scouts could complete their required fifty-mile wilderness hikes.

The Silver Arrow Trail started at Sylvan Lake and climbed Harney Peak before descending to Horsethief Lake and joining the present route of the Centennial Trail. It mostly followed BHNF roads to Boxelder Creek. Alert hikers may notice some of the Silver Arrow Trail

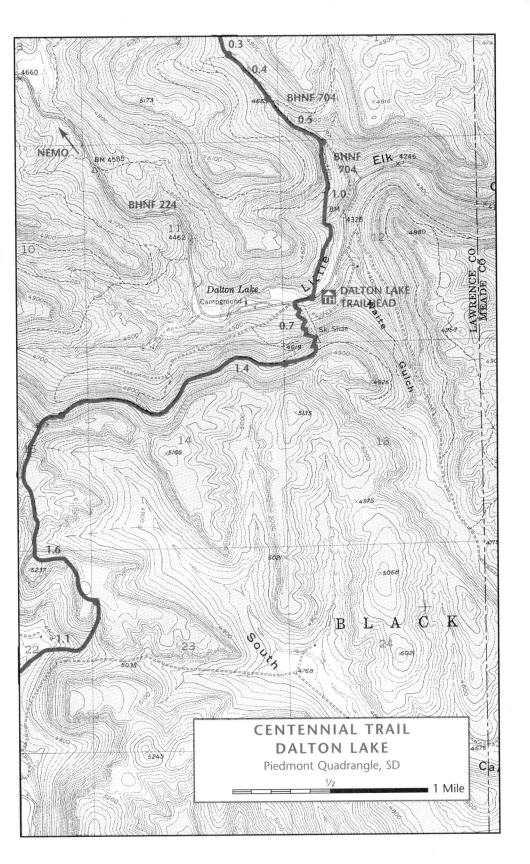

CENTENNIAL TRAIL
DALTON LAKE
Piedmont Quadrangle, SD

½   1 Mile

markers still in place. As the Centennial Trail is gradually removed from roads onto constructed trail, fewer of the arrows will remain along the route to remind hikers of their place in history.

Boxelder Creek to Dalton Lake Campground
SPEARFISH RANGER DISTRICT,
BLACK HILLS NATIONAL FOREST

Description: A moderately difficult trip between Boxelder Creek and Little Elk Creek.

General Location: Near the town of Nemo, South Dakota.

Highlight: Views into Little Elk Creek Canyon.

Access: From Nemo, drive west on gravel BHNF Road 140 for 0.9 mile to the Centennial Trail crossing. To reach *Dalton Lake Campground*, drive 0.5 mile north on the Nemo Road to paved BHNF Road 26. Drive 3.6 miles north to gravel BHNF Road 224. Turn right onto Road 224 and stay on the main road for 4.1 miles to Dalton Lake. The trailhead and sign are 0.1 mile beyond the campground.

Distance: 6.6 miles one way.

Maps: Trails Illustrated Black Hills Northeast and pages 46 and 49.

The Centennial Trail between Boxelder Forks and Dalton Lake Campground is far more diverse and scenic than the trail sections immediately to the south. This hike features steep canyons and choice overlooks that serve as the hiker's reward for the climbs out of the canyons. On this hike you will also leave the Precambrian schist and slate of the central Black Hills behind, and enter the younger Phanerozoic sedimentary rocks that rim the Black Hills.

Pick up the Centennial Trail on BHNF Road 140 where it leaves the road on the north side 0.9 miles west of the Nemo Road. Head west on BHNF Road 140 for .25 mile before turning north onto BHNF Road 140-1B. Follow Road 140-1B over the crest of a small divide, then descend to a four-way junction with BHNF Road 678 at 1.0 mile. Continue straight through the intersection on BHNF Road 678-1A for .5 mile. Then turn onto a cattle path which leads to the intersection of the paved Nemo and Dalton Lake roads at 1.8 miles.

Cross the Nemo Road then hike alongside paved BHNF Road 26 for

.25 mile to a gate. Beyond the gate, climb steadily. The next 2.4 miles of the Centennial Trail are difficult riding on mountain bikes because of steep grades and loose rocks. Finish your climb at 2.9 miles on a rocky, heavily-logged limestone ridge. Follow the ridge northwest, then north while enjoying the views down into the open valleys north of Nemo. Leave the ridge at a switchback just short of a powerline. Descend two switchbacks to reach a dirt road at 4.5 miles.

Follow the smooth, two-track road east along contour and enjoy the many views down into Little Elk Creek Canyon. At 5.9 miles reach the start of an older relocation. Continue on the dirt road east for .25 mile, then descend a series of steep rutted switchbacks on the west side of the abandoned Dalton Lake Ski Slide. At 6.6 miles, reach BHNF Road 224 and the Dalton Lake Trailhead.

The Dalton Lake Ski Slide and Jump was built in 1935 by the Civilian Conservation Corps based in Nemo. This was the first ski area built in the Black Hills. One look down the steep, narrow runs is enough to convince anyone that downhill skiing in the 1930s was a more committing endeavor than it is today. Much of the ski slide is becoming overgrown, but it is still possible to imagine pioneer skiers on the slopes. The same CCC crew also built the Dalton Lake Dam and Campground.

The first sale of timber from the U.S. government was made to Homestake Mining Company in 1898. The Case One Timber Sale was located south of Nemo and just east of the Centennial Trail. The company bought all timber eight inches in diameter and over from a site on Estes Creek. At that time, Homestake's mining operations in Lead used nearly five million board feet and twenty thousand cords of wood in a single year. At this rate, logging on Case One lasted only until 1908. Homestake operated sawmills in Estes and Nemo until 1939. By 1988 two billion board feet of timber had been cut in the Black Hills National Forest, with half of that cut in the last twenty years. In 1996 alone, forty-nine million board feet of timber were cut from the forest.

The Black Hills National Forest plans a number of improvements to the Centennial Trail north of the Nemo Road. Most of the work will involve improving the treadway and installing erosion control. The new route will extend east from the rim of Little Elk Creek Canyon into Waite Gulch, descend the gulch and then turn west to the Dalton Lake Trailhead.

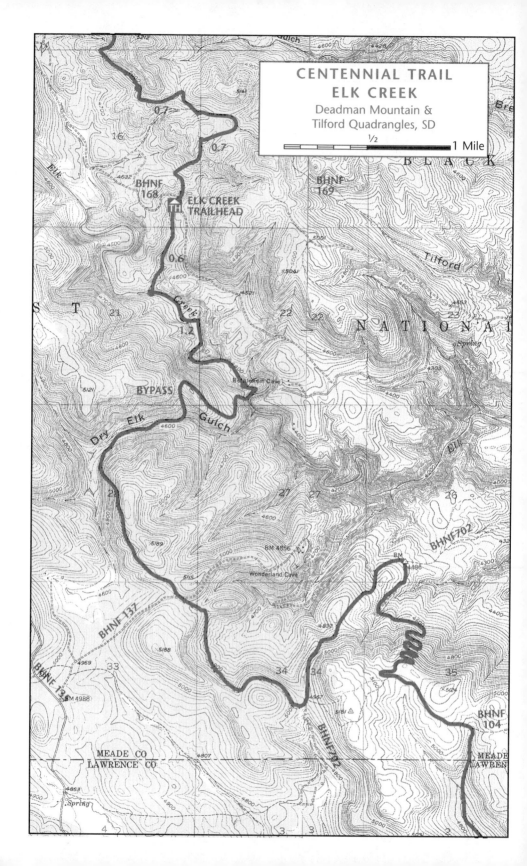

CENTENNIAL TRAIL
ELK CREEK
Deadman Mountain &
Tilford Quadrangles, SD

½   1 Mile

Dalton Lake Campground to
Alkali Creek Trailhead

SPEARFISH RANGER DISTRICT,
BLACK HILLS NATIONAL FOREST

Description: A rugged and remote trip through the northeast corner of the Black Hills. Includes an option loop hike via Elk Creek Canyon and an optional mountain bike loop via BHNF Road 139.

General Location: Two miles south of Sturgis, South Dakota.

Highlight: The sheer limestone cliffs of Elk Creek Canyon.

Access: To reach *Dalton Lake* from Nemo, drive 0.5 mile north to paved BHNF Road 26. Follow Road 26 north for 3.6 miles to BHNF Road 224. Turn right on Road 224, and drive 4.1 miles, past the Dalton Lake Campground, to the trailhead. To reach the *Elk Creek Trailhead* from Sturgis, take Exit 32 off Interstate 90. Turn south and follow the signs for Wonderland Cave on BHNF Road 170. At 3.2 miles, turn south onto gravel BHNF Road 135 for 2.8 miles. Then turn left onto dirt BHNF Road 168 and drive 2.4 miles to the trailhead. Elk Creek Trailhead can also be reached from I-90 on exit 40. Turn south on the frontage road for 2.3 miles, then turn west onto unmarked BHNF Road 168. Drive 5.5 miles on road 168 to reach a four-way junction before Bethlehem Cave. The trailhead is 1.5 miles farther on Road 168, which is signed "road closed in one mile."

Distance: This section is 23.3 miles one way. A 10.6-mile loop hike can be made by connecting the Centennial Trail with an off-trail scramble through Elk Creek Canyon from the Elk Creek Trailhead.

Maps: Trails Illustrated Black Hills National Forest Northeast and pages 49, 52, 54, and 56.

One of the most isolated sections of the Centennial Trail lies between Dalton Lake and the Black Hills National Cemetery. Within this isolation is Elk Creek Canyon, and perhaps the wildest and most rugged hiking in the Black Hills. Hikers can combine the main Centennial Trail and a rugged bushwhack along the floor of Elk Creek Canyon to form an exciting loop.

From the Dalton Lake Trailhead, cross Little Elk Creek and turn north onto the slope above the creek. The Centennial Trail follows a mix of dirt roads and trails until it reaches a spring and stock tank. Just beyond, at 1.0 mile, turn north onto gravel BHNF Road 704. At 1.5 miles, where Road 704 turns east out of the gulch, continue northwest on a dirt road. Another side road leads west at 1.9 miles, where the dirt road up the main fork is blocked by sandstone boulders.

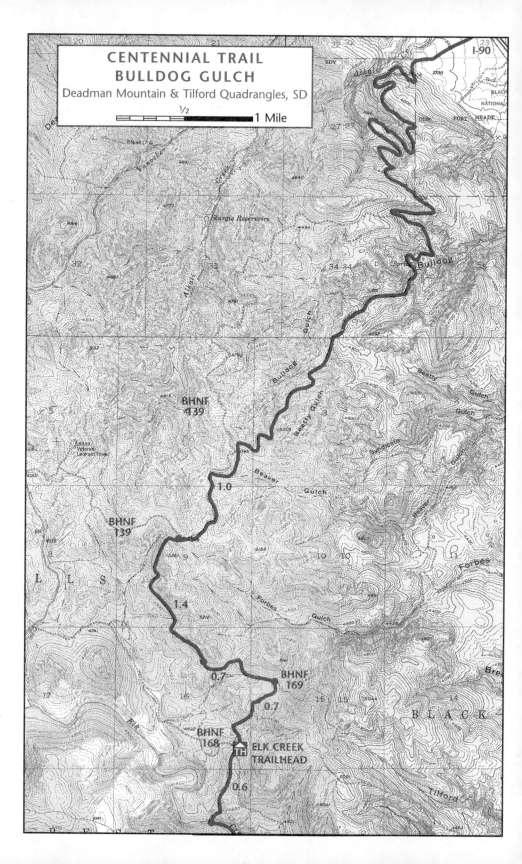

CENTENNIAL TRAIL
BULLDOG GULCH
Deadman Mountain & Tilford Quadrangles, SD

½   1 Mile

At 2.2 miles, go right at a fork to begin a relocation built in 1995. At 2.6 miles the Centennial Trail rejoins BHNF Road 704. Follow Road 704 to 3.2 miles, then turn north on a series of switchbacks down a steep slope. Cross a small gully before reaching a junction with BHNF Road 702 at 4.7 miles.

The Centennial Trail no longer descends directly into Elk Creek Canyon, but swings west in a long detour. Continue west on BHNF Road 702 and enter a recently logged area. Go straight through a four-way intersection at a sign for the Big Elk management area. Pass a spring on the south side adjacent to a stone foundation and crumbling log cabin. Then pass side roads to the right, left, then right again in an area with few trail markers. Pass one more side road leading south before reaching the Wonderland Cave Road (BHNF Road 137) at 6.2 miles. Paved BHNF Road 26 is 1.0 mile southwest on Road 137.

Cross BHNF Road 137 and follow a logging road along the crest of a ridge to the north. Descend the ridge to reach an old road along contour at 7.0 miles. Hike west along the road for about 100 feet and then follow a trail down switchbacks to the bottom of beautiful Dry Elk Gulch. Head east down Dry Elk Gulch, then climb steeply up the north side. Gain the crest of the north ridge, then descend again to reach the bottom of Elk Creek Canyon, just below Bethlehem Cave at 9.6 miles. The original route of the Centennial Trail continued directly down the canyon from this point.

Continue up the canyon along a long-abandoned railroad grade beside the creek bed. At 10.8 miles turn north up a side draw. Follow a trail and old dirt road to reach the Elk Creek Trailhead and BHNF Road 168 at 11.4 miles.

From the Elk Creek Trailhead, follow a jeep road north to 11.5 miles, then turn left onto a trail. Climb over a small divide and follow old logging roads north to reach dirt BHNF Road 169 at 12.1 miles. At 12.3 miles, turn north onto a grassy road and then left onto a trail along contour. The trail merges with a rough dirt road at 12.8 miles and continues generally north.

Leave the contour road by taking three consecutive right turns ending up at a BHNF Road 139 at 14.2 miles. Follow Road 139 to 15.2 miles at the head of Beaver Creek. Follow a 1995 relocation down the south side of Bulldog Gulch, across a slope then along the bottom of the gulch. Turn north and follow a gravel road to return to BHNF Road 139 at 18.2 miles. Cross Road 139 and follow a difficult and intricate section of new trail to the boundary of the Fort Meade National Recreation Area at 22.2 miles.

From the Fort Meade Boundary, hike northeast on an overgrown

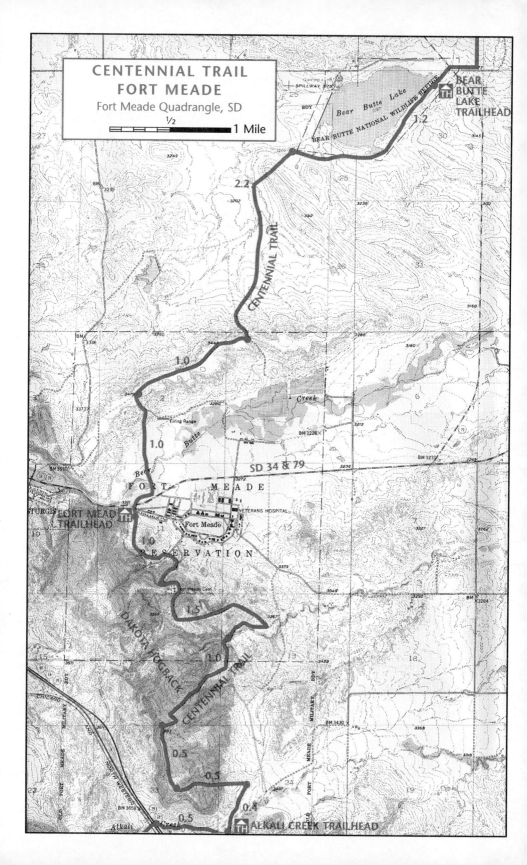

two-track road to a culvert under Interstate 90 at 22.8 miles. Continue east through a cut in the Dakota Hogback to reach the Alkali Creek Trailhead at 23.3 miles.

Two loop trips are possible in conjunction with this section of the Centennial Trail. The *Elk Creek Canyon Route* is a rugged off-trail scramble that begins at the junction with BHNF Road 702 4.7 miles north of the Dalton Lake Campground. Descend a steep series of switchbacks down obliterated trail north to the floor of Elk Creek Canyon in about 0.6 mile. Turn west to hike up the canyon. For the next 1.5 miles the route winds through the deep canyon of Elk Creek. There is no pretense of a trail here, only a route along, across and finally in the creek bed. High water every spring washes away any footway that develops. The canyon is choked with oak, ash and willows. Steep limestone cliffs rise from the creek bed isolating the canyon floor. The bushwhack through the cobbles and boulders in the creek bed is very slow. Elk Creek is usually flowing at the east end, but is usually dry at the junction with the main Centennial Trail at the west end. From the Dalton Lake Trailhead, the Elk Creek Canyon route and Centennial Trail form a 13.6-mile round trip.

Anyone who has seen Elk Creek will find it difficult to imagine that a railroad once ran through the bottom of the canyon. But, in 1881, Homestake Mining Company started construction on a line down the canyon that reached Piedmont in 1890. The line was built to supply the underground gold mine in Lead with timber, but eventually added freight and passenger service. After frequent damage from fire and flood, the line was destroyed by a flood caused by heavy rain and melting snow in 1907. A few rough ties remain on the grade at the west end of the canyon, and one old rail survives near the mouth of Dry Elk Gulch.

Mountain bike riders seeking a long, rugged loop can ride the *Bulldog Gulch Route* that combines the Centennial Trail with BHNF Road 139. From the junction of the Centennial Trail and Road 139 14.2 miles north of Dalton Lake, turn north and follow Road 139 north along the Alkali Creek–Bulldog Gulch divide for 3.8 miles back to the Centennial Trail in Bulldog Gulch. The first 2.7 miles are smooth with rolling terrain that is perfect for mountain bikes, but the next 1.1 miles of this road is rough and rocky. An added feature of the ridge top route are the cool breezes that seldom penetrate into the gulches. Several overlooks along the ridge provide views southwest to the radio towers on top of Veterans Peak, the most prominent summit in this part of the Black Hills. From the Alkali Creek Trailhead, this is a 18.9-mile loop ride.

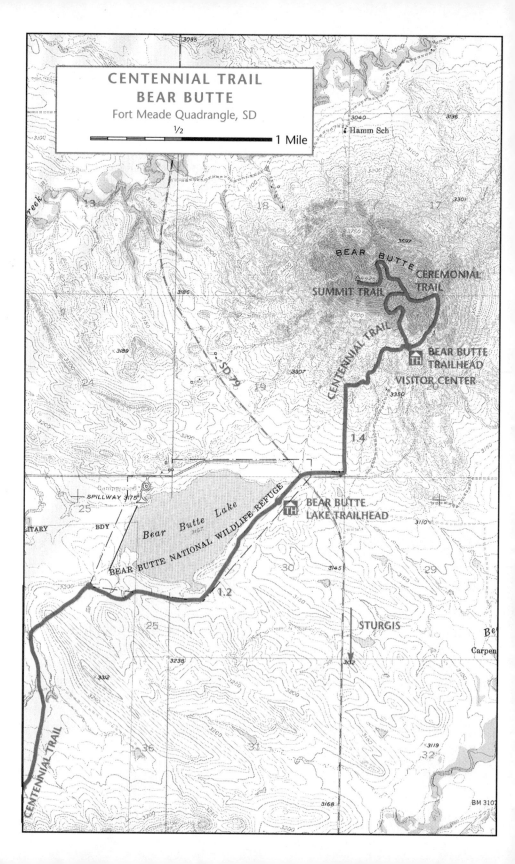

CENTENNIAL TRAIL
BEAR BUTTE
Fort Meade Quadrangle, SD

½   1 Mile

Hamm Sch

BEAR BUTTE

CEREMONIAL TRAIL

SUMMIT TRAIL

CENTENNIAL TRAIL

BEAR BUTTE TRAILHEAD

VISITOR CENTER

1.4

SD 79

SPILLWAY

Campground

MILITARY

BDY

Bear Butte Lake

BEAR BUTTE NATIONAL WILDLIFE REFUGE

BEAR BUTTE LAKE TRAILHEAD

1.2

STURGIS

Carpen

CENTENNIAL TRAIL

BM 3107

The Black Hills National Forest plans to relocate the Centennial Trail between BHNF Road 702 at 4.7 miles, and Elk Creek Canyon at 9.6 miles. The new route will hug the canyon rim and have far more overlooks than the current route. The new route will have a gentler grade from rim to canyon bottom. Pending funding, this work is planned for 1999 or 2000.

A hike north from Dalton Lake illustrates the diversity of geology in the Black Hills. Downstream from Dalton Lake is a small outcrop of Archean Little Elk Granite. At 2.5 billion years old, these are some of the oldest rocks in the Black Hills. To the north, around Elk Creek, the bedrock is Paleozoic sedimentary rocks, mostly massive beds of gently dipping Paha Sapa limestone. North of the Elk Creek Trailhead are Tertiary igneous quartz latite rocks of the Vanocker Laccolith, which are some of the youngest rocks in the Black Hills.

The Bulldog Gulch–Beaver Park area has been only lightly logged, leaving a forest of ponderosa pine, aspen and oak. The purple berries of Oregon grape are especially common in the understory. This corner of the Black Hills is steep and very rugged. Off-trail hiking along the bottoms of the gulches is difficult, but rewarding. BHNF Road 139 forms the northwest boundary of the Beaver Park RARE II area, a proposed Wilderness.

~

Alkali Creek Trailhead to Bear Butte Lake Trailhead
BLM, FORT MEADE RECREATION AREA

Description: A moderate hike or mountain bike ride from the Dakota Hogback to Bear Butte Lake.

General Location: One mile east of Sturgis, South Dakota.

Highlight: Outstanding views of Bear Butte and the Black Hills.

Access: For the *Alkali Creek Trailhead*, take Exit 34 from Interstate 90 to the frontage road east of the highway. Follow a gravel road 0.3 mile north into Fort Meade to the trailhead. The *Fort Meade Trailhead* is located one mile east of Sturgis, south of South Dakota 34, just inside the Fort Meade boundary. To reach the *Bear Butte Lake Trailhead*, drive three miles east of Sturgis on South Dakota 34, then three miles north on South Dakota 79. Turn left onto a gravel road which starts opposite of the entrance to Bear Butte State Park. The trailhead is 0.2 mile down this road.

Distance: 10.3 miles one way.

Maps: Trails Illustrated Black Hills Northeast and pages 56 and 58.

The Fort Meade section of the Centennial Trail offers hikers and mountain bike riders two distinct areas. To the south of South Dakota 34, the trail follows the high sandstone ridge known as the Dakota Hogback. In early spring this is some of the best mountain bike riding in the Black Hills. The sandy soil dries quickly and the elevation is too low to hold significant snowfall. This area can be ridden when much of the northern Black Hills is still snow-covered or muddy. North of South Dakota 34 lies the only true prairie along the Centennial Trail. This section can be impassable when wet, but is usually clear by late spring.

From the Alkali Creek Trailhead, cross the gravel Fort Meade Road and head north through the prairie along the east side of the Dakota Hogback. After 0.4 mile turn west and climb steeply on a rough trail for 0.5 mile to the top of the Hogback Ridge. Catch your breath and then head north along the ridge top, enjoying views to the west of Bulldog Gulch and Beaver Park. Turn northeast off the ridge at 1.4 miles and descend on a rutted two-track jeep road to intersect the Fort Meade Road at 2.4 miles.

Cross the gravel road and follow a two-track road, first northeast along the bottom of a small draw, then northwest up a steep hillside. The hilltop offers commanding views of Fort Meade and Bear Butte to the north. Cross a steep gulch just before reaching the Fort Meade Cemetery. Just beyond the cemetery at 3.9 miles, the Centennial Trail skirts the gravel road once more. Reach the Fort Meade Trailhead at 4.9 miles through an old barracks or stable area.

After leaving the Fort Meade Trailhead, the Centennial Trail crosses South Dakota 34 and 79, crosses Bear Butte Creek, crosses a gate and reaches the top of a gravel-covered hill at 5.9 miles. The trail follows the flat ridge top northeast and crosses another gate at 6.9 miles. Leave the ridge at a small saddle and follow a faint path north to a gate at 9.1 miles that marks the boundary between Fort Meade Recreation Area and Bear Butte State Park. The path is a portion of the historic Bismarck–Deadwood Trail. The Centennial Trail here is marked only by carsonite posts that are easily knocked down by cattle. If you lose the trail, just continue generally towards the fence that marks the boundary, and then head toward the gate.

Once into Bear Butte State Park, go east to the often muddy dirt access road at 9.3 miles. Follow the road to 10.0 miles where a trail turns east to reach the Bear Butte Lake Trailhead at 10.3 miles. A small area around the lake is maintained as a National Wildlife Refuge.

Once the home of a major cavalry outpost, Fort Meade now houses a veterans' hospital named in honor of Civil War hero Major General George B. Meade. Also on the grounds is a museum dedicated to the story of the western cavalry. The town of Sturgis was founded in 1878 in the shadow of the fort's protection and is named after Lt. Jack Sturgis, who died at the Little Bighorn under the command of Lieutenant Colonel George Armstrong Custer. The Bureau of Land Management manages 6,700 acres of the former Fort Meade Military Reservation as the Fort Meade Recreation Area. The improved gravel road through Fort Meade is designated as a National Backcountry Byway. There is a self-guided tour brochure for the byway.

The ridge known as the Dakota Hogback circles the entire Black Hills and is separated from the hills by the Red Valley. Rapid erosion of the soft red-colored rocks of the Spearfish formation created the Red Valley. The hard sandstone of the Dakota formation resists erosion, consequently the sandstone outcrops form ridges.

The Alkali Creek Trailhead contains a six-unit fee campground with water and toilets open from May 15 to September 30. The other trailheads have parking only. There is a campground on the north side of Bear Butte Lake within the state park. No drinking water is found along the trail.

Any trip on the Centennial Trail north of South Dakota 34 and 79 requires preparation for the sun and wind typical of the prairie. Mid-afternoon summer thunderstorms are common.

Bear Butte Lake Trailhead to
Bear Butte Summit
BEAR BUTTE STATE PARK

Description: A moderate hike to the north end of the Centennial Trail on top of Bear Butte.

General Location: Nine miles northeast of Sturgis, South Dakota.

Highlight: An exhilarating climb to the northern end of the Centennial Trail.

Access: Drive three miles east of Sturgis on South Dakota 34, then three miles north on South Dakota 79 to the park entrance. The trailhead is located past the visitor center at the top of the loop road. From South Dakota 79 turn left on the gravel road to Bear Butte Lake and drive 0.2 mile to the Bear Butte Lake Trailhead.

Distance: 5.9 miles round trip from the Bear Butte Lake Trailhead or 3.1 miles round trip from the upper trailhead. This hike includes the final 3.0 miles of the Centennial Trail.

Maps: Trails Illustrated Black Hills Northeast and page 58.

Bear Butte is the most interesting of the short summit hikes in the Black Hills region and the climb to the top is one of the most popular hikes in the area.

From the Bear Butte Lake Trailhead head east 0.2 mile on the gravel road to South Dakota 79. Then follow the park road on the north side to 0.4 mile. Turn north away from the road and begin climbing a two-track dirt road which parallels a fence. Cross a gate at 0.7 mile and reach another gate at 0.9 mile. The second gate is the north limit of horse travel on the Centennial Trail. From the gate, climb to the paved park road at 1.2 miles and follow the road to the Bear Butte Trailhead at 1.4 miles. This trailhead is the north limit for mountain bike travel on the Centennial Trail.

Most day hikers will skip the preceding 1.4 miles and begin their climb of Bear Butte from the upper trailhead. The Centennial Trail follows the west side of the Ceremonial Trail to 2.15 miles, then the Summit Trail to 3.0 miles to finish at the top of Bear Butte. Observation platforms are located at the junction of the Ceremonial and Summit trails, at the summit and at an overlook 0.45 mile from the top. The climb is persistently steep and the summit a worthy end to the region's premiere hiking trail.

Bear Butte is located outside of the Dakota Hogback, the prominent ridge that circles the main part of the Black Hills. Thus it offers a unique perspective. Deadman Mountain, Custer Peak, Terry Peak and Spearfish Peak are the highest summits visible. At low light, a series of "circus rings" are apparent to the southwest. These rings are formed by the uplift of more resistant strata during the intrusion of the igneous rocks that formed Bear Butte. The rings are exposed by erosion like the layers of an onion with the top sliced off.

The *Ceremonial Trail* forms a loop along the southern slopes of Bear Butte. Although the east loop is longer than the west loop, most hikers use the east loop to return to the parking area. The Ceremonial Trail was designated a National Recreational Trail by Congress in 1971 for its scenic, historic, and recreational opportunities. Bear Butte was likewise registered as a National Landmark in 1965 by the U.S. Department of the Interior.

A free self-guiding interpretive booklet for the Ceremonial Trail highlights the natural and cultural history of the area. The booklet is particularly helpful in the spring and summer when woody plants, wildflowers, and grasses are in bloom and easy to identify.

The South Dakota Department of Game, Fish, and Parks maintains a visitor center below the trailhead. Displays focus on the geology of the mountain and the rich culture of the Plains Indian people for whom Bear Butte is a religious shrine. The park also maintains a small bison herd on the prairie below the visitor center. In winter, park trails may be closed due to the build up of ice and snow on the steep slopes.

Many Indian people continue to come to Bear Butte to participate in religious ceremonies. Prayer flags tied to trees are a common sight along the trails. Please do not disturb them. Also, to avoid conflicts with ceremonies, hiking off-trail is prohibited in the park. Hikers are asked to avoid making unnecessary noise and to refrain from taking photographs or video taping individuals along the trail or near the camp area.

In the summer of 1996 an 856-acre fire, which began in the religious use area, burned across the slopes of Bear Butte. Over 90 percent of the trees, mostly ponderosa pine, were killed. The fire consumed about two-thirds of the trail and burned steps, railings, and an observation platform. The trails have been restored, but the forested slopes, which are too steep for salvage logging, still bear the scars of the fire.

Trails in the park are short, but they are also steep, rocky and have numerous switchbacks. However, the trails are suitable for family groups with children. It is easy to gauge your progress while climbing, and the interpretive sites offer an excuse to stop and learn while resting. A family group should be able to hike to the top and complete the Ceremonial Trail in two to three hours. No water or toilet facilities can be found along the trail, but they are available at the trailhead or visitor center from May to mid-September.

A park entrance fee is required to enter Bear Butte State Park. A daily permit costs $2.00 per person, 12 years of age or older. An annual entrance permit costs $20.

Wind Cave National Park and Jewel Cave National Monument

Rankin Ridge Trail
WIND CAVE NATIONAL PARK

Description: An easy loop hike to the tower on the highest point in Wind Cave National Park.
General Location: Thirteen miles north of Hot Springs, South Dakota.
Highlight: Interpretive guide and summit views.
Access: From Hot Springs, drive north on U.S. 385 to South Dakota 87. Drive north on South Dakota 87 for 5.2 miles then turn east onto the Rankin Ridge Road. Follow the Rankin Ridge Road 0.4 mile to a parking area.
Distance: A 1.0-mile loop.
Maps: Trails Illustrated Black Hills Southeast and page 26.

Rankin Ridge is the most popular trail on the surface of Wind Cave National Park. The trail is short, easy and suitable for families with small children. There is an interpretive guide for the trail, which is keyed to numbered posts along the trail. The guide is an excellent means of educating yourself and your children about the natural history of the park.

To follow the numbered posts, hike the loop clockwise. The lookout tower is about half-way along. Be sure to climb the tower to fully appreciate the view from Rankin Ridge. Beyond the tower, the trail follows the access road back to the parking area.

The interpretive guide provides details of the ecology of the ponderosa pine forest atop Rankin Ridge and the geology of the granite that forms the ridge.

Although Wind Cave has an excellent trail system, the hiking trails will always be a secondary attraction in the park. The National Park

Service offers five different tours of the cave in the summer. The *Garden of Eden Tour* is the shortest, easiest and best for small children. The *Fairgrounds Tour* highlights the larger rooms found on the tour routes. The *Natural Entrance Tour* is the only one that does not access the cave by the elevator. The *Candlelight Tour* lets visitors see the cave as it was before electric lights were installed along the popular cave routes. This tour requires reservations and is limited to groups of ten, since it does not follow a paved path.

For the adventurous, there is the *Caving Tour*. This four-hour trip visits an undeveloped part of the cave and introduces novices to the basics of safe caving. Special equipment is used as much of the trip involves crawling and wriggling through narrow passages. The trip is offered only once a day in the summer and reservations are needed. The advance planning is well worth the effort because the caving tour is perhaps as spectacular an afternoon as you can spend in the Black Hills. Year-round temperature in the cave is about 53 degrees, so many visitors often hike in the cooler mornings and take a cave tour in the afternoon to avoid the summer heat.

Bison Flats to Lookout Point Trails
WIND CAVE NATIONAL PARK

Description: A prairie hike through the southern part of Wind Cave National Park.
General Location: Six miles north of Hot Springs, South Dakota.
Highlight: Bison and prairie dog towns.
Access: The *Gobbler Pass Trailhead* is a pullout at the south park boundary on U.S. 385 which is 3.9 miles south of the Visitors Center. The hike ends at the Centennial Trail *Norbeck Trailhead*, which is a small parking area on the east side of South Dakota 87, located 0.6 mile north of the junction of South Dakota 87 and U.S. 385.
Distance: 7.7 miles one way.
Maps: Trails Illustrated Black Hills Southeast and page 67.

The Bison Flats Trail crosses open prairie at the south end of Wind Cave National Park. It's a hike for those who love open spaces, grassland and wildlife, and for those undeterred by bright sun and strong wind. The Bison Flats Trail begins by following the park boundary east

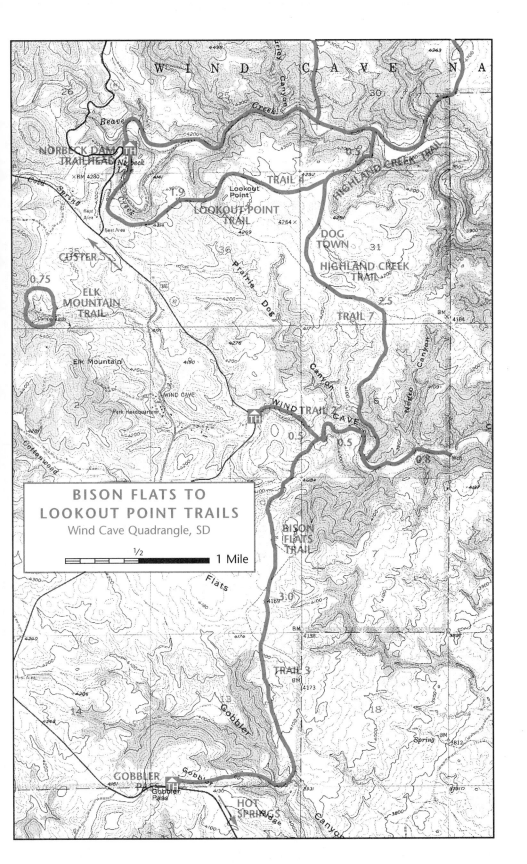

BISON FLATS TO
LOOKOUT POINT TRAILS
Wind Cave Quadrangle, SD

½   1 Mile

into Gobbler Canyon where deer, rose hips and poison ivy flourish. The trail then exits the canyon to the north and continues to follow the park boundary along a poorly-defined trail.

Once reaching the broad top of Bison Flats, pass through a prairie dog town. The dogs have dug up some quartz pebbles indicating that Tertiary-age gravel deposits overlie the limestone bedrock here. Enjoy views north to the tower on top of Rankin Ridge, at the park's north end, and Mt. Coolidge, in Custer State Park. Descend into Wind Cave Canyon at 3.0 miles where the Bison Flats Trail ends at the intersection with the *Wind Cave Canyon Trail*. Turn east to follow Wind Cave Canyon for 0.5 mile to the junction with the *Highland Creek Trail*. For a shorter trip you have the option of turning left on Wind Cave Canyon to reach the Wind Cave Canyon Trailhead on U.S. 385 in 0.5 miles.

To continue to Lookout Point, turn north on the Highland Creek Trail and climb out of Wind Cave Canyon in the welcome shelter of ponderosa pine groves. Of the park's 28,000 acres, 75 percent is mixed grass prairie and only 25 percent ponderosa pine forest. Once back on the prairie, the route crosses a small prairie dog town and then a larger one. Besides the ever-vigilant dogs, bison, who love to roll in dust around the burrows, are usually found here. Keep an eye out for coyotes and part of the park's small herd of skittish pronghorn. After hiking 2.5 miles north, reach the junction with *Lookout Point Trail*. To complete the trip, hike west 1.9 miles on Lookout Point. The Lookout Point Trail has been relocated so that it crosses Beaver Creek, at a perfect spot for cooling hot dusty feet, and ends at the *Centennial Trail* Norbeck Trailhead.

Bison Flats is one of Wind Cave's lesser used trails. The park plans to maintain the trail at a lower level compared to more travelled trails such as the Centennial Trail.

Highland Creek & Lookout Point Trails
WIND CAVE NATIONAL PARK

Description: A moderate hike through the northern part of Wind Cave National Park.
General Location: Eleven miles north of Hot Springs, South Dakota.
Highlight: Wildlife along the way includes bison and elk.

Access: From the intersection of U.S. 385 and South Dakota 87 turn north on South Dakota 87. Drive 8.0 miles, nearly to the park boundary, and turn east onto gravel NPS Road 5. Drive 1.3 miles to the Centennial Trail Highland Creek Trailhead and then 1.4 miles farther to the start of the Highland Creek Trail.

Distance: This hike is 7.8 miles one way and requires a car shuttle. Alternatively, this route can be combined with the Centennial Trail to form a 14 mile loop.

Maps: Trails Illustrated Black Hills Southeast and pages 26 and 28.

The Centennial and Highland Creek trails form the backbone of the trail system in Wind Cave National Park. Because of its length, Highland Creek is the most diverse trail in the park, traversing prairie, forest and riparian habitats as well as a prairie dog town. Combine the Highland Creek and Lookout Point trails to make a superb one-day trip.

Begin hiking south from the trailhead. After about 0.5 mile, begin to descend from the prairie toward the valley of Highland Creek. Cross Highland Creek near a prairie dog town where you may also see bison.

Loop around the north and west sides of two side draws to Highland Creek as the old road follows a crest of a ridge. Descend south from the ridge to reach the junction with the *Sanctuary Trail* in the bottom of a side draw at 3.3 miles. From this intersection, the *Centennial Trail* is 1.5 miles northwest.

To continue south on the Highland Creek Trail turn left. The trail next climbs to the divide between Highland and Beaver creeks. Reach a corner of the park, turn southwest and descend into Limestone Canyon. Follow Limestone Canyon a short distance downstream to reach Beaver Creek at 5.0 miles.

Hike upstream along Beaver Creek, making one crossing just before the trail leaves the south side of the valley at 5.4 miles. At this point, an unmarked route leads upstream 0.5 mile to the Centennial Trail. Climb to a prairie, which is the north limit of Bison Flats. Then continue west on the *Lookout Point Trail* from a junction at 5.9 miles near a prairie dog town. The Lookout Point Trail reaches South Dakota 87 at 7.8 miles at the Norbeck Dam Centennial Trail Trailhead.

Along the Highland Creek Trail you'll see prairie dogs and bison and will probably see mule deer and elk if you are quiet and careful. Forty species of grasses have been identified in the mixed grass prairie of the park. Blue gramma is the most common and western wheatgrass, little bluestem and threadleaf sedge are also abundant.

While much of the original trails in Wind Cave National Park followed two-track dirt roads, the park is in the process of rehabilitating the trails to footpaths. Most trail junctions are marked with large posts with trail numbers carved in the top. Cross-country travel in the park is easy, so carry your topographic map with you.

To camp overnight in the backcountry camping zone, which is bounded by SD 87, NPS Road 5, the Highland Creek Trail and Beaver Creek, you must obtain a free Backcountry Use Permit from the Visitors Center or a Centennial Trail access point. All plants, animals and cultural features in the park are protected and cannot be disturbed. No open fires are allowed and there is no drinking water in the backcountry. Campsites must be located at least .25 mile from any maintained roads and must be at least 100 feet from water sources or archaeological sites.

~

Other Wind Cave National Park Trails

The *Elk Mountain Nature Trail* is a .75-mile interpretive loop located next to the Elk Mountain Campground. The interpretive guide focuses on the ecology of the prairie in Wind Cave National Park. See map on page 67.

The *Cold Brook Canyon Trail* leads 1.4 miles from U.S. 385 to the park's western boundary. It follows an overgrown dirt road along the bed of Cold Brook. The Park Service hopes to someday extend this trail to form a loop.

The *Wind Cave Canyon Trail* leads 1.8 miles east from U.S. 385 to the park's eastern boundary. The trail is still used by park vehicles to access a pumphouse. Still, the trail is a favorite of birders and the section from 0.5 to 1.0 mile is a useful connector between the Bison Flats and Highland Creek trails. See map on page 67.

The *Sanctuary Trail* leads 3.6 miles from South Dakota 87 into the heart of the park. Try it if you're looking for bison or elk. The trail intersects the Centennial Trail at 2.1 miles, and the Highland Creek Trail at 3.6 miles. See map on page 26.

The *Boland Ridge Trail* leads to the remote northeast corner of the park. It winds 2.7 miles from NPS Road 6 along a route that sees more bison than humans and may be hard to follow. Bull bison near the ridge tend to be aggressive and have treed NPS rangers. The Park Service plans to shorten this trail so that it ends at the ridge top about 1.4 miles from NPS Road 6.

Canyons Trail

JEWEL CAVE NATIONAL MONUMENT

Description: The Canyons and Walk-on-the-Roof trails are the only hiking trails at Jewel Cave National Monument.

General Location: Twelve miles west of Custer, South Dakota.

Highlight: The limestone cliffs in Hell and Lithograph canyons and the historic entrance at Jewel Cave.

Access: From the junction of U.S. 16 and 385 on the west side of Custer, drive 12.0 miles west on U.S. 16 to the entrance of Jewel Cave National Monument. The loop can be accessed from either the Visitor Center or the Historic Area.

Distance: A 3.5-mile loop.

Maps: See page 72.

For a small monument, Jewel Cave is blessed with many attractions. The cave contains over 118 miles of passageways and is now the third longest cave known in the world. On the surface, the Canyons Trail and Walk-on-the-Roof trails are a perfect complement to the wonders of the cave below.

Start with a Walk-on-the-Roof. This .25-mile interpretive trail provides an excellent introduction to the ponderosa pine forest above the cave, and is a great way to pass some time while waiting for your cave tour. Be sure to pick up a copy of the interpretive guide at the visitors center before starting your hike.

The Canyons Trail starts and ends on the Walk-on-the-Roof. To walk the loop counterclockwise, start by the sign near the visitor center restrooms. The trails soon split with the Canyons Trail leading towards Jewel Cave's Historic Entrance. At the Historic area, pass a picnic area and historic cabin before following a concrete walkway to the Historic Entrance, which is closed by a steel gate. Next descend the limestone cliffs to the floor of Hell Canyon. Hell Canyon is an easy walk through pine and birch. Look for a small wood-framed tunnel on the west wall of the canyon. Near a sharp U-turn to the left look for smooth worn

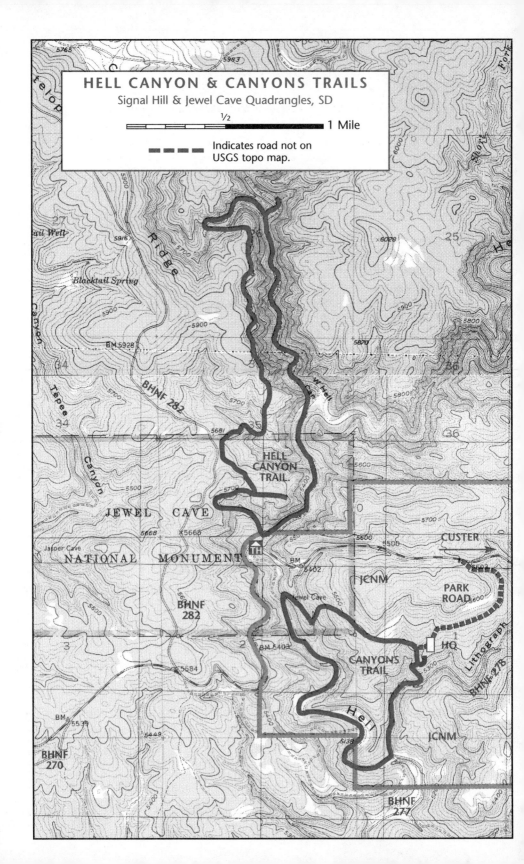

HELL CANYON & CANYONS TRAILS

Signal Hill & Jewel Cave Quadrangles, SD

½ | 1 Mile

– – – – Indicates road not on
USGS topo map.

HELL
CANYON
TRAIL.

JEWEL CAVE

NATIONAL MONUMENT

JCNM

CUSTER

PARK
ROAD

HQ

CANYONS
TRAIL

Hell

JCNM

BHNF
282

BHNF
270

BHNF
277

Blacktail Spring

Jasper Cave

Ridge

Canyon

Tepee Canyon

stones that look like river rock. These rocks were indeed left by ancient rivers, during deposition of the Tertiary Age White River Formation.

Reach a gate across the gravel Lithograph Canyon Road (BHNF Road 278). The trail follows the road below sheer 30-foot walls for 0.5 mile before turning sharply left onto a footpath. The last .25 mile climbs steeply to the visitors center. At the top of the sixth switchback rejoin the Wall-on-the-Roof near the observation platform.

Only the claustrophobic will visit the monument without going into the cave. Three different tours are offered with a full schedule in summer and less frequent tours out of season. The *Scenic Tour* enters the cave by an elevator shaft and follows a paved path with 723 stairs. It is a 0.5 mile, one hour and twenty minute introduction to Jewel Cave, its history and formations. The *Historic Candlelight Tour* uses the historic entrance and hand-held candle lanterns to give visitors an experience similar to that of early tourists. The *Spelunking Tour* is a difficult four-hour introduction to caving that requires advance reservations.

Jewel Cave is unusual among caves for more than just its size. Many of the cave's rooms are coated with jewel-like pointed crystals of calcite which probably formed during a time when the cave was filled with water. The lure of the thick coat of crystals led to early commercial development of the cave and its eventual protection by President Theodore Roosevelt. Flowstone, stalactites, and frostwork are some of the other underground cave formations visitors can see.

Much of the early exploration of Jewel Cave was done by a couple who originally came to the Black Hills to rock climb. Herb and Jan Conn first tried caving as a winter alternative to climbing. Soon the thrill of opening new, undiscovered passages became as compelling as establishing new climbing routes in their beloved Needles. From 1959 through the 1970s they helped map more than sixty miles of tortuous passages and helped transform Jewel Cave from a seemingly small cave to the third longest known in the world.

Custer State Park

Prairie Trail

Description: A short, easy loop hike through the grasslands in the southern part of Custer State Park.
General Location: Eighteen miles southeast of Custer, South Dakota.
Highlight: Interpretive guide and bison.
Access: From Custer, drive east on U.S. 16A to South Dakota 87. Turn south on South Dakota 87 and drive to the southwest end of the Wildlife Loop Road (CSP Road 1). Drive 4.5 miles east on the Wildlife Loop Road and park at a small lot on the south side of the road.
Distance: Custer State Park lists the loop as 3.5 miles around, but it is probably closer to 2.5 miles.
Maps: Trails Illustrated Black Hills Southeast and page 28.

Most hikers in Custer State Park follow the popular trails that leave from the parking area at Sylvan Lake. For those seeking solitude, and different terrain, the park offers a variety of short loop trails that are ideal for family outings. The most unusual of these trails is the Prairie Trail.

Our route starts by crossing the valley of the south fork of Lame Johnny Creek, and then climbs to Hay Flats. The trail then descends to Flynn Creek before the loop closes just south of the parking area. Hikers must climb two fences on stiles. The fences are used to separate winter and summer pastures for the park's bison herd.

The Custer State Park Interpretive Guide for the Prairie Trail is an invaluable addition to your hike. It is available from the Peter Norbeck Visitor Center or the Blue Bell entrance station. Numbered posts along the trail are keyed to specific features that are discussed in the booklet. The trail is marked by these posts and generally follows a well-defined footway.

The Prairie Trail is an excellent place to study the dry grasslands of the southern Black Hills. Wheatgrass, buffalograss, green needlegrass, bluestems and grammas are the most common grasses. Scattered groves of ponderosa pine have begun to invade the plains grasslands.

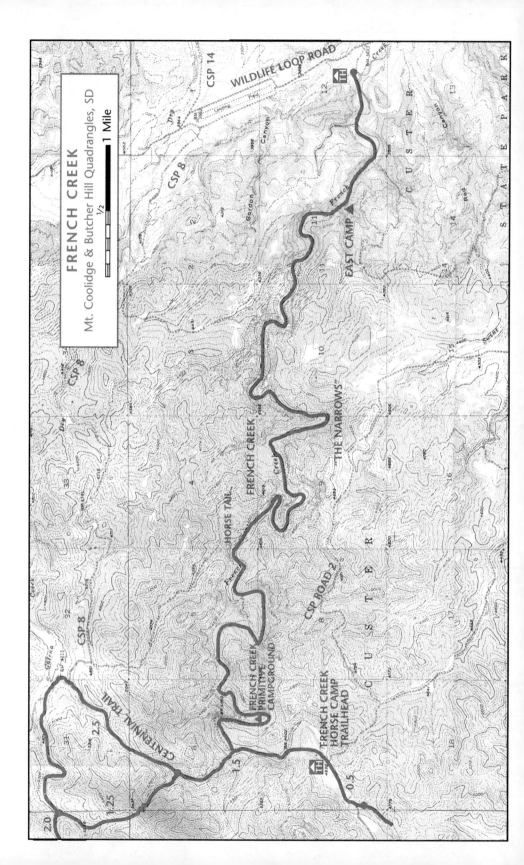

FRENCH CREEK

Mt. Coolidge & Butcher Hill Quadrangles, SD

½ 1 Mile

Bur oak, the only oak species native to the Black Hills, is found near Flynn Creek along with green ash and American elm.

"Edge Areas," where forests meet grasslands, are biologically very productive and are often the best places for observing Custer State Park's diverse wildlife population. Western meadowlarks and black-billed magpies are common birds seen and heard along the trail. Mule deer, white-tailed deer, pronghorn, raccoon and coyotes are common in the southern part of the park.

Lucky hikers may spot part of the park's bison or elk herds. Elk will generally flee from people, but bison should be avoided. They are huge, fast and not always as docile as they appear.

Hikers should be prepared for the grasslands environment. This preparation should include protection from the sun and a good supply of water. Afternoon storms are common; be sure to take cover in the event of lightning, but do not use trees for shelter in an electrical storm.

French Creek Natural Area

Description: A one- or two-day off-trail hike along beautiful French Creek.
General Location: Ten miles southeast of Custer, South Dakota.
Highlight: The high, sheer walls of the narrows.
Access: From Custer, drive east on U.S. 16A. To reach the *West Trailhead*, turn south on South Dakota 87 and drive 4.8 miles to Blue Bell Resort. From the resort drive 2.6 miles east on CSP Road 4 to a marked trailhead. To reach the *East Trailhead*, drive east on U.S. 16A to the Wildlife Loop Road and then 3.8 miles south to the trailhead. A car can be left at both ends for a one way hike. The hike is done west to east, which is downstream.
Distance: About 12.0 miles one way.
Maps: Trails Illustrated Black Hills Southeast and page 76.

Hidden in the center of Custer State Park is the French Creek Natural Area. Twenty-two hundred acres are managed to minimize human impact around the creek and its canyon. A hiking route meanders through woodlands alongside French Creek as the creek cuts through the eastern slope of the Black Hills to reach the grasslands beyond.

This hike is much different than trips on the maintained trails in Custer State Park. As a day hike, the journey can take up to eight hours. French Creek is one of the few hikes in South Dakota that is commonly done as an overnight backpack trip. Designated campsites for overnight stays are located near each end of the trail. The route through French Creek is not maintained between the two campsites. However, the way is obvious in most places and not difficult to follow until the narrows are reached.

Permits are necessary for overnight camping and the fee is two dollars a night. There is a limit of fifteen people per night per campsite. Advance reservations are not accepted, the sites are first come, first served. Camping is allowed only in the designated campsites and fires must be confined to established fire grates at the campsites. Water from French Creek must be treated before drinking. Poison ivy is very common along the route and prairie rattlesnakes are sighted occasionally.

The French Creek narrows are the highlight of the trip and easily the wildest area in Custer State Park. There is just enough challenge in walking and scrambling among the granite boulders to make the mouth of the narrows a little intimidating for hikers inexperienced at travelling off-trail. Working your way downstream alongside steep cliff walls without any sign of previous hikers gives a feeling of exploration that is rare in the Black Hills. High water may require that the narrows be bypassed by climbing up the steep canyon walls and following the creek from the plateaus above. At lower water, hikers can follow beside or in the creek, stopping occasionally to refresh themselves in some of the larger pools of water. A wide, steel aqueduct on a trestle above the canyon marks the normal limit of summer stream flow. Downstream, the water runs underground when it reaches permeable sedimentary rocks and the stream bed most often is dry.

Horseback riders use the western part of French Creek. There is a well-defined footway on the western side until Horse Trail 1 leaves French Creek Canyon to climb to the north rim from Lockwood Springs. Horseback riders are restricted to the marked trail in the Natural Area.

Wildlife watching is the other attraction of this walk. Bighorn sheep, elk, and occasionally bison can be seen along the French Creek. On one spring attempt to bypass the narrows, a friend and I came upon a newborn mountain goat kid and its mother. The kid wobbled as it tried to walk and still had its umbilical cord attached. With a little more vigor in our climb, we would have disturbed its birth. Instead, we took a few quick pictures and left the pair in peace. French

Creek is also noted for excellent bird watching and trout fishing. Bird species along French Creek include the lazuli bunting, black-and-white warbler and western tanager. Brook, brown and rainbow trout live in French Creek.

The first documented discovery of gold in the Black Hills was made along French Creek by miners with Custer's 1874 Black Hills Expedition. The diggings near the present town of Custer never amounted to much, but word of the find triggered a gold rush throughout the Black Hills. It is ironic that French Creek is now one of the few areas in the Black Hills to be managed as a wild area, and that the only sign of mining activity along the creek is a small tunnel driven into pegmatite.

Lovers Leap Trail

Description: A short loop trail suitable for family groups that leads to a spectacular overlook above Galena Creek.

General Location: Ten miles east of Custer, South Dakota.

Highlight: Spectacular views from the overlook.

Access: From Custer drive east on U.S. 16A to Custer State Park. Continue east on U.S. 16A to the Peter Norbeck Visitor Center. One-tenth of a mile east of the Visitor Center there is a parking area beside an old schoolhouse on the south side of the road. The trail begins beyond a sign, in the woods to the southeast.

Distance: Four-mile loop, moderately difficult.

Maps: Trails Illustrated Black Hills Southeast and page 80.

The massive granite cliffs above Galena Creek are the site of a Native American legend about two young lovers who leapt to their deaths. Today, hikers follow the popular Lovers Leap Trail to the cliffs for less compelling reasons. They are drawn by the spectacular views to the north of Harney Peak, the Needles and the Cathedral Spires and by the beautiful, quiet walk along Galena Creek.

The trail begins by climbing steeply along switchbacks to a ridge high above Grace Coolidge Creek. Don't panic, this is the only difficult part of the hike. Once on the ridge, the trail follows an old jeep trail west to a short side trail that leads to the overlook at Lovers Leap. From Lovers Leap, the trail continues to follow the ridge, which now

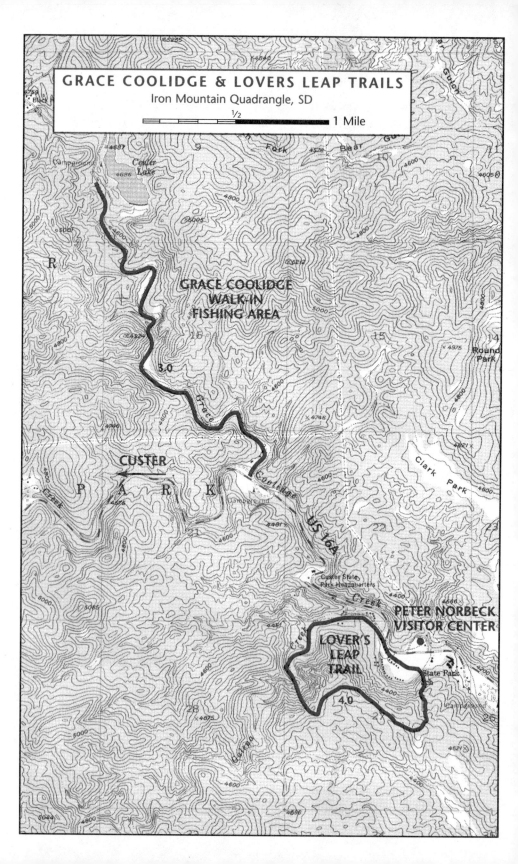

GRACE COOLIDGE & LOVERS LEAP TRAILS

Iron Mountain Quadrangle, SD

½   1 Mile

GRACE COOLIDGE
WALK-IN
FISHING AREA

CUSTER

P A R K

LOVER'S
LEAP
TRAIL

PETER NORBECK
VISITOR CENTER

trends southwest. A steep descent then brings hikers alongside Galena Creek. After crossing Galena Creek many times, the trail merges with a road along an unnamed tributary of Galena Creek. The gravel road leads to the Coolidge Inn. From the Inn, a walkway leads past the park chapel back to the old schoolhouse.

The trail is easy to follow. The footway is well worn and marked by black arrows set in orange blazes. There is no drinking water along the route, so carry water along with your lunch.

The Lovers Leap Trail is short and diverse enough to be suitable for family groups. The only difficult part is the climb at the beginning. The ridge-line hiking that follows is particularly scenic. The ponderosa pine dominated forest along the ridge is typical of Custer State Park. The west side of the ridge was burned in the 1988 Galena Fire. The fire began on July 4, 1988, and burned out of control for five days. Over 16,000 acres and $4.4 million worth of timber were lost in the blaze. Over one thousand fire fighters fought the blaze, but it was not controlled until a large rain and hail storm doused the area. Damage from the fire is visible along the trail and from Lovers Leap.

The final section of trail along Galena Creek is cool and shaded from the sun. There are no holes large enough for swimming, but hikers can use the many creek crossings to look for small brook trout. You may see red-tailed hawks from the trail or belted kingfishers by Galena Creek. Be sure to watch for poison ivy along the creek, and remember that high runoff in springtime can lead to difficult stream crossings.

Grace Coolidge Walk-In Fishing Area

Description: An easy walk or mountain bike ride along Grace Coolidge Creek.

General Location: Ten miles east of Custer, South Dakota.

Highlights: A premiere trout stream.

Access: From South Dakota 87 take the Black Hills Playhouse Road (County 359 or BHNF Road 753) northeast to the Center Lake access road. The south end of the trail is across the road from the Grace Coolidge Campground on U.S. 16A, just 0.4 mile west of park headquarters.

Distance: Three miles one way.

Maps: Trails Illustrated Black Hills Southeast and page 80.

Custer State Park was the favorite summer retreat of Calvin Coolidge, the nation's thirtieth president. He came primarily to escape the summer heat of Washington, but also for the fishing, which still attracts visitors today. The walk-in fishing area is used primarily by fisherman to access pools and riffles, but it is a pretty place, whether or not you chase the rainbows. The easy access to water and gentle terrain make the trail ideal for easy hiking and mountain bike rides. Just be sure to watch for poison ivy and realize that the trail can be wet in spring.

The trail follows an abandoned roadway, which crosses the stream fourteen times. There still remains a series of dams along the creek. If you're not fishing, keep an eye out for other wildlife. I've seen ducks, deer and bighorn sheep nearby. Observant hikers may still see remnants of the 1988 Galena fire that obliterated the Center Lake Trail, formerly looping around a ridge to the west.

~

Sunday Gulch and Sylvan Lakeshore Trails

Description: Two short loop trails that circle Sylvan Lake and descend into Sunday Gulch.

General Location: At Sylvan Lake, six miles north of Custer, South Dakota.

Highlight: The fantastic granite spires near the outlet of Sylvan Lake.

Access: From Custer, drive 6.3 miles north on South Dakota 89, turn east onto South Dakota 87, then drive 0.3 mile to the Sylvan Lake parking area. From Hill City, drive three miles south to the junction of U.S. 385 and South Dakota 87. Turn east on South Dakota 87 and after 6.1 miles reach the parking area at Sylvan Lake.

Distance: About 3.5 miles long for Sunday Gulch and 1.0 mile for the Lakeshore Trail.

Maps: Trails Illustrated Black Hills Southeast, Sierra Club Hiking Map of the Norbeck Wildlife Preserve and page 83.

Three trails leave Custer State Park's most popular trailhead at Sylvan Lake. The two most popular lead east and north to Harney Peak. A less travelled route leads west down into Sunday Gulch. This streamside route explores a vastly different landscape than the trails to the east.

From the parking area, follow the Sylvan Lakeshore Trail to a point just below the Sylvan Lake Dam where the Sunday Gulch Loop begins

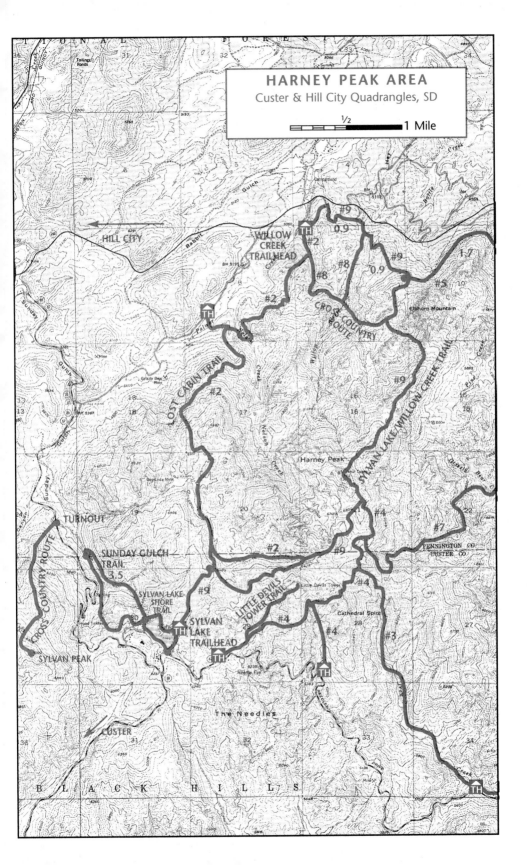

by a prominent trail sign. The trail begins with a steep descent down the boulder-strewn canyon of Sunday Gulch. Concrete steps and handrails make the descent into the upper canyon easier. As the trail descends further into the gulch, hikers pass through a diverse forest of ponderosa pine, white spruce, paper birch and quaking aspen, which are supported by the cool, moist environment along the stream.

At the low point of the route, the Sunday Gulch Trail turns southwest and begins a steady climb. A short stretch of the trail skirts the shoulder of South Dakota 87 before the trail reenters the woods. The final section of trail passes behind the Sylvan Lake Lodge before the loop closes at Sylvan Lake Dam. Remember not to cross South Dakota 87 and to pass behind Sylvan Lake Lodge. Hike downhill between some granite boulders to return to the Sylvan Lakeshore Trail. Hikers can return to the parking area via the north half of the Sylvan Lakeshore Trail.

Custer State Park publishes an interpretive guide for the trail that is available at the Peter Norbeck Visitor Center and the Sylvan Lake Entrance Station. Discussions of the natural history of the area are keyed to numbered posts along the route.

Custer State Park supports a small population of mountain goats, some of which may be seen from the trail. White-tailed deer are common along the trail and brook trout may be seen in the stream.

The area below the Sylvan Lake Dam is one of the most popular rock climbing areas in the Black Hills. The spires directly behind the dam are known as "the outlets." Below the outlets lies "Middle Earth," where the spires, walls and climbing routes derive their names from the J.R.R. Tolkien trilogy *Lord of the Rings*. As you hike through this area, check above you on the rocks, for all the wildlife does not wear thick white coats nor have long shaggy beards.

No drinking water is available on the route, but there is a small store at Sylvan Lake that is open in summer. Poison ivy grows along the trail and is especially common in spring and early summer. Avoid any plants with the distinctive cluster of three shiny leaves. The stream and much of the trail in Sunday Gulch is frozen from late fall through early spring, making for very difficult hiking.

Little Devils Tower Trail

Description: A short hike to one of the most spectacular overlooks in Custer State Park.

General Location: Seven miles northeast of Custer, South Dakota.

Highlight: Unobstructed views of Harney Peak and The Needles.

Access: From Sylvan Lake, drive about .75 mile east on South Dakota Highway 87 to the Little Devils Tower parking area on the north side of the highway.

Distance: Three miles round trip.

Maps: Trails Illustrated Black Hills Southeast, Sierra Club Hiking Map of the Norbeck Wildlife Preserve and page 83.

Most of the hiking trails in the Norbeck Wildlife Preserve are long, and difficult at best for families with small children. The exception is the Little Devils Tower Trail, which is short, but requires a steep climb at the end. However, the rewards at the summit far outweigh the effort spent on the climb. From the top you can see Harney Peak and rugged ridges that extend east above Nelson Creek. The tower has perhaps the best views of the Cathedral Spires and Needles, both close by to the south. Sylvan Peak is prominent to the west, and much of the Norbeck trail system is visible. At night the stars and the lights of Rapid City are especially impressive.

Start from the Little Devils Tower parking area, and hike east on the *Cathedral Spires Trail*. The trail follows the north side of a creek through a forest of spruce, birch, aspen and willow. The trail here can be submerged during spring thaw. Reach a signed junction and take the left fork to the tower. The right fork is the Cathedral Spires Trail that continues east to the Cathedral Spires.

There are fewer blazes beyond the junction, but the footway is well defined as the trail stays on the north side of the valley. Pass an old fence that ends on the south side of the trail. Begin to climb steadily beyond the fence. Just before reaching a divide, look for a red arrow painted onto a blaze in a tree. The arrow marks a cleft between two granite monoliths. Exit the cleft up hill and follow more painted arrows up to, and about twenty feet beyond, a narrow divide. Follow arrows painted on rocks through another cleft and then up a route that scrambles to the summit.

Return by retracing your route. Little Devils Tower can also be combined with the Harney Peak via Sylvan Lake and Cathedral Spires Loop described in this guide.

The scrambling at the end of the climb will be difficult for smaller children, but this section is very short. Once on top, be sure to pay attention where you step. The drop-off of the north face is every bit as vertical as the one at the "real" Devils Tower.

Other Custer State Park Trails

The *Legion Lake Trail* provides a short alternative to the Centennial Trail north of Legion Lake and U.S. 16A. Combined with the Centennial Trail, it makes a 1.5-mile loop. See map on page 32.

The *Badger Clark Historic Trail* starts from CSP Road 9 south of Legion Lake. This 1.0-mile loop honors South Dakota's first poet laureate and the man who built much of the trail that begins behind his cabin. Interpretive stops are paired with selections from Clark's poems. The interpretive guide is available at the Visitor Center. See map on page 32.

The *Stockade Lake Trail* is a 1.5-mile loop that starts near U.S. 16A near the park's west entrance. The trail climbs a ridge east of the lake through an area logged in the 1980s. An open ridge top provides views of Harney Peak and the Cathedral Spires.

Custer State Park offers *mountain bikers* other routes besides the Centennial Trail and walk-in fishing area. Four horse trails are open to bikes along with a network of gravel roads found between French Creek and the Wildlife Loop Road. The park's mountain bike brochure also recommends a 15.5-mile loop through Robbers Roost Draw that combines CSP Road 4, Horse Trail 2 and the Centennial Trail. Near CSP Road 4, north of French Creek, the loop passes the world's second largest known ponderosa pine.

The Wildlife Loop Road is perhaps the Black Hills finest *road bike* ride. The 31-mile loop packs in lots of climbs and sharp turns, but compensates with wildlife and scenery.

Black Hills National Forest: South Dakota

Hell Canyon Trail

CUSTER RANGER DISTRICT,
BLACK HILLS NATIONAL FOREST

Description: A moderate loop along both the bottom and rim of Hell Canyon for hikers and mountain bikers.

General Location: North of Jewel Cave National Monument, and twelve miles west of Custer, South Dakota.

Highlight: Views from rocky canyon walls and aspen colors in fall.

Access: From the junction of U.S. 16 and U.S. 385 on the west side of Custer, drive 13.2 miles west on U.S. 16. At the northwest corner of Jewel Cave National Monument, park at a small lot on BHNF Road 284-2L. The trail begins beyond a gate across the road.

Distance: A 5.5-mile loop with a 0.5-mile side trip to an overlook.

Maps: Black Hills National Forest Hell Canyon Trail and page 72.

Hell Canyon's claim to fame is that it is the place where Jewel Cave was discovered. Because the cave was declared a National Monument in 1908, when little of it was explored, the monument protects only 1,275 acres of surface land above the cave. To the north of the monument, Hell Canyon and its upper reaches have carved narrow, steep-walled canyons in the same Paha Sapa limestone in which the cave has formed.

One of the Black Hills National Forest's newest trails follows a loop across the canyon's middle reaches. Most hikers will travel this loop clockwise, electing to gain all their elevation in the first one-half mile of trail. Once the west rim of Hell Canyon is gained, a side trail leads another 0.5 mile east to an overlook high above the canyon floor. As it winds along the west rim, the Hell Canyon Trail passes two other overlooks before reaching an intricately built section that hugs the edge of the rim. Look here for solution cavities and other cave features in the limestone cliffs.

Descend to the bottom of West Hell Canyon at 3.0 miles and turn east. At the next junction at 3.5 miles, go south passing a small pocket cave on the west side. At 4.8 miles, reach the junction with the main branch of Hell Canyon before returning the trailhead at 5.5 miles.

Though the Hell Canyon route is open to hikers and mountain bikers, many riders will find the cliffside trail along the west rim too narrow and exposed. A better alternative is to combine the main and west forks of Hell Canyon in a ten-mile loop. Begin by riding up West Hell Canyon. Where the Hell Canyon Trail climbs to the rim, continue north along the canyon bottom. At about 4.7 miles reach a small stock pond and go right on an old jeep trail. At 4.9 miles reach another fork and go right. Cross a cattle guard at 5.2 miles, then go due east cross-country to a jeep trail at 5.4 miles. Turn north, then wind down the Short Fork of Hell Canyon until reaching the main canyon at about 7.4 miles. Follow a grassy two-track road along the canyon bottom to a junction with the Hell Canyon Trail at 9.7 miles. The trailhead is only another 0.7 mile down the trail.

~

Harney Peak via Sylvan Lake and Cathedral Spires

CUSTER RANGER DISTRICT, BLACK HILLS NATIONAL FOREST

Description: A moderate loop hike to the top of Harney Peak, the highest point in South Dakota, and a return leg through the Cathedral Spires.

General Location: Nine miles north of Custer, South Dakota.

Highlight: Probably the most popular hike in South Dakota.

Access: From Hill City, drive 3.0 miles south to the junction of U.S. 385 and South Dakota 87. Turn east onto South Dakota 87 and drive 6.1 miles to reach Sylvan Lake. Park in the day-use area located just past the parking area at Sylvan Lake. The trail starts at the northwest corner of the day-use loop road, next to a large trail sign. From Custer, drive 6.3 miles north on South Dakota 89, turn east on South Dakota 87, then drive 0.3 mile to reach Sylvan Lake.

Distance: Seven miles round trip, including the Cathedral Spires on the return leg.

Maps: Trails Illustrated Black Hills Southeast, Sierra Club Hiking Map of the Norbeck Wildlife Preserve and page 83.

Harney Peak is the highest point in South Dakota, and a popular goal for all Black Hills hikers. The peak can be reached from any one of eleven trailheads that surround the Black Elk Wilderness and Norbeck Wildlife Preserve, but by far the most popular route is via Sylvan Lake. Adventurous hikers can make a loop via the Cathedral Spires, the most spectacular of the granite pinnacles that surround Harney Peak.

From the trail sign at the northwest corner of the day use area, hike about 100 feet on the Sylvan Lakeshore Trail before turning north onto *Sylvan Lake–Harney Trail*, (9). It is a three-mile climb from the lake to the summit. From the lake, climb steadily to a junction with the south fork of *Lost Cabin Trail* (2), then turn east onto a gentle ridge which offers good views to the north.

Immediately after crossing into the Black Elk Wilderness, the Sylvan Lake–Harney Trail reaches a junction with the east fork of the Lost Cabin Trail at the site of the old Midway Picnic Ground. The Sylvan Lake–Harney Trail continues east at a moderate grade to reach a junction with *Cathedral Spires Trail* (4), and the end of a recent relocation.

Continue on the Sylvan Lake–Harney Trail as it resumes a steady climb and gains over 600 feet in less than a mile. Leave the main trail at the summit junction, climb over a small ridge and navigate a maze of trails to the tower on top of Harney Peak.

The view from the top of Harney Peak may be the finest in the Black Hills. To the east, Rapid City and Ellsworth Air Force Base are visible. Off in the distance is Badlands National Park. To the north, beyond Hill City, are Custer Peak, Terry Peak and Bear Butte. On the west side are Bear Mountain and the high Limestone Plateau. Odakota Mountain, at 7,200 feet on the plateau, is the second highest point in South Dakota. To the south is Mount Coolidge, the highest point in Custer State Park, and closer to the peak are the Needles, Cathedral Spires and Little Devils Tower.

To complete a loop back to Sylvan Lake, retrace the Sylvan Lake–Harney Trail back to the junction with the Cathedral Spires Trail. Follow the Cathedral Spires Trail south past the junction with the *Grizzly Creek Trail* (7) to a junction with *Willow Creek–Rushmore Trail* (3), which is about a mile from the peak. Continue on the Cathedral Spires Trail a short distance to reach the north side of the Cathedral Spires.

The spires are actually a series of vertical slabs with highpoints on their northwest sides. The summits are numbered 1 through 9 from west to east. All are technical rock climbs. Spire 4 is the highest, and Spire 5 is the easiest to climb. Mountain goats have been sighted on the top of Spire 5. Custer's 1874 expedition originally named the spires the "Organ Pipes."

After passing between the spires and the "Picket Fence," which is the group of spires to the north of the trail, the Cathedral Spires Trail forks. The south fork leads between the spires and the spectacular wall of Bartizan to the Needles Highway (South Dakota 87). Limber Pine, an uncommon species in the Black Hills, grows between the split in Trail 4 and the Needles Highway.

To complete the loop, follow the west fork, which passes a side trail to Little Devils Tower before reaching a different parking area on the Needles Highway. Hike through the parking area, and continue on the Cathedral Spires Trail for one-half mile before reaching the day use area at Sylvan Lake.

Harney Peak is roughly the center of a large outcrop of granite of Precambrian age. Granite weathers and erodes to form the spectacular needles and spires common in the area between Sylvan Lake and the Needles Highway. Associated with the granite is an especially coarse-grained form called pegmatite, which contains crystals ranging in size from inches to feet. Pegmatites also concentrate rare elements such as lithium and beryllium, which are mined along with the more common minerals feldspar, rose quartz and mica from numerous mines around Keystone and Custer.

The Norbeck trails are among the best marked and maintained in the Black Hills. Trails are marked with blazes that may have the trail number carved in the center. However, the loop described here is very heavily used and the trails are deeply eroded in some spots. Because of overuse, the Black Hills National Forest urges hikers to consider alternate hikes between May 1 and September 30. Horseback riding is permitted on most trails and mountain bikes are allowed on all trails outside the Black Elk Wilderness and Mount Rushmore. Camping in the area does not require a permit. Remember that no camping is allowed at Harney Peak.

The Black Elk Wilderness receives less snow than the northern Black Hills, so year-round hiking is possible for the hardy. Sandy soils formed by weathering of granite drain quickly, so the trails are often dry while the roads and trails in the northern Black Hills are still muddy.

Harney Peak via Willow Creek and Lost Cabin Trails

CUSTER RANGER DISTRICT, BLACK HILLS NATIONAL FOREST

Description: A long hike or overnight backpack loop to the top of Harney Peak from the north side.

General Location: Six miles east of Hill City, South Dakota.

Highlight: A more secluded, but more difficult route to South Dakota's highest point.

Access: From Hill City, drive 3.0 miles south to the junction of U.S. 16 and South Dakota 244. Follow South Dakota 244 east for 3.0 miles to a sign for the Willow Creek Horse Camp. Turn south onto the gravel road and park at the day use area which is located just before the Horse Camp.

Distance: About 12 miles round trip, with 2,200 feet of elevation gain.

Maps: Trails Illustrated Black Hills Southeast, Sierra Club Hiking Map of the Norbeck Wildlife Preserve and page 83.

My favorite route up Harney Peak starts from the north side. The trailhead at Willow Creek is closer to the northern Black Hills and Rapid City, so is more convenient than the Sylvan Lake approach. Still, fewer people use the north approach, and you may have the trail to yourself until you reach the summit. This is a long dayhike, or a moderate backpack trip with potential campsites on upper Lost Cabin Creek or near the crossing of Elkhorn Mountain. The route treats hikers to the wildly exotic granite formations that make the Black Elk Wilderness such a special place. The added distance and elevation gain on the north side give Harney the feel of a much larger mountain.

The route is simple and easy to follow. From Willow Creek take the *Sylvan Lake–Harney Trail* (9) to the east shoulder of the peak and then follow a short spur trail to the summit lookout. The north end of this trail is the least interesting part of the trip. Here it follows an old dirt road, which is parallel to South Dakota 244, to a junction with the *Willow Creek Trail* (8) at 0.9 mile. Climb steadily away from the road to a junction with the *Willow Creek–Rushmore Trail* (5) at 1.8 miles. Beyond the junction with the Willow Creek–Rushmore Trail, the trail enters the Black Elk Wilderness and leaves the road behind.

Once into the Wilderness, cross a small spring and hike among the impressive display of granite spires which form the southwest side of

Elkhorn Mountain. A small knob just beyond Elkhorn Mountain offers a spectacular view of the backside of Mount Rushmore. From the knob, follow the open northeast ridge of Harney Peak at a gentle grade to reach 6,800 feet. From this point, the Sylvan Lake–Harney Trail climbs steadily on switchbacks to the summit lookout tower.

The small spring on the northwest side of Elkhorn Mountain marks the start of an alternate off-trail route to return to Willow Creek Horse Camp, if you hike the loop in reverse. Bushwack alongside a branch of Willow Creek for about 0.5 mile to the confluence with the main stem of Willow Creek. A dam completely filled by sediment is located near the confluence. Two short spur trails lead from the dam to the Willow Creek Trail. Follow the Willow Creek Trail west to the *Lost Cabin Trail* (2) and then back to the trailhead. Hikers should be cautious on this trail, as it is the most popular horse trail in Norbeck.

To complete the loop from Harney Peak continue to follow the Sylvan Lake–Harney Trail south toward Sylvan Lake (see Harney Peak from Sylvan Lake hike). Pass a junction with the *Cathedral Spires Trail* (4) and turn onto the *Lost Cabin Trail* at the junction with its eastern end. Pass through a series of narrow fissures below high granite walls to reach the junction with the south fork of the Lost Cabin Trail in a meadow which contains some camping spots. Beyond this point much of the trail has been recently relocated to provide better footing and to decrease erosion around the trail.

Near the site of the long-abandoned Gap Lode Mine, the Lost Cabin Trail rises to a ridgetop 100 yards beyond the Black Elk Wilderness boundary that has a dry campsite. Pass a signpost and an abandoned trail leading west before reaching a maintained side trail leading west to the Palmer Creek Trailhead near Nelson Creek.

In summer, blue aster, blue bells and bunchberry grow here along with the birch and aspen so common along Black Hills streams. Leaving Nelson Creek behind, look out for black-eyed susans and prairie coneflowers on the way to the junction with Willow Creek Trail. From this junction, it is short walk on the heavily-used horse trail back to Willow Creek Horse Camp.

Harney Peak was named for General William S. Harney in 1857, by members of an early military expedition led by Kemble Warren and the renown geologist Ferdinand V. Hayden. The first attempt to climb the peak was made by part of Custer's 1874 expedition. Like many parties to follow them, Custer's group ran out of daylight just below the summit, and was forced to abandon their attempt. The Custer expedition was more successful in leaving their mark on the geography of the Black Hills, naming both Custer Peak, for their leader, and Terry Peak, for General Alfred H. Terry.

Numerous prehistoric ascents of Harney were undoubtedly made by Native Americans. In 1875 Dr. Valentine T. McGillycuddy was part of the Jenney Scientific Expedition to the Black Hills and made the first recorded ascent by a white man. Dr. McGillycuddy's ashes now rest at the base of the steps in the lookout tower. The tower was completed shortly before the doctor's death and was manned as a fire lookout from 1938 to 1967. The tower stands as a monument to both depression era construction workers, and the fire lookouts who followed. The tower was placed on the National Register of Historic Places in 1982.

The Harney Peak area has long been a focus of conservation efforts. Peter Norbeck, who was later to become governor and United States Senator from South Dakota, was instrumental in creating the Custer State Forest, which later became Custer State Park. The Norbeck Wildlife refuge was created in 1920 to protect game animals and birds and to provide a breeding place for them. Norbeck's conservation legacy also includes the creation of Grand Teton and Badlands national parks.

In 1980, Congress created the 9,824-acre Black Elk Wilderness that protects the heart of the Norbeck Wildlife Preserve. The legislation came about, at least in part, due to opposition to a proposal to build an aerial tramway from Keystone, near Mount Rushmore, to the top of Harney Peak.

Grizzly Creek Trail Loop
CUSTER RANGER DISTRICT,
BLACK HILLS NATIONAL FOREST

Description: A one- or two-day hike through the east side of the Black Elk Wilderness and Norbeck Wildlife Preserve, which combines the Centennial, Grizzly Bear Creek and Horsethief Lake trails.
General Location: Three miles south of Keystone, South Dakota.
Highlight: Wilderness trails and granite spires.
Access: From Keystone, drive 1.0 mile south on U.S. 16A. Turn west onto South Dakota 244 and drive 1.8 miles to Mount Rushmore

National Memorial. The unmarked Mount Rushmore trailhead is located south of the parking area across South Dakota 244. Look for a trail leading up from the east end of the guardrail along the road.
Distance: About 12.0 miles.
Maps: Trails Illustrated Black Hills Southeast, Sierra Club Hiking Map of the Norbeck Wildlife Preserve and pages 34 and 36.

The eastern side of the Norbeck Wildlife Preserve contains some of the most scenic areas in the Black Hills. None of the famous granite spires are here, but a less-known group that extends southwest from Horsethief Lake is nearly as impressive as the Needles or Cathedral Spires. Many hikers will savor the streamside sections of trails along Grizzly Bear and Iron creeks.

A loop extending west from Mount Rushmore along the *Horsethief Lake* (14) and *Grizzly Creek* (7) trails, along with the Centennial Trail, covers most of the northeast part of the preserve. This hike can be done in one long day, but is better as an easy overnight hike.

From the parking area at Mount Rushmore, hike south down the Centennial Trail Spur for 0.5 mile to the boundary of the Black Elk Wilderness. Just beyond the boundary, cross a side draw of Grizzly Bear Creek and come to the junction with the Centennial Trail. Turn right onto the Centennial Trail, cross a corner of the Mount Rushmore National Memorial, and hike north to the junction with Trail 14 at a spectacular group of granite spires. Turn south onto Trail 14 to hike alongside the spires. After crossing through the spires, reach a junction with Trail 7 in the valley of Grizzly Bear Creek. Several good campsites can be found on the high ground above the beaver dams which flood the valley. This is a good midway point of the trip for groups planning an overnight hike.

From the Trail 14-7 junction hike southeast on Trail 7. Cross over a divide into the drainage of Iron Creek. After about 1.0 mile, leave the Black Elk Wilderness where the trail becomes a two-track dirt road. Trail 7 has been relocated to follow this road for 1.1 miles to the intersection of the Centennial Trail just west of a prominent granite tower.

Turn northeast onto the Centennial Trail and hike for 0.6 mile to a four-way junction with the Centennial Trail Mountain Bike Bypass (89B) and BHNF Road 347. Continue north on the Centennial Trail for 1.1 miles to the Black Elk Wilderness boundary, then over the divide and into the Grizzly Creek Drainage back to Mount Rushmore.

The trails in the Norbeck Wildlife Preserve and Black Elk Wilderness are well-marked and easy to follow. A number of loop trips are possible in addition to the one described here. Several are suitable for overnight trips, in fact the area is ideal for novice backpackers. Camp sites in Norbeck must be at least 200 feet from trails or streams. Giardia is found in some Black Hills water, so be sure to treat all your water by boiling or filtering with a filter designed to remove giardia bacteria. Camp stoves are allowed, but open fires are not allowed due to high fire danger.

~

Other Norbeck Trails

Trail 3 extends 4.4 miles west from the Iron Creek Horse Camp to *Trail 4*. Combined with *Trail 7*, it provides a loop of more than 9.5 miles through the sparsely-travelled heart of the Black Elk Wilderness. See maps on pages 34 and 83.

The south end of *Trail 4* connects the Cathedral Spires Trailhead with the popular trail from the Cathedral Spires to Harney Peak. This short but steep feeder is a popular access point for rock climbers. See map on page 83.

Trail 5 connects Elkhorn Picnic Area with *Trail 9* and is seldom hiked on its own. It makes possible a loop that encircles the Upper Pine Creek Natural Area via trails 9, 7, 14 and 89. From the short spur leading from Elkhorn Picnic Area it is 1.7 miles to *Trail 9* and 0.2 mile east to the *Centennial Trail*. See maps on pages 36 and 83.

Trail 7 is 5.1 miles long and is split by a short section of the *Centennial Trail*. From BHNF Road 345, it follows an old roadbed before joining the *Centennial Trail* for 0.2 mile. Trail 7 then turns west and follows an often muddy old roadway for 1.1 miles before reaching the boundary of the Black Elk Wilderness. The trail stays near Grizzly Creek, intersects the south end of *Trail 14*, then ends at *Trail 4* just south of Harney Peak. See maps on pages 34 and 83.

Trail 8 is a favorite of horse riders based out of the Willow Creek Horse Camp. It is a pretty route, but badly overused. The loop is 1.5 miles. See map on page 83.

Trail 14N connects Horsethief Lake with the *Centennial Trail*. Remember that the junction of trails 14 and 89 is an offset four-way intersection. To continue south of *Trail 14* heading from Horsethief Lake it is necessary to turn west of the Centennial Trail for a short distance. See map on page 36.

Trail 15 connects the east end of BHNF Road 345 to the Iron Mountain Road. It follows an abandoned roadway along Iron Creek for 2.0 miles. See map on page 34.

Trail 16 is the last remaining segment of a once extensive trail system in the southeast corner of the Norbeck Wildlife Preserve. The trail now connects BHNF Road 345 with the *Centennial Trail* bypass (89B). This 1.4 mile trail is closed May 15 through July 15. See map on page 34.

Trail 89B is the Centennial Trail mountain bike bypass. It leads 1.8 miles east to Iron Mountain picnic area on U.S. 16A. To regain the Centennial Trail, turn north on U.S. 16 to Mount Rushmore, then turn west on South Dakota 244 to reach the Big Pine Trailhead. See map on p. 34.

Sylvan Peak Route

Description: A rugged off-trail hike to the top of a 7,000-foot peak.
General Location: Six miles south of Hill City, South Dakota.
Highlight: Unique views of Harney Peak and the Norbeck Wildlife Preserve from a little-visited summit.
Access: From Hill City, drive three miles south on U.S. 16. Turn east onto South Dakota 87 and drive three miles to a prominent left turn where Johnson Canyon crosses the road. Park at a turnout just beyond the next right turn. The route is unmarked, but begins on the slope southwest of the turnout.
Distance: 3.5 miles round trip with a 1,400-foot climb.
Maps: USGS Custer, SD 7.5-minute quadrangle and page 83.

From the top of Harney Peak you can see most of the Black Hills. As South Dakota's highest point, Harney Peak offers a glimpse of most of the state's other 7,000-footers including Terry Peak, Bear Mountain, Odakota Mountain and the large area of the Limestone Plateau which climbs over the 7,000-foot mark. But often confused with Bear Mountain, or simply overlooked, is a small range to the west that is bounded by U.S. 16 and South Dakota 89, and anchored by Buckhorn Mountain on the south and St. Elmo Peak to the north.

The high point of this range checks in at an even 7,000 feet, making it the seventh highest peak in South Dakota. By a quirk of geography, it never received an official name, but was called "Sylvan Peak" in the first edition of this guide, the name that was adopted on the 1996 Black Hills National Forest map.

There is no trail to the top of Sylvan Peak, but access to the area is possible from anywhere on Black Hills National Forest land on South Dakota 87. However, the north ridge of the peak is the most prominent. A start near the mouth of Johnson Canyon requires an elevation gain of 1,400 feet, one of the largest required to reach any summit in the Black Hills. This obvious and challenging route is entirely on Black Hills National Forest land.

From the turnout, hike southwest to gain the north ridge at an elevation of 6,000 feet. Continue due south on the crest of the ridge, cross an old logging road and reach the north sub-peak at 6,880 feet. It is the cliffs on this sub-peak that appear to be the summit when viewed from near Sylvan Lake. The scramble to the top of the rocky sub-peak is well worth the effort. There are excellent views of Sylvan Lake and Harney Peak. The group of spires around the dam at Sylvan Lake, called the "outlets," are especially prominent.

Cross another old logging road in the saddle between the north and main peaks, and continue southeast to the summit. The lack of a summit cairn or marker post on top indicate that this peak is rarely climbed.

Sylvan Peak is a difficult climb, not recommended for hikers unfamiliar with travelling off-trail. A topographic map and compass, along with the ability to use these tools, are essential for route finding. There is a lot of fallen timber on the north ridge, and some easy scrambling may be necessary. Hikers looking for a little added adventure in their Black Hills hikes will find these qualities attractive rather than discouraging.

Flume Trail
PACTOLA RANGER DISTRICT,
BLACK HILLS NATIONAL FOREST

Description: A hike along an abandoned flume from Spring Creek to Rockerville, and a climb to the top of Boulder Hill.
General Location: Eight miles north of Hill City, South Dakota.
Highlight: Easy walking on a National Recreation Trail.

Access: To reach the *Upper Spring Creek Trailhead*, leave U.S. 385 on the Sheridan Lake Road and drive 1.9 miles east before turning south at a sign for the trailhead. Drive 0.4 miles on a dirt road to reach the parking area. To reach the *Boulder Hill Trailhead*, leave U.S. 16 2.5 miles west of Rockerville, and turn right on County Road C233 which is paved for 0.1 mile. Turn left on BHNF Road 358 and continue to the trailhead. To reach the *Flume Trailhead*, drive 1.7 miles on U.S. 385 from the junction with U.S. 16. Turn east on paved BHNF Road 192 for 0.7 mile. Then turn left onto a paved road toward the South Marina and reach the Flume, or Calumet Trailhead at 1.5 miles. The *Coon Hollow Trailhead* is located just west of U.S. 16 at Rockerville on the north side of Storm Mountain Road, which is BHNF Road 676.

Distance: The trail is 14 miles long, including a spur to Boulder Hill and the Spring Creek Loop.

Maps: Black Hills National Forest Flume Trail Map and page 39.

One of the most interesting hiking trails in the Black Hills follows the route of an historic flume from Sheridan Lake to the old town of Rockerville. If you have time for only part of the trail try the section from the Upper Spring Creek Trailhead to Boulder Hill.

From the Upper Spring Creek Trailhead, the Flume Trail follows a dirt road that winds upstream to the face of the Sheridan Dam. Along the way, it crosses Spring Creek five times, and also passes a point where a torrent of water pours out of a cliff. Creek crossings may be difficult in spring and early summer due to high water. Most crossings can be made on large rocks placed in the stream, but these do not guarantee dry feet.

Intersect the *Centennial Trail* just south of the dam. From this intersection the Centennial Trail leads southwest 1.0 mile to the Flume (or Calumet) Trailhead and the west end of the Flume Trail, or 1.3 miles north to the Dakota Point Trailhead.

From the dam, follow the Flume Trail east along the old flume bed to a long tunnel, then a shorter tunnel. The tunnels are interesting breaks from typical hiking scenery and are great places to escape the sun on a hot day, or to take shelter on a rainy day. If you need to return to the Upper Spring Creek Trailhead, take a short cut that leaves the main Flume Trail from the site of tunnel base camp, located between the tunnels, and leads to Spring Creek. From the tunnels, continue east to the Baker Park Vista for a view of Boulder Hill.

From the Baker Park Vista, continue east along the flume bed to the west end of the Spring Creek Loop. The south branch of the loop is only a half mile long, while the north branch is 2.75 miles. From the east end of the loop continue south on the Flume Trail to a side trail that leads .75 mile to the top of Boulder Hill, where a lookout tower once stood. Boulder Hill offers the best view of the Black Hills from the Flume Trail.

From the Boulder Hill side trail, continue east to Air Force Vista, cross BHNF Road 676 and pass Coon Hollow Vista before reaching trails end at the Coon Hollow Trailhead.

The Black Hills gold rush was booming in 1880 when prospectors discovered placer gold near what was to become the town of Rockerville. Processing of the gold ore was hampered by a lack of water until the Black Hills Placer Mining Company constructed a flume to divert water from Spring Creek, above the old townsite of Sheridan, for use at the Rockerville diggings. Construction of the flume was a massive engineering project that involved the construction of 17.5 miles of canals and troughs, digging two tunnels, building a dam near Sheridan and the construction of trestles that were up to eighty feet high. Lack of maintenance on the flume by the late 1880s reduced its flow, and the diggings at Rockerville slowly withered.

The builders of the flume left their legacy to future Black Hills residents in the flume bed that has an overall grade of two per cent. From the outlet of Sheridan Lake to Coon Hollow near Rockerville, the Flume Trail generally follows the bed. A few sections are located away from the flume bed to avoid private land or places where trestles bypassed steep gullies.

The Flume Trail was designated a National Recreation Trail in 1979 primarily for its historic significance. In order to preserve the flume bed, it is open to foot travel only. Motorized vehicles, horses, and mountain bikes are not allowed. The trail is an ideal route for a family hike and is the most popular trail in the Black Hills National Forest outside of the Harney Peak area. The terrain is level and it is one of the best marked and maintained trails in the BHNF. There are numerous interpretive signs and trail maps located along the way. An unusual feature of the trail is the patches of scrub oak amid the pines, spruce, aspen, and birch, which are more typical of the Black Hills.

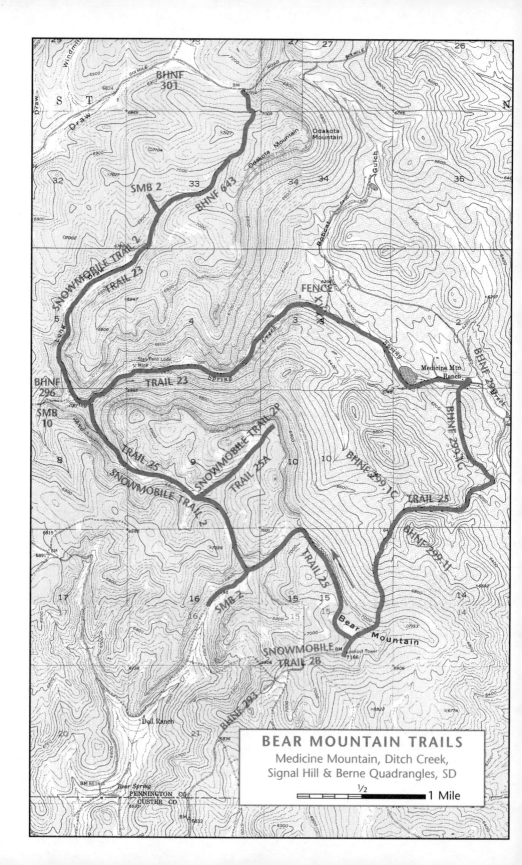

BEAR MOUNTAIN TRAILS
Medicine Mountain, Ditch Creek,
Signal Hill & Berne Quadrangles, SD

½   1 Mile

Bear Mountain Trails

HARNEY RANGER DISTRICT,
BLACK HILLS NATIONAL FOREST

Description: A long cross-country ski or mountain bike loop over the third highest point in South Dakota.

General Location: Twelve miles southwest of Hill City, South Dakota.

Highlight: Views of the Black Elk Wilderness and Limestone Plateau from the tower on top of Bear Mountain.

Access: To reach the Medicine Mountain Boy Scout Camp from Hill City, drive 1.3 miles south on U.S. 385 to Pennington County Road T317, which is also called BHNF Road 303 or the Reno Gulch Road. Turn west on T317, which is paved for about a mile. After 9.8 miles, turn left onto BHNF Road 297. Follow Road 297 for 1.6 miles, then turn right onto BHNF Road 299. Reach the Medicine Mountain Boy Scout Camp 1.8 miles later. Drive through the gate and park beside a trail sign in a small lot on the left side of the entrance road. The road is plowed in winter to the scout camp via Medicine Mountain.

Distance: The Bear Mountain loop is 9.5 miles long. The entire trail system is 16.0 miles. It is 2.75 miles one way from the Boy Scout Camp to the summit of Bear Mountain.

Maps: Black Hills National Forest Bear Mountain Ski Trails and page 100.

Anchoring the northern end of the Bear Mountain Cross Country Ski Trails is Odakota Mountain (7,200 feet), the second highest point in South Dakota. Merely the highest point on the highest ridge of the Limestone Plateau, Odakota, and the views from it, are not that impressive. Bear Mountain (7,166 feet) at the south end of the trail system, is the third highest point in the state, and a much more interesting summit.

The Bear Mountain ski trails form a figure 8. Bear Mountain and Trail 25 form the south loop. Odakota Mountain and Trail 23 form the north loop. The south loop, while more difficult, is more scenic and a more popular route. Trail 25 leaves the scout camp by heading west through a meadow and then turning south to pass through a gate in a fence. Keep a close eye on the carsonite posts which mark the route here, or ask the scout camp caretaker if you have problems finding the start of the trail. Trail 25 is a narrow, winding hiking trail until it merges with BHNF Road 299.1G.

Follow Road 299.1G until it reaches a prominent draw, then turn west up the draw onto BHNF Road 299.1C. Pass a side trail leading south, and stay left on Road 299.1J at a fork where Road 299.1C leads right. Continue straight at another fork where Road 299.1J goes left. The climb up Bear Mountain begins in earnest from this junction.

Trail 25 steepens considerably and adds a few switchbacks before reaching the summit ridge of Bear Mountain. Once on the ridge, a side road merges from the left, and you then pass a gate in an open meadow. From the gate, follow the main road to the Bear Mountain lookout tower.

The summit rocks are the same massive limestone that forms the plateau, but Bear Mountain is the center of an uplift of Archean-age granite and gneiss, some of the oldest rocks in the Black Hills.

The lookout tower is closed in winter and views from it are limited. When open, views from the tower extend north and south along the rim of the Limestone Plateau, and east to Harney Peak. A well-used spur from Snowmobile Trail 2 reaches the tower, and there are also restrooms adjacent to it.

Return to the gate and Trail 25. The section of trail beyond the gate follows the rim of the Limestone Plateau and is perhaps the most scenic section of ski trail in the Black Hills. There are several spectacular overlooks with views extending east to Harney Peak. The trail winds through open timber and can be difficult to find. If in doubt, just remember that the trail stays very close to the rim.

After about a mile on the rim, Trail 25 turns west near some slash piles, then follows a fence downhill into Grand Vista Draw and a forest service road. From this point to Spring Creek, skiers and snowmobilers share the same route, as cross-country ski Trail 25 coincides with Snowmobile Trail 2. For a reprise of the views from the rim of the Limestone Plateau, ski side Trail 25A (also Snowmobile Trail 2-P) for a .75-mile side trip northeast to the Grand Vista Overlook.

Reach a junction with Trail 23 at Spring Creek, turn east down Trail 23. From this junction, Trail 23 and Snowmobile Trail 2 continue north. Enjoy some well deserved downhill skiing as Trail 23 follows Spring Creek. Cross a fence, and about 200 yards later reach an intersection with Trail 23A, which enters from the north. Past this intersection the trails are not marked and skiers are on their own back to the scout camp. Just follow Spring Creek and stay to the south side of the large pond, just upstream from the camp.

There is much less snow at Bear Mountain than in the area of Lead-Deadwood. Don't be surprised if there is little snow at the scout camp, but snow conditions improve markedly with elevation. Nevertheless, keep in mind the option of skiing Trail 23 from BHNF Road 301 south along Long Draw to Odakota Mountain and Spring Creek. This area is higher and holds snow well into the spring. As a last resort, consider hiking up Bear Mountain from the scout camp.

Bear Mountain is not a trip for beginners. Trail markers are sparse and the ability to use a topographic map is a necessity. The loop along trails 23 and 25 is long and snow conditions may be poor. But for skiers willing to make a little extra effort to climb Bear Mountain or Odakota Mountain via routes away from the snowmobile trail, this area provides an exciting alternative to the easier and more reliable trails at Big Hill and Eagle Cliff.

In summer, Bear Mountain is excellent for mountain biking. To avoid parking at the scout camp, start at BHNF Road 299.1G, about .75 mile south of the scout camp. You can ride the ski loop, or try a loop farther north around Odakota Mountain. The north loop combines Trail 23 with BHNF roads 299, 301, and 693. To climb Odakota Mountain, hike east at a small saddle near the north end of BHNF Road 693. There is a faint blazed trail to the top, but no marker on the flat summit.

The mountain pine beetle has found Bear Mountain to its liking. Pine beetles reach epidemic proportions in the Black Hills about every twenty years attacking 7- to 13-inch ponderosa pines in crowded stands. By 1993 the pests destroyed over 5,100 acres of forest between the scout camp and Bear Mountain. Noting that beetle damage ends near open, recently logged stands, the BHNF counterattacked by awarding emergency timber contracts. This timber salvage should reduce the spread of the infestation to healthy trees and reduce fuel and fire danger. Ironically, it was the absence of natural fire and the inability of previous logging contractors to thin ponderosa pine stands that contributed to the epidemic. Pines infested with mountain pine beetles remain green in the winter, but can be recognized as they turn yellow in the spring, then red in the summer.

Lake Loop Trail

HARNEY RANGER DISTRICT,
BLACK HILLS NATIONAL FOREST

Description: An easy trail which circles Deerfield Lake.
General Location: Sixteen miles northwest of Hill City, South Dakota.
Highlight: Deerfield Lake and great swimming.

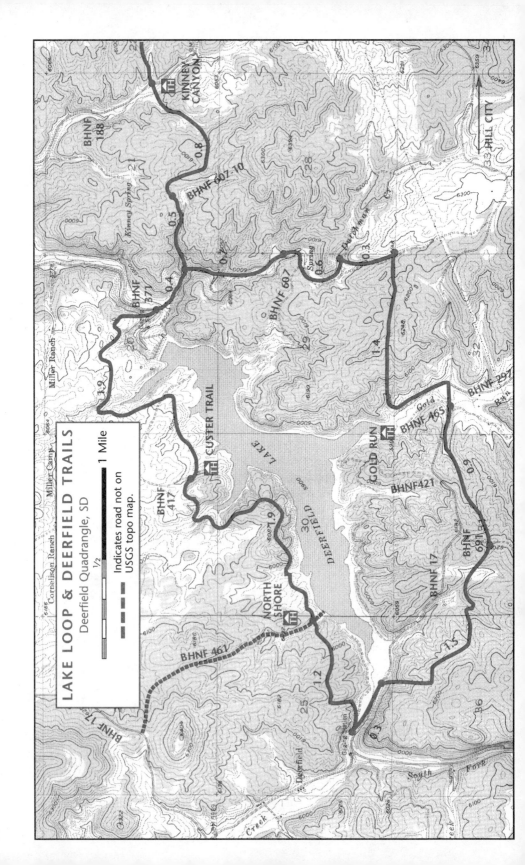

LAKE LOOP & DEERFIELD TRAILS
Deerfield Quadrangle, SD

1/2   1 Mile

Indicates road not on
USGS topo map.

Access: From Hill City, drive west on Pennington County Road C308 (BHNF Road 17) 14 miles to BHNF Road 465. Turn north onto Road 465 for 0.1 mile to the *Gold Run Trailhead.* From Rochford, drive 0.6 miles south on Pennington County Road C306 (BHNF Road 231). Turn left on C306 (BHNF Road 17), and drive 9.2 miles to BHNF Road 417. Turn left onto Road 417 and drive 1.5 miles south to the *Custer Trail Campground.*

Distance: The loop is 11.1 miles around.

Maps: Black Hills National Forest Deerfield Trail and Lake Loop Trail and page 104.

Few Black Hills Recreation Areas boast the luxurious combination of trails and swimming found at Deerfield Lake. Most of the four campgrounds spread around the lake have good swimming, and best of all, an eleven-mile trail links them together. The trail is open to horseback riders, hikers, and mountain bikers, with horses and bikes being the most popular. Much of the trail follows old two-track dirt roads, but new trail has been constructed from about the North Shore Trailhead to Castle Creek, below the Deerfield Dam. The trail could be good for cross-country skiing, although from Gold Run to the gauging station at the head of Castle Creek the trail follows the Black Hills Snowmobile Trail 2.

From the Gold Run Trailhead, cross BHNF Road 17, then follow a two-track road to the west. At 0.9 mile cross a gate and gravel BHNF Road 691. Descend to a meadow where a side trail leads north to the Hilltop Trailhead. At 1.3 miles a side road leads south and at 1.6 miles, go left at a T-junction. Another side road leads left at 1.8 miles, then the trail descends to reach BHNF Road 17 at 2.4 miles.

Follow BHNF Road 17 and Snowmobile Trail 2 west. Cross a bridge over Castle Creek, then follow a two-track dirt road along the north shore of Deerfield Lake into a area logged in 1991–1992. At 3.2 miles, cross a gate, then go right at a junction with BHNF Road 461-1F. At 3.4 miles, pass a side road left and then go straight through a T-junction onto a foot trail. A side road leads north to the North Shore Trailhead at 3.9 miles.

Continue through timber on the north shore to reach gravel BHNF Road 417 and Custer Trail Trailhead at 5.8 miles. The trail then enters Reynolds Prairie, climbs in and out of numerous gullies and crosses fences at 6.4 and 7.2 miles.

At 7.7 miles descend to a gravel road below the spillway of Deerfield Dam. Continue straight ahead on a dirt road to reach a junction at 8.1 miles with the *Deerfield Trail,* which follows BHNF Road 607-

1D for 1.3 miles east to the Kinney Canyon Trailhead. The Lake Loop Trail stays right and follows BHNF Road 607-1C. At 8.5 miles, a side trail leads west to Dutchman Campground and at 8.8 miles BHNF Road 607-1E leaves to the east.

Climb south alongside gravel BHNF Road 607 past a junction with BHNF Road 607-1A. At 9.7 miles, cross Road 607 and turn west onto a ridge in an area logged in 1991. Follow a series of old logging roads on the ridge before descending to Gold Run Gulch at 10.8 miles. Head south along a fence to BHNF Road 17 and the close of the loop at 11.1 miles.

The Lake Loop Trail is well-marked with brown carsonite posts labeled "L-40" and with gray plastic diamonds. Most of the trailheads have a signboard with a map of the trail. Old horse trails which intersect the Lake Loop Trail on the east side are marked with carsonite posts with a picture of a horse and gray reflective diamonds. These horse trails can be confused with the main trail.

Drinking water is available at the many campgrounds and picnic areas around the lake. The best feature of the trail, and an unusual one for the Black Hills, is the proximity to good swimming. A cool swim after a long hike is hard to beat. The trail is ideally situated for use by campers since it passes through, or adjacent to, Custer Trails and Dutchman campgrounds. The full loop should take about six hours of hiking, but shorter out-and-back hikes could be made from any of the campgrounds.

Deerfield Dam was built in 1942–1946 by conscientious objectors to World War II. About 500 men, mostly Mennonites, were assigned to the project by their draft boards because their religious beliefs prohibited them from bearing arms.

~

Deerfield Trail

BLACK HILLS NATIONAL FOREST

Description: A trail for hikers and mountain bikers that links the Lake Loop, Mickelson and Centennial trails.

General Location: The western end is sixteen miles northwest of Hill City and the east end is two miles east of Silver City.

Highlight: The scenic canyons of Slate and Rapid creeks.

Access: See the Centennial Trail for directions to the *Deer Creek Trailhead* and the Mickelson Trail for directions to the *Mystic Trailhead*. To reach the Silver City Trailhead from U.S. 385 drive 4.6 miles on paved BHNF Road 141 to Silver City. Before crossing Rapid Creek, turn right at a sign for the trailhead onto a gravel road and drive 0.5 miles to a parking area at a locked gate. The *Kinney Canyon Trailhead* is located on BHNF Road 188 about one mile west of the junction with BHNF Road 187.

Distance: 18.0 miles one way.

Maps: Black Hills National Forest Deerfield Trail and Lake Loop Trail and pages 104, 108, and 109.

The Deerfield Trail now connects the Centennial Trail to the Lake Loop Trail and George S. Mickelson Trail. The route is designed for hikers, mountain bikers and horses and is closed to motorized vehicles. The primary uses are mountain biking and fishing access. The Black Hills National Forest describes the trout fishing in Rapid Creek as "some of the best and most challenging" in the Black Hills.

The Deerfield Trail along Slate and Rapid creeks is ideal for a hot summer day. The route follows an old railroad bed on the floor of the canyon of Rapid Creek. The Black Hills National Forest has built bridges across Rapid Creek so that getting wet is now an option rather than a certainty. There are a few pools near the crossings to relax in, and the water is often warmer than expected.

The Deerfield Trail begins east of Deerfield Lake at a junction with the Lake Loop Trail. Head east to reach a junction with BHNF Road 188-1D at 0.4 miles, then turn north onto BHNF Road 188-1G at 1.0 mile. Reach the Kinney Canyon Trailhead on gravel BHNF Road 188 at 1.3 miles.

Continue east, crossing BHNF Road 187 before intersecting BHNF Road 429. Turn right onto Road 429, then continue northeast on BHNF Road 443, where Road 429 exits to the right. Turn east off Road 443 and follow the upper reaches of Crooked Creek before leaving the creek on a gated dirt road that leads to the Mystic Trailhead at 6 miles.

From the Mystic Trailhead, the Deerfield Trail currently crosses the creek and follows new trail, dirt roads and part of the Mickelson Trail to a dirt road in Lind Gulch. With the completion of the Mickelson Trail, the two trails will follow the same path between the Mystic Trailhead and Lind Gulch. Follow a dirt road southeast along Lind Gulch, then crest a small divide to drop alongside Slate Creek. While crossing the many bridges over Slate Creek keep an eye out for signs of

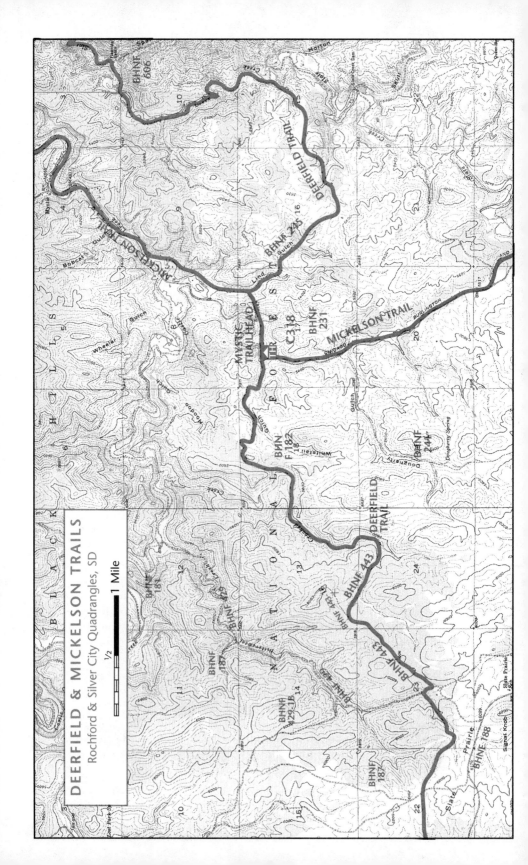

DEERFIELD & MICKELSON TRAILS
Rochford & Silver City Quadrangles, SD

½ 1 Mile

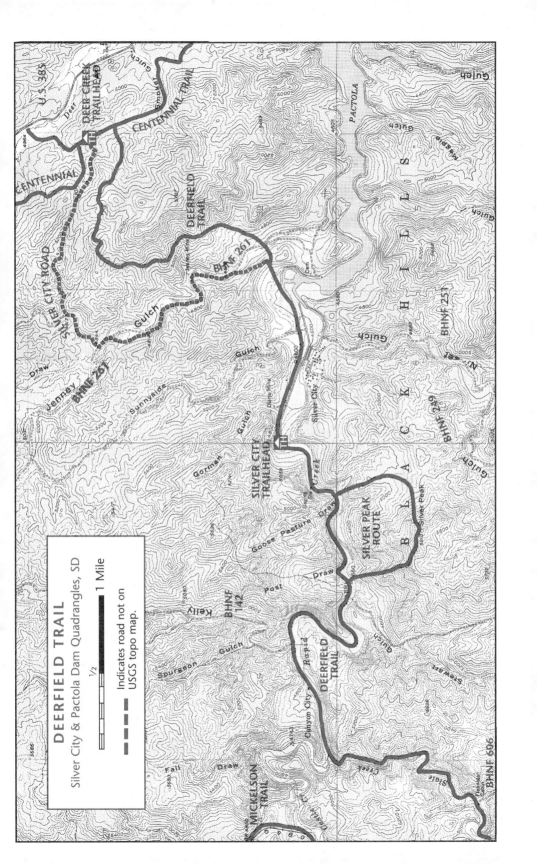

DEERFIELD TRAIL

Silver City & Pactola Dam Quadrangles, SD

½   1 Mile

Indicates road not on USGS topo map.

long-abandoned mining operations in the valley. Quartz veins, which cut the Precambrian slates around Mystic, contained small amounts of gold. These operations left behind short tunnels, shallow shafts and small piles of waste rock.

At 12 miles Slate Creek joins Rapid Creek and the Deerfield Trail turns east once more. In any season, the canyon of Rapid Creek is a beautiful walk. It is deep with steep walls and heavily covered in spruce. Mining first brought men to Rapid Creek. They took little ore from the narrow veins, but left small adits and prospect pits scattered throughout the canyon. Many of their cabin sites would make excellent campsites today. Do not disturb any historic sites or relics you encounter.

The north ridges of 5,810-foot Silver Peak can be reached from Rapid Creek between Stewart Gulch and Goose Pasture Draw for those interested in an adventurous side trip. There is a large cairn on the summit and a good view to the south of Scruton Mountain and the Seth Bullock Fire Tower. Plan on taking over an hour for this 1,200-foot off-trail climb, and try to avoid using a slab of slate as a surfboard to speed your descent.

After a cool refreshing trip along Rapid Creek reach the Silver City Trailhead at 15 miles. Continue east along the Silver City Road, then cross it. Ascend a small hill, then cross BHNF Road 450. The next three miles to the *Centennial Trail* pass through dense ponderosa pine forest as the trail turns gradually from north to east. At 18 miles reach the trail's end at a junction with the Centennial Trail. To reach the Deer Creek Trailhead turn north on the Centennial Trail for 0.2 mile.

Swede Gulch Route

Description: An easy cross-country ski trip or mountain bike ride.
General Location: Six miles northwest of Rochford, South Dakota.
Highlight: An isolated trip through pleasant terrain.
Access: From Rochford, drive 5.1 miles north on the Rochford Road to BHNF Road 259. Drive 0.4 miles south on Road 259, cross Swede Gulch and the Mickelson Trail to park at the junction of BHNF roads 259 and 367. Or, drive south from Lead on U.S. 85, and turn south on the Rochford Road. Then drive 10.0 miles south to the abandoned town of Nahant, and turn right onto BHNF Road 259.

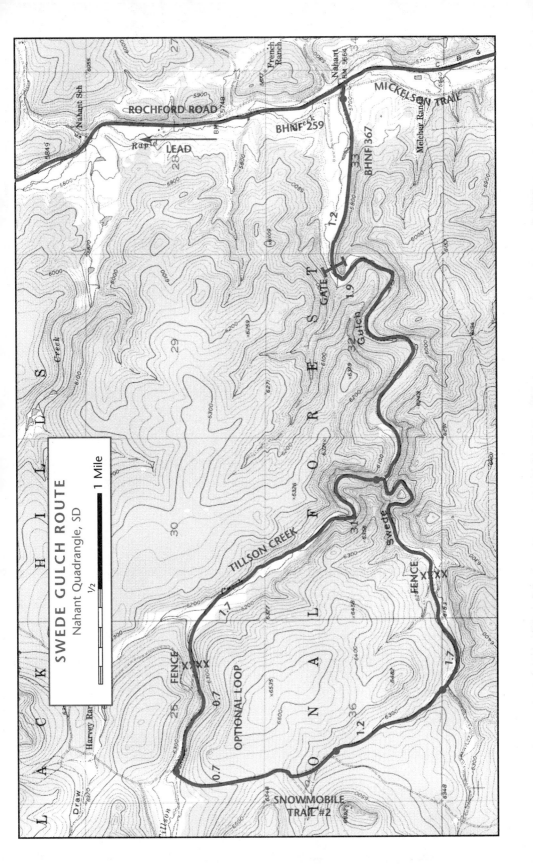

SWEDE GULCH ROUTE
Nahant Quadrangle, SD

½   1 Mile

Distance: 6.2 miles round trip, and an optional 6.0 mile extra loop.
Maps: USGS Nahant, South Dakota 7.5-minute quadrangle and page 111.

If you're looking for a quiet, easy place to do some off-trail skiing, Swede Gulch is the place. This little-used area offers a creekside route through some of the prettiest terrain in the central Black Hills. Even when snow conditions are poor elsewhere, the sheltered canyons of Swede Gulch and Tillson Creek hold their snow against the onslaught of sun and warm temperature.

From the junction of BHNF roads 259 and 367, head west for 1.2 mile on BHNF Road 367, which is not maintained in the winter. Beyond the gate at the end of Road 367, snowmobiles and motorized vehicles are prohibited. Go around the gate, turn south and enter the narrow canyon of Swede Gulch. From the gate it is 1.9 miles to the confluence of Swede Gulch and Tillson Creek. Along the way, you'll pass steep, heavily wooded slopes and dramatic rock walls. You'll see the tracks of deer and wild turkeys and pass a chain of abandoned beaver ponds.

Most skiers will turn around at the junction, but ambitious and strong skiers can make a 6.0 mile loop from this point. To ski the loop clockwise, continue up Swede Gulch crossing through a gate in a fence. At a prominent fork, 1.7 miles past the confluence and just before crossing a creek, turn northwest and follow the fork to Snowmobile Trail 2. Follow Snowmobile Trail 2 north over a saddle, then reach Tillson Creek 2.9 miles past the confluence. At the bottom of the hill, turn east off Snowmobile Trail 2 to follow the narrow, overgrown canyon of Tillson Creek. Deep snow and dense timber make this descent difficult, even though it is a gentle downhill grade. Skiers surviving this section will emerge into a meadow just after crossing a fence at 4.3 miles. From the meadow, continue to follow Tillson Creek southeast back to the junction with Swede Gulch for a total distance of 6.0 miles.

The Black Hills National Forest manages the Swede Gulch area with an emphasis on semi-primitive non-motorized recreation. Hiking, horseback riding, hunting, and cross-country skiing are allowed activities, but no improvements have been made. Despite this management emphasis, Swede Gulch is a place for solitude; the area is seldom travelled.

The long ski loop which connects the upper ends of Swede Gulch and Tillson Creek makes an excellent mountain bike ride in the summer. Riders will probably want to start at the gate across BHNF Road 267 to avoid 1.2 miles of gravel road each way. Livestock graze in Swede Gulch, but roads are closed to the public.

Custer Peak Route

Description: A difficult cross-country ski trip or a long, moderate mountain bike trip.

General Location: Seven miles south of Lead, South Dakota.

Highlight: Views from the tower on top of Custer Peak.

Access: From U.S. 85 at Brownsville turn west onto the Englewood Road (BHNF Road 227). Drive 2.1 miles west, then turn south onto BHNF Road 229. Drive 1.4 miles to the end of the plowed road and park. To approach the peak from the west via Snowmobile Trail 7, drive 7.2 miles south of Lead on the Rochford Road and park at the Dumont Lot, which also serves the Mickelson Trail. To approach from the east, drive south of Brownsville on U.S. 385 for 1.8 miles. Turn west onto BHNF Road 216 and drive a short distance to the Custer Lot which is opposite a large gravel pit.

Distance: From the north it is 2.7 miles one way to the summit. From the west it is 5.3 miles one way to the summit. The two routes on the east side can be combined to form a 10.0 mile loop.

Maps: USGS Deadwood South, Lead, Minnesota Ridge and Nahant, South Dakota 7.5-minute quadrangles and page 114.

A trip to the top of Custer Peak is a challenging and rewarding climb to one of the most scenic vistas in the northern Black Hills. The flat cone of Custer Peak is one of the most recognizable landmarks in the Black Hills, and a climb to the top can be made in any season.

The *North Approach* begins by following an unmarked extension of BHNF Road 229 south along Elk Creek. Continue south on a lesser fork where the Road 229 turns west. At the end of the meadows along the headwaters of Elk Creek, turn left again at another stream junction and begin to climb steadily. At 1.3 miles reach a prominent saddle on the west shoulder of Custer Peak.

At the saddle turn left and north onto Snowmobile Trail 7 and follow the trail for 0.1 mile. Then turn right and east, then follow an

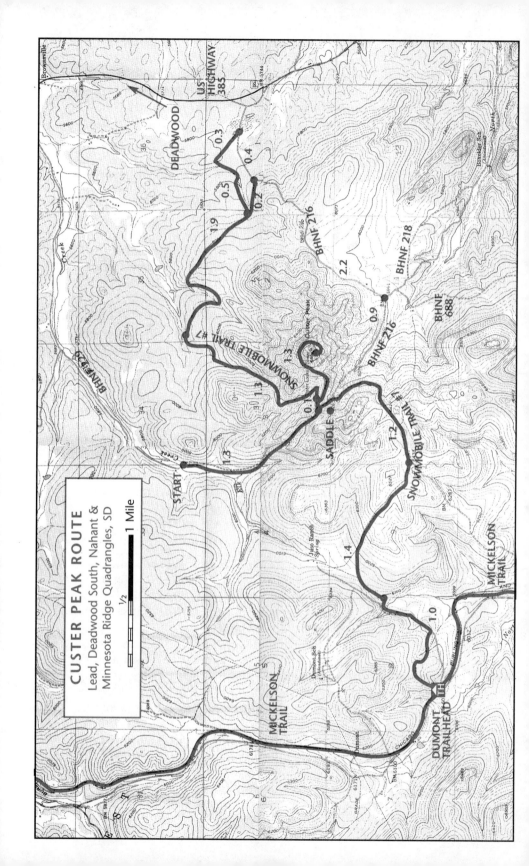

CUSTER PEAK ROUTE
Lead, Deadwood South, Nahant &
Minnesota Ridge Quadrangles, SD

obvious dirt road that spirals up the summit cone of Custer Peak to end just short of the summit lookout tower. The Custer Peak Lookout Tower is staffed throughout the summer.

The tower is an excellent spot to rest, eat lunch and enjoy the views. Bear Butte, Harney Peak, Deer Mountain and Terry Peak are particularly prominent. To return, follow your tracks back to Elk Creek. The steep narrow trail from the meadows on Elk Creek to the shoulder of Custer Peak can be very difficult to descend on skis, especially on icy snow.

Snowmobile Trail 7 leads to Custer Peak from the Rochford Road on the west side. The *West Approach* follows a route toward Juso Ranch before climbing east just below ridge 6,527. Trail 7 then leads northeast to point 6,427 before turning north to reach the west saddle.

The *East Side Mountain Bike Loop* combines Snowmobile Trail 7 with BHNF Road 216, which is plowed in the winter. From the Custer Lot follow Road 216 west 3.3 miles to the west shoulder, then to the summit. Return to the west shoulder and follow Snowmobile Trail 7 east.

Snowmobile Trail 7 winds down the north slope of Custer Peak to a fork 1.3 miles from the west shoulder of Custer Peak to the Snowmobile Custer Parking Lot. Old Snowmobile Trail 5 used to follow BHNF Road 213 down the left fork, but Road 213 is now blocked by private land. Snowmobile Trail 7 follows the right fork along BHNF Road 213 southeast for 1.9 miles. Just before Road 213 crosses a fork of Bear Butte Creek and reaches Road 216, turn left and east onto a rough dirt road. Follow the dirt road for 0.5 mile and turn right off the road just before reaching a gate. The right fork leads 0.3 mile to the Custer Lot.

Custer's 1874 expedition to the Black Hills named the peak for its leader. Surprisingly the group made no attempt to scale the peak.

Ward Draw Route

Description: A long loop over moderate terrain suitable for skiers and mountain bikers.

General Location: Ten miles south of Lead, South Dakota.

Highlight: Reliable winter snow and cool summer riding.

Access: From the junction of U.S. 85 and the Rochford Road, (BHNF 17) drive 2.5 miles south on the Rochford Road to a sign for the Lead

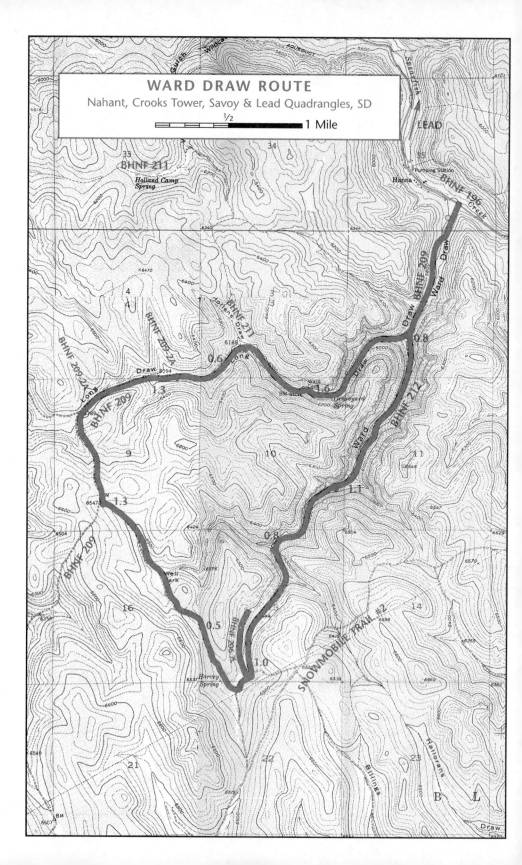

WARD DRAW ROUTE

Nahant, Crooks Tower, Savoy & Lead Quadrangles, SD

½ 1 Mile

Country Club. Turn right onto the Hanna Road, which becomes BHNF Road 196, then drive 2.4 miles to the junction with BHNF Road 209. Park here, or in a small parking area which is on the west side of the road 0.1 mile south.

Distance: The loop is 9.4 miles around.

Maps: USGS Lead, Savoy, Crook's Tower, and Nahant, SD 7.5-minute quadrangles and page 116.

Ward Draw, and the area surrounding Hanna, are among the coldest areas in the Black Hills. This is a place to be if you are looking for good late season snow, and for excellent cross-country ski terrain. The high elevation here makes for pleasant mountain biking on sweltering summer days.

From the junction of BHNF roads 196 and 209, go south on Road 209 for 0.8 mile along Ward Draw to a junction with BHNF Road 212. Stay left on Road 212, and continue to follow Ward Draw, which enters a steep, narrow canyon. The slopes of the draw are covered in spruce and ponderosa pine similar to Dead Ox Gulch in the Eagle Cliff ski area.

Continue up Ward Draw for 1.1 mile, past a building used by the City of Lead Water Department. In upper Ward Draw, the canyon becomes even steeper and narrower. Once in the upper draw there are several ways to complete the loop. The simplest is to continue to follow the main draw until it merges with BHNF Road 206-2L near Harvey Spring, 1.8 miles from the cabin. An alternate route leaves the main draw 0.6 mile beyond the water building, and leads directly to Well Park.

BHNF Road 206-2L quickly leads to a major road. Turn right and follow this road past Well Park to a four-way junction with BHNF Road 209 which is 1.8 miles from Road 206-2L. This intersection is the highest elevation on the loop, and a good spot to stop for lunch after nearly six miles of gradual uphill. Turn right at the intersection onto BHNF Road 209 and enjoy a fast, well-deserved descent into the bottom of Long Draw. Follow Long Draw past the Ward Cemetery and Graveyard Spring back to the junction of Roads 209 and 212. From this junction, retrace your route on Road 209 back to the Hanna Road.

Mountain bikers will find the Ward Draw loop varied and challenging. To avoid repeating the start of the loop, bikers can park at the junction of BHNF roads 209 and 212. Beyond the Lead Water Supply Building, Ward Draw can be a difficult slog on cattle trails. Once into the headwaters, in section 15, many riders will be forced to dismount and push their bikes. But, there is plenty of easy downhill riding on gravel BHNF Road 209.

Although Ward Draw loop is long, all the climbing comes at the beginning, so skiers have a reasonably easy return route. Route finding is easy. The only complicated area is at the head of Ward Draw, and if you do get confused here any side draw will lead eventually to the road that connects Harvey Spring to Well Park on the way to BHNF Road 209.

The scenery is fabulous. Ward Draw is the prettiest of the many north-south trending canyons located south of U.S. 85. This is a cold, snowy place that offers good skiing even when other trails have spring conditions at best. The south part of the area is close to Snowmobile Trail 2, so snow machines may be found along the route from Harvey Spring to Hanna via BHNF Road 209. Ward Draw is not passable by snowmobile.

~

Eagle Cliff: Holey Rock–Clifftop Trails Loop
SPEARFISH RANGER DISTRICT,
BLACK HILLS NATIONAL FOREST

Description: A moderate mountain bike or cross-country ski loop through the heart of the Eagle Cliff trails.
General Location: Fifteen miles southwest of Lead, South Dakota.
Highlight: The view of Intake Gulch from atop Eagle Cliff.
Access: From Cheyenne Crossing, drive southwest 8.4 miles on U.S. 85 to the Eagle Cliff Trailhead. Park in the lot located on the north side of the highway. This lot is plowed in winter by the South Dakota Department of Transportation.
Distance: A 6.1-mile loop with many optional side trips.
Maps: Black Hills National Forest Eagle Cliff Trails Map and page 119.

The arrival of summer at Eagle Cliff used to signal a respite for the trails from their avalanche of winter visitors. However, the Black Hills National Forest now keeps the trails open for summer use by hikers, mountain bikers and horseback riders. Mountain biking is by far the most popular use, and once the trails have dried out in early summer, the tracks of fat tires replace those of skinny skis.

A loop from the Holey Rock–Lily Park Trailhead to Clifftop best illustrates the fun of mountain biking or hiking at Eagle Cliff. The start of both the Holey Rock and Lily Park trails are narrow, steep and

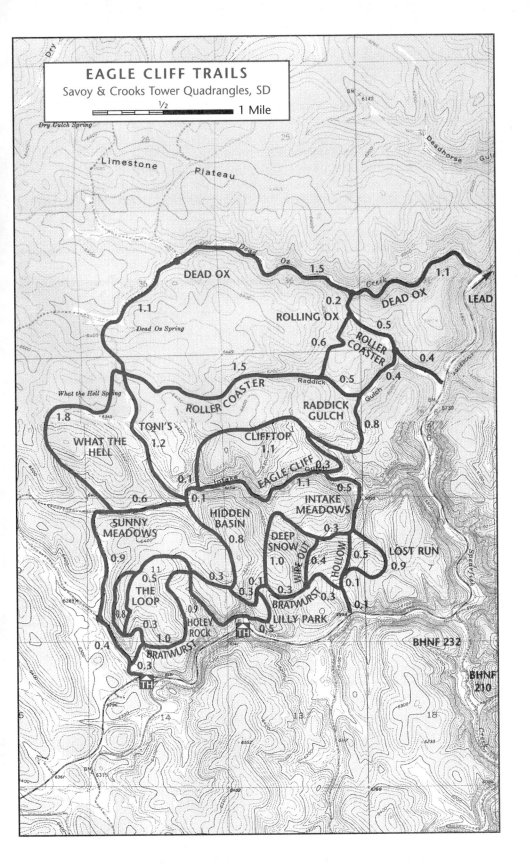

winding. Beginning skiers struggle on these sections, which are the most difficult at Eagle Cliff. However, the trails are navigable by novice hikers and bikers.

To follow the loop counterclockwise, begin on the Lily Park Trail. Cross a fence through a gate and follow Lily Park for 0.5 mile to the Bratwurst Trail which is also BHNF Road 179. Turn east on Bratwurst and go 0.4 mile to Wipe Out which is BHNF Road 179.1B. Not surprisingly, Wipe Out is a steep descent which leads to Intake Meadows after 0.4 mile. Follow Intake Meadows for 0.8 mile passing through a gate in a fence just past the junction with Lost Run. Turn east onto Eagle Cliff and head 0.3 mile to the east end of the Clifftop Trail.

The gentle grades of Intake Meadows and Eagle Cliff become just fond memories as the climb to Clifftop begins. After a level section on Clifftop, the descent back to the Eagle Cliff trail is just as steep, so be careful to control your speed over the many berms on the trail in this narrow canyon. Once back on the Eagle Cliff Trail go west, then south for 0.2 mile to a gate and the start of the Hidden Basin Trail.

Hidden Basin climbs steadily over a small knob, then descends gradually to reach Bratwurst after 0.8 mile. Turn west on Bratwurst and go 0.3 miles to the Holey Rock Trail. A gate across the Holey Rock Trail marks the beginning of a difficult descent along switchbacks to the trailhead which is 0.9 mile from Bratwurst.

This basic route has many simple variations. For a longer trip, use Lost Run or Deep Snow between Bratwurst and Intake Meadows. To shorten the loop from the east end of Intake Meadows, head directly west on Eagle Cliff all the way to Hidden Basin, instead of using the Clifftop Trail.

The Black Hills National Forest has worked hard at opening Eagle Cliff for year-round recreation. The trails are well blazed, easy to follow and almost every intersection is marked by a sign. Maps of the trail system are available at Black Hills National Forest offices. With the exception of Bratwurst, which is a well-used road, the other trails on this loop are two-track dirt roads well suited to mountain bikes. Eagle Cliff is a multiple use area. Trail users may encounter grazing cattle or logging activities, which could pose hazards.

Eagle Cliff: Dead Ox–
Roller Coaster Trails Loop
SPEARFISH RANGER DISTRICT,
BLACK HILLS NATIONAL FOREST

Description: A moderate cross-country ski tour or mountain bike ride in the north side of the Eagle Cliff trails.

General Location: Thirteen miles southwest of Lead, South Dakota.

Highlight: Steep and narrow Dead Ox Gulch and a thrilling descent down the Roller Coaster.

Access: From the junction of U.S. 14A and 85 at Cheyenne Crossing drive 4.0 miles southwest on U.S. 85 to a Black Hills National Forest picnic area on the southeast side of the road. The Dead Ox Trail starts directly across the highway in the yard of a summer home. In the winter, this trailhead is maintained by the Northern Hills Cross Country Ski Club and BHNF, which has an easement through the cabin property.

　　Mountain bike riders who wish to ride the loop in the summer can start from the unmarked Raddick Trailhead located 0.7 further west on U.S. 85 on the north side of the road.

Distance: The ski loop is 7.1 miles long and the mountain bike loop is 6.5 miles long.

Maps: Black Hills National Forest Eagle Cliff Trails and page 119.

The Dead Ox–Roller Coaster loop may be the best ski trip on marked trails in the Black Hills. It has all the features required for a good tour. The snow is deep and dependable, and is well shaded in Dead Ox and Raddick gulches. The loop is uphill on the way out and downhill on the return, so there is no long climb to finish your tour. Both trails are rolling and include some tight downhill turns that should be challenging, but not impossible for most skiers.

　　From the cabin, ski up the valley of Dead Ox Creek 1.1 miles to a gate and the junction with the Rolling Ox Trail. The tight, winding canyon in lower Dead Ox may be the prettiest part of Eagle Cliff. Steep limestone walls are covered with dense coats of spruce and ponderosa pine. Further up the canyon, forested area is mixed with open meadows. Continue up the canyon 1.5 miles to a fork in Dead Ox Creek, a point where snowmobiles may illegally penetrate the Eagle Cliff trails. Take the left fork to where the trail turns south near an old stock tank onto an abandoned logging road. After another obscure left turn, the trail crosses Boland Ridge and reaches a junction with the Roller

Coaster and What The Hell trails, 1.1 miles from the fork. Both of these turns are easy to miss, but are marked with arrows on wood signs.

The reward for all this climbing is a rollicking descent down the aptly named Roller Coaster. After 1.5 miles of well-deserved downhill skiing, turn left at the junction with the Raddick Gulch Trail, then climb a small ridge. Descend a short distance to the junction with the Rolling Ox Trail 0.6 mile from the junction. The toughest 0.2 mile of the entire loop lies just ahead. Rolling Ox is a steep, narrow descent down a heavily wooded slope that leaves little room for error. Two switchbacks make the descent to Dead Ox Gulch a little easier. From Dead Ox, the trail leads a gradual mile downhill back to U.S. 85.

Experienced Black Hills skiers learn to start their trips early in the morning. Afternoon temperatures, particularly in mid to late winter, often climb above freezing. As temperatures climb, the top of the snowpack begins to melt, producing perfect "snowball" snow that clings to the bottom of skis, nullifying any glide. After a mile or so of walking on skis caked with six inches of wet snow, some skiers have been known to sleep away the rest of the afternoon and resume their tours only after the snow has refrozen.

Of course, starting early means that your party is more likely to have to break trail, but remember that part of the fun of cross-country skiing is the exercise and that breaking trail is far easier than skiing through sticky snow.

The Black Hills National Forest does not sanction either the Dead Ox or Raddick trailheads, both of which are on private land. Summer trail users should use Raddick or another trailhead in place of Dead Ox, since the cabin at the head of the gulch may be occupied in the summer. To access the loop from the Raddick Trailhead, ride 0.4 mile up the gulch to a fence and the start of the Roller Coaster Trail. Ride up the northwest fork of Raddick Gulch on Roller Coaster to the junction with Rolling Ox. Ride down the Rolling Ox Trail into the valley of Dead Ox Creek to a junction with the Dead Ox Trail.

To return to Raddick, exit Roller Coaster onto the Raddick Gulch Trail. Follow the Raddick Gulch Trail 0.9 mile to the gate at the end of Roller Coaster. Then ride 0.4 mile back down the gulch to U.S. 85. Both Roller Coaster and Raddick Gulch are two-track dirt roads that are fun riding. Dead Ox, however, is simply a cattle track. The northwest fork of Dead Ox (1.1 miles from the four-way junction, or 1.5 miles from the Rolling Ox junction) is a two-track dirt road. BHNF Road 733.1A is a two-track gravel road which runs along the top of Boland Ridge.

Black Hills National Forest trail ratings at Eagle Cliff are conservative and are based in part on trail length. Although rated most difficult, the terrain along Dead Ox is moderate and suitable for intermediate, or strong beginner skiers, although almost anyone can "face plant" here if their attention wavers at the wrong moment.

Eagle Cliff: Sunny Meadow Trails Loop

SPEARFISH RANGER DISTRICT, BLACK HILLS NATIONAL FOREST

Description: An easy cross-country ski or mountain bike loop.
General Location: Seventeen miles southwest of Lead, South Dakota.
Highlight: A short, sunny loop for less experienced skiers.
Access: From Cheyenne Crossing, drive 9.4 miles southwest on U.S. 85. Park on the north side of the highway at the entrance to Sunny Meadow. The lot is plowed in winter by the Black Hills National Forest and Northern Hills Cross Country Ski Club.
Distance: The short loop is 4.2 miles around. A longer loop that adds the Toni's and What The Hell trails is 6.6 miles around.
Maps: Black Hills National Forest Eagle Cliff Trails and page 119.

Some of the easiest terrain at Eagle Cliff is on the west side of the area. The small parking area on U.S. 85 allows access to a variety of loop trips perfect for those looking for a gentle tour of the high country.

To ski the short loop counterclockwise, take your first right onto the Bratwurst Trail, after crossing the cattleguard. Climb gently to the east on Bratwurst for 1.3 miles to the Hidden Basin Trail. Follow Hidden Basin for 0.8 mile north over a small knob, and then descend a moderately steep grade to rejoin the Sunny Meadows Trail. Return to the trailhead by skiing 2.0 miles west, then south, on Sunny Meadow.

If you desire a longer route, follow the Hidden Basin Trail to the junction with Toni's Trail. Toni's leads 1.2 miles north up a small draw to a four-way intersection. At the intersection, turn left onto the What The Hell Trail and follow it for 1.8 miles west, then south to a junction with the Sunny Meadow Trail. From this junction it is 1.4 miles south on Sunny Meadow back to the trailhead.

These two loops are equally attractive as mountain bike rides in the summer or fall. The What The Hell Trail is on rough, two-track dirt roads and trails, but the rest of the trails follow easier two-track roads. Cattle graze at Eagle Cliff in the summer, and seem to particularly favor the north end of the Sunny Meadow Trail. Remember that the soil developed on the Paha Sapa limestone is very slick when wet, so avoid this trail in the spring, and any time after a rain. The trailhead, and most of the first 1.5 miles of the Sunny Meadow Trail, are on private land. So be careful to respect private property rights as you ride or ski through the area.

Sunny Meadow could just as well been named "Windy Meadow." Without the pervasive tree cover found elsewhere at Eagle Cliff the wind can howl across the meadow. A windshell and sunscreen are handy to have while skiing here.

~

Other Eagle Cliff Trails

SPEARFISH RANGER DISTRICT,
BLACK HILLS NATIONAL FOREST

Eagle Cliff is a dense network of trails perched near the top of the Limestone Plateau at elevations exceeding 6,000 feet. In winter, this is the Black Hills' premier ski area. In summer, the terrain is ideal for mountain biking. The ski area has something for nearly everyone. The gentle grades of Bratwurst and Sunny Meadow are ideal for beginners. The hard climbs and challenging downhill runs between Holey Rock and Clifftop will challenge experienced skiers. Remote Dead Ox Gulch and the Roller Coaster Run will excite anyone who skis them. Three tours are recommended here to show the variety of the area. In reality few groups arrive at Eagle Cliff with a precise route planned out. There are so many trails and conditions are so variable that it is often best just to follow whatever trails look fun to you. The trails described below are those not used in the three tours described above.

Deep Snow (1.0 mile) is BHNF Road 179.1G. It is one of four connections between Bratwurst and Intake Gulch.

Hollow (0.5 mile) is the shortest route between Bratwurst and Intake Gulch. It is the steepest and narrowest of the four trails.

Lost Run (0.9 mile) is the least used trail between Bratwurst and Intake Gulch. The trail includes parts of BHNF Roads 179.1A and 179.1D. The northern end of this trail is very steep.

Eagle Cliff (1.1 miles between Intake Meadows and Toni's) provides a shorter, and easier, alternative to Clifftop along the bottom of Intake Gulch.

Raddick Run (0.8 mile) connects Eagle Cliff and Clifftop with Raddick Gulch. The steep slope at its south end is ideal for practicing downhill runs. The hill is wide and open with an easy run-out.

The Loop (1.6 miles for the outer part and 1.3 miles for the inner) connects with Bratwurst for a short trip from Sunny Meadow over easy terrain.

Roughlock and Spearfish Canyon Floor Trails
SPEARFISH RANGER DISTRICT,
BLACK HILLS NATIONAL FOREST

Description: Two short, scenic walks suitable for families.
General Location: Nine miles south of Spearfish, South Dakota.
Highlight: Spearfish and Roughlock Falls are two of the Black Hills most scenic waterfalls.
Access: From Cheyenne Crossing, drive 5.5 miles north on U.S. 14A. Drive a short way up BHNF Road 222 to a gravel parking lot on the east side of the road.
Distance: 1.0 mile one way for Roughlock Falls. The Spearfish Canyon Floor Nature Hiking Trail is a 0.75 mile loop.
Maps: USGS Savoy, South Dakota 7.5-minute quadrangle and page 126.

Most tourists who have visited the Black Hills will tell you that the drive through Spearfish Canyon was one of the highlights of their trip. The lush valley floor, steep limestone cliffs and sparkling waters of Spearfish Creek provide some of the Black Hills' most memorable scenes. Two exciting new trails to canyon waterfalls are perfect for family groups.

The BHNF's Roughlock Trail connects the Cultural Center at Savoy with the picnic area at Roughlock Falls. The path is wide and easy with

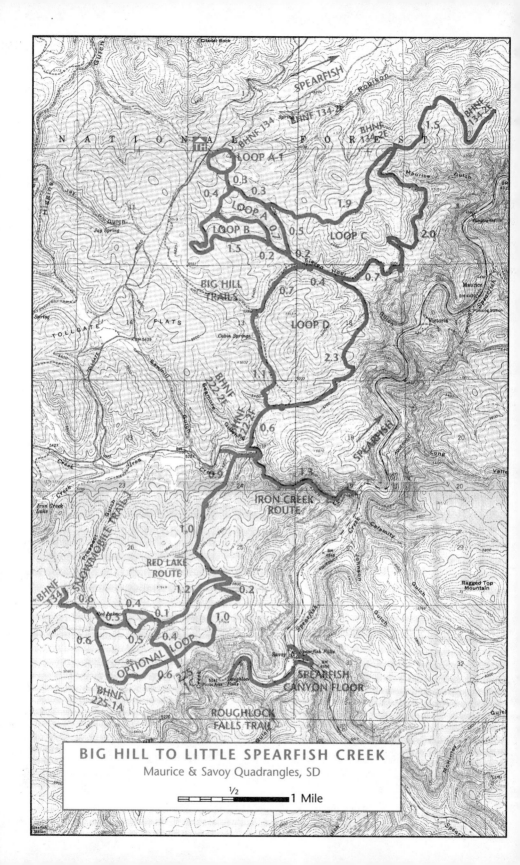

BIG HILL TO LITTLE SPEARFISH CREEK

Maurice & Savoy Quadrangles, SD

½

1 Mile

one bridged crossing of Little Spearfish Creek. Along the way you'll pass through a flower-filled meadow with views of the canyon walls, but the real attraction is the waterfall. A lower eight-foot drop is separated from the main thirty-foot drop by a small cascade. Many casual trails lead from the viewing area at the base of the falls to a picnic area owned by Homestake Mining Company. At the picnic ground visitors will find picnic tables, bathrooms and the upper trailhead.

The Spearfish Canyon Floor Nature Hiking Trail is a three-quarter mile interpretive loop around Spearfish Falls built by the Spearfish Canyon Foundation, The Friends of Spearfish Canyon, Homestake Mining Company and the South Dakota Department of Game, Fish and Parks. It begins by a sign at the north end of the Latchstring Cultural Center. Follow a gravel path to Spearfish Falls, a fifty-foot tall free-falling column of water. For many years this spectacular falls was dry, its water diverted by Homestake Mining Company to run the hydroelectric plants located down the canyon. From the overlook at the bottom of the falls pass by the old aqueduct and return to the south end of the parking area.

These are two of the most kid-friendly hikes in the Black Hills. The waterfalls are high pay-off sites guaranteed to be worth the walk. Both trails are closed to mountain bikes.

Little Spearfish and Rimrock Trails

SPEARFISH RANGER DISTRICT,
BLACK HILLS NATIONAL FOREST

Description: Two easy loop trails along Little Spearfish Creek for hikers, mountain bike riders, and cross-country skiers.

General Location: Sixteen miles southwest of Spearfish, South Dakota.

Highlight: Prime fall foliage.

Access: From Cheyenne Crossing drive 5.5 miles north on U.S. 14A. Turn left onto BHNF Road 222 and drive 4.8 miles to the trailhead, which is located just beyond Timon Campground.

Distance: The Little Spearfish loop is 5.9 miles around. The Rimrock Trail is 6.5 miles around.

Maps: Black Hills National Forest Little Spearfish and Rimrock Trail Map and page 128.

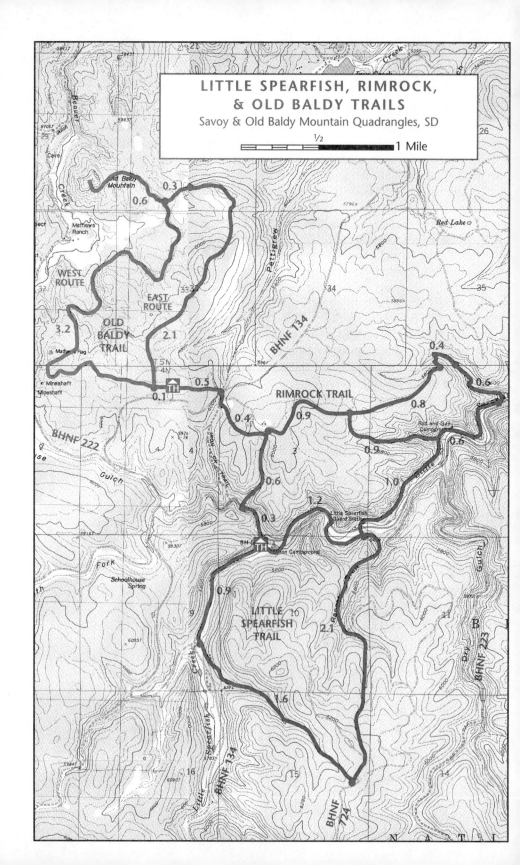

LITTLE SPEARFISH, RIMROCK, & OLD BALDY TRAILS

Savoy & Old Baldy Mountain Quadrangles, SD

½

1 Mile

Old Baldy
Mountain

0.3

0.6

5796x

Red Lake

Beaver

Cave

Mathews
Ranch

WEST
ROUTE

EAST
ROUTE

OLD
BALDY
TRAIL

3.2

Pettigrew

BHNF 134

34

35

5886x

5896x

2.1

Mathews Flag

T 5 N
4 N

TH

0.5

0.4

RIMROCK TRAIL

0.8

0.4

0.6

0.1

Mineshaft
Mineshaft

BHNF 222

0.4

0.9

Rod and Gun
Campground

0.9

0.6

se

Gulch

0.6

1.0

1.2

Little Spearfish
Guard Station

0.3

BM

TH

Canyon Campground

Fork

Schoolhouse
Spring

0.9

LITTLE
SPEARFISH
TRAIL

16

2.1

BHNF 223

60957

6200

1.6

Creek

BHNF 134

16

15

14

BHNF
724

N   A   T

The Black Hills National Forest has constructed two exciting loop trails from its popular Timon and Rod & Gun Campgrounds in Little Spearfish Canyon. The Little Spearfish Trail leads south, while the upper and lower loops of the Rimrock Trail lie to the north. Mountain bikers especially will welcome the diverse terrain and scenery, as well the chance to ride some relatively short loops. In early fall with the aspen covered in bright gold the trail is a little bit of heaven.

From the trailhead at Timon Campground, the *Little Spearfish Trail* leads gradually up the valley of Little Spearfish Creek. After 0.9 mile, the trail crosses the creek on a bridge that is within sight of BHNF Road 134, then begins to climb to the ridge that divides Little Spearfish Creek from Ranger Draw at 1.6 miles. This climb starts steeply, then becomes more gentle closer to the divide. On the divide, reach a dirt road that is adjacent to a fence at 2.5 miles. Follow the dirt road for 0.2 mile where the trail turns north and enters Ranger Draw. A fast descent along Ranger Draw is the well-deserved reward for the climb to the divide.

Ranger Draw joins Little Spearfish Creek and BHNF Road 222 at 4.6 miles where the trail turns to the west. Follow the combined trails for 1.3 west miles back to Timon Campground.

To follow the *Rimrock Trail* clockwise from Timon Campground, head west alongside BHNF Road 222 for 0.3 mile. Then turn north and begin a steep climb out of the canyon. At 0.9 mile reach a junction with a side trail that leads further west 0.9 mile to the *Old Baldy Trailhead*. From this intersection ride east to enjoy a windy descent to the intersection of the upper and lower loops at 1.8 miles. To follow the *Lower Loop*, ride along the rim then down into a small draw to a gate at 3.0 miles. Continue down the draw to reach BHNF Road 222 at 3.6 miles. Ride up the canyon to the Rod and Gun Campground at 4.2 miles, then follow single-track on the north side of Road 222 to the junction with the Little Spearfish Trail at 5.2 miles. To return to Timon Campground at 6.5 miles follow the combined trails west.

The upper and lower loops of the Rimrock Trail are divided by a 0.9 mile connector that climbs to the canyon rim from just west of the Rod and Gun Campground. The connector is the easiest of the three trails that climb from the floor to rim.

The terrain along this route is difficult for beginning cross-country skiers. The route may be too long for children or novices, especially if they have to break trail. The trails are well marked and easy to follow, even when snow covered. Experienced skiers will have no problems, and may want to explore some of the other forest roads that the trail intersects. Snow conditions should be similar to the Eagle Cliff area since the terrain and elevation are similar.

Little Spearfish is one of the best cross-country ski trails in the Black Hills. But all good things have a catch, and for this trail the catch is winter access. BHNF Road 222, which reaches Timon Campground from the east, is part of Snowmobile Trail 4A, and is closed to wheeled vehicles beyond Savoy after December 1, when maintenance begins on the state snowmobile trail system. BHNF Road 134, which provides access from the west, is not plowed between the 134-222 junction and the 134-733 junction to the south. Access will change every winter based on logging needs and the decision of the County Commission, so it is best to check beforehand for information. Generally, the county plows Road 134 for the entire length. Skiers determined to try the Little Spearfish Trail can either ski up the road from Savoy or ski south from the BHNF Road 134-222 junction.

Old Baldy Trail

SPEARFISH RANGER DISTRICT, BLACK HILLS NATIONAL FOREST

Description: A moderate loop hike or bike ride to the top of Old Baldy Mountain.
General Location: Fifteen miles southwest of Spearfish, South Dakota.
Highlights: Summit views and exceptional trail riding.
Access: From U.S. 14A at Savoy leave Spearfish Canyon on BHNF Road 222. After 6.0 miles, turn north on BHNF Road 134. Follow Road 134 for 1.2 miles to a parking area on the west side of the road. The trailhead can also be reached by driving south from Spearfish on BHNF Road 134 for 15.6 miles.
Distance: 6.9 miles, including the spur trail to the summit.
Maps: Black Hills National Forest Old Baldy Trail and page 128.

The Old Baldy Trail is one of the Black Hills' most scenic trails and remains a favorite of BHNF Recreation Specialist Galen Roessler, a man who knows them all. Built for hikers, mountain bikers and cross-country skiers, the Old Baldy Trail consists of a loop trail south of Old Baldy Mountain and a side trail to the summit. Deer and wild turkeys are common along the trail.

The loop begins 150 yards from the trailhead. The west route follows a ridge west, then north, before dropping into the valley of a tributary of Beaver Creek. After descending along the tributary, the trail turns northeast and follows a fence that is the property boundary of Lap Circle Ranch. Beyond the ranch boundary is a rolling section of trail. Just after crossing Snowmobile Trail 3, the west route intersects the east route and the summit spur trail in a meadow 3.3 miles from the trailhead.

The summit spur follows the divide west, then finishes with a steep climb up the cone of Old Baldy Mountain. From the intersection, the east route leads 0.3 mile to Baldy Lake, a glorified stock pond in a heavily-grazed meadow. The trail turns south and leads 2.2 miles back to the trailhead on overgrown jeep roads and single track.

The top of Old Baldy offers a few surprises. The first is a scattered covering of ponderosa pines and bur oak, illustrating the power of revegetation on the Limestone Plateau. The best surprise is the view east over Spearfish Canyon to Terry Peak, Ragged Top, and Spearfish Peak. Crow Peak to the north, and the Cement Ridge Lookout, only three miles west, are visible. Open-pit gold mines at Richmond Hill and Annie Creek–Foley Ridge lie on the north and west sides of Terry Peak.

The east route is underlain primarily by rocks of the Mississippian-Age Paha Sapa limestone while the west route is underlain mostly by Tertiary-Age intrusive igneous rocks. Old Baldy is one of the many prominent summits in the northern Black Hills formed from these hard, resistant intrusive rocks.

While the loop trail alone is an easy hike, the extra distance and elevation gain of a summit trip make this hike moderately difficult. The full loop with a trip to the summit should take three to four hours. No water or other facilities are available along the trail or at the trailhead. Cattle graze in the area so bring your own water. The trail is in excellent condition, and is well marked with posts and blazes.

Red Lake Route

Description: A moderately difficult trip over unmarked trails.
General Location: Fourteen miles southwest of Spearfish, South Dakota.
Highlight: Reliable winter snow.
Access: From Spearfish, follow the Iron Creek Road (BHNF Road 134) to the south. After 7.0 miles, pass the Big Hill Cross Country Ski Area,

and after 11.2 miles pass the side road to Iron Creek Lake. Red Lake is two miles past the Iron Creek Lake Road. The trailhead is unmarked so you must park on the roadside.

Distance: There are 6.1 miles of trails for cross-country skiing.

Maps: USGS Savoy, South Dakota 7.5-minute quadrangle and page 126.

The Red Lake Cross-country Ski Routes have been developed by outdoor education majors of Black Hills State University under the supervision of Everett Follette. The unmarked trails are designed as an alternative to the Big Hill Trails for winters when Big Hill has insufficient snow for ski touring. Red Lake is higher in elevation than Big Hill, so it receives more snow and holds it longer. For those seeking to complete some long trips in the northern Black Hills, Red Lake and Iron Creek provide a useful connection between the Big Hill trails and the Little Spearfish and Rimrock trails.

There are three main loops at Red Lake. The short loop is located just east of Red Lake, and the long loop extends farther east. An optional route that follows BHNF roads is located south of the other two loops. All three loops start from the same main feeder trail, and all are best skied clockwise.

The Red Lake routes start downhill and east of BHNF Road 134, just across Snowmobile Trail 1. Follow a forest road over a ridge, then across a small draw to a junction at 0.6 mile. The road to the south is BHNF Road 225-1A and the end of the optional loop. The next junction at 0.9 mile is the start of the short loop.

Turn left onto the short loop and pass the stockpond that is Red Lake at 1.1 miles. Then turn right off the main road into a gentle draw. A 0.4 mile downhill stretch connects the short loop to the long loop. To complete the short loop, turn right onto BHNF Road 225-1D and ski back up the draw for 0.5 miles.

To follow the long loop from the junction with BHNF Road 225-1D, ski northeast into a large meadow for 1.2 miles. The Iron Creek Route leads north from the meadow at this point. To continue on the long loop, turn back up the meadow, then climb the hillside to the south for 0.2 mile. This turn can be very difficult to find when there are no ski tracks on it. Mountain bikers may be forced to simply bushwhack up the ridge. The grade is steep at first, but soon becomes more gentle as the trail follows a broad ridge. At the top of the loop, a break in the trees offers a view over Little Spearfish Creek. Just before reaching BHNF Road 225-1C, a faint path leads north off of the ridge. The faint path is the long loop. Follow it for 0.4 mile down a steep descent to the head of the large meadow. To close the long loop, continue east down the meadow to a point just east of the junction of the long and short loops.

To follow the optional loop, continue southwest on the ridge past BHNF Road 225-1C. In 0.6 mile, turn north onto BHNF Road 225-1A. Follow Road 225-1A for 0.6 mile to the junction located west of Red Lake.

The Red Lake routes cover excellent ski terrain and should have enough snow, even after snow has melted off other ski trails. None of the hills are especially long or difficult. There is a good mix of hills and flatter sections.

Red Lake is also an interesting area for a summer mountain bike ride. Without ski tracks to follow, the turns both onto and off of the ridge that forms the south side of the long loop are tough to find. Otherwise, most of trails follow two-track dirt roads. Mountain bikers can connect to routes at Iron Creek or the BHNF Rimrock Trail for extended trips.

Iron Creek Route

Description: An easy and popular off-trail hike leading from Spearfish Canyon to the Limestone Plateau.

General Location: Eleven miles south of Spearfish, South Dakota.

Highlight: A gentle grade up a narrow canyon.

Access: From Cheyenne Crossing, drive 7.2 miles north on U.S. 14A to Iron Creek or drive 12 miles south down the canyon from Spearfish. A small parking area is located on the west side of the road.

Distance: 1.3 miles one-way. An additional 0.6-mile route leads north to connect to the Big Hill Trails or an additional 1.9 mile route leads south to connect to the unmarked Red Lake cross-country ski routes.

Maps: USGS Maurice and Savoy, South Dakota 7.5-minute quadrangles and page 126.

In the dry climate of the Black Hills it is easy to underestimate the power of floods in shaping the landscape. But what rain does fall offers clear evidence of the power of storms. The Black Hills are rarely soaked by long gentle rains. Instead, rain here comes hard and quickly as afternoon thunderstorms in the summer, or powerful storms such as the one that flooded Rapid City in 1972.

A good road once led from Iron Creek Lake, high on the Limestone Plateau, to Savoy at the bottom of Spearfish Canyon. This road was destroyed by the 1972 flood and abandoned soon after. The route has since overgrown and eroded to the point that only a rough foot trail remains. Because this path is the only easy way to climb out of lower Spearfish Canyon on foot or by mountain bike, it has become one of the more popular hikes in the Black Hills.

From the parking area at U.S. 14A in Spearfish Canyon, cross through a rock barricade and head west up Iron Creek. The route is unmarked, but the trail is obvious. The old road is rocky and eroded, but still easy walking. After 1.3 miles reach another rock barricade at the end of the steep and narrow part of Iron Creek Canyon.

To reach the *Big Hill Trails* from the second barricade, continue alongside Iron Creek where the trail becomes a road. After 0.2 mile turn right (north) onto BHNF Road 222-2F which is blocked by a locked gate to prevent motor vehicle access to Big Hill. Climb another 0.4 mile to a small divide and the southern limit of loop D at Big Hill.

To reach the unmarked *Red Lake Routes* from the second barricade, turn left off the main road at the barricade. After 0.1 mile turn left at a wood and gravel barricade across an old road. Follow a faint trail 0.1 mile into a meadow where the trail forks just before reaching a fence. Take the right fork into the trees and begin a steady climb up the nose of a ridge. After crossing a powerline, drop off the southeast side of the ridge. Turn right at a junction 0.9 mile from the barricade and continue for another 0.5 mile to a junction beside an abandoned stock pond. From the stock pond junction the left fork leads another 0.5 mile to a junction that marks the northeast corner of the Red Lake Trails.

Fall is the best time of year for this trip. Much of the area is covered by mixed aspen and ponderosa pine. Most overlooks feature patches of golden aspen framed in the dark green of ponderosa pine.

Spearfish Canyon is a botanical crossroads containing species from a wide variety of ecosystems. Low elevation and abundant water combine to produce some of the best conditions in the Black Hills for the growth of trees typical of eastern hardwood forests such as birch, aspen, elm, willow and oak. On cool, shaded north-facing slopes grow white spruce, which is a relict of ice age boreal forests. Biologists also recognize more common plants from the Rocky Mountain and Great Plains vegetative regions.

A hike along Iron Creek gives one the sense of what a roadless

Spearfish Canyon must have been like. The canyon repelled road builders until the Black Hills gold rush was well under way. It wasn't until 1893 that a railroad from Deadwood to Spearfish penetrated the entire length of the canyon. The railroad provided most of the transportation in the Spearfish Canyon until 1933, when the rail line and most of the thirteen bridges along it were destroyed by flood. The line was replaced by a highway (now U.S. 14A) that uses much of the old railroad bed.

Big Hill Trails

SPEARFISH RANGER DISTRICT, BLACK HILLS NATIONAL FOREST

General Description: Many loop trips are possible ranging from short, easy family trips to long, difficult tours. The area is best for cross-country skiing and mountain biking.

General Location: Eight miles south of Spearfish, South Dakota.

Highlight: The only non-commercial groomed ski trails in the Black Hills.

Access: From Black Hills State University in Spearfish, drive 0.8 mile west on West Oliver Street, past the Pope and Talbot Sawmill, to the Iron Creek Road (BHNF Road 134). An alternate route to the start of BHNF Road 134 leaves from the junction of North Avenue and Utah in Spearfish. Drive 1.6 miles west on Utah to a 4-way stop. From the stop sign drive 0.5 mile south on a gravel road to the start of BHNF Road 134. Drive south on Road 134 for 7.8 miles to the Big Hill Trailhead.

Distance: The A Loop is the shortest at 2.7 miles. A 10.9 mile loop combines the outer parts of A, C and D loops.

Maps: Black Hills National Forest Big Hill Trails and page 126.

Five interconnected loops comprise the Big Hill Trails. The trails traverse rolling terrain on the Limestone Plateau west of Spearfish Canyon, through stands of aspen, birch and ponderosa pine. Big Hill is the most popular area with groomed trails in the Black Hills region. During the winter, loops A, A1, C and D are groomed with a track setter by the Northern Hills Cross Country Ski Club in cooperation with the South Dakota Department of Game, Fish and Parks and the Black

Hills National Forest. Funds for trail maintenance are raised by the club and Black Hills National Forest, partially through a donation box which is located at the trailhead.

Loop A.1 is 0.6 miles around and is designed primarily as a warm-up trail for skiers. Loop A is the main feeder trail, and is 2.0 miles around. A and A.1 can be combined for an ideal family ski trip. If you are a novice skier, plan on sticking to Loop A on your first trip out.

Loop B is 2.2 miles around and a total of 3.6 miles from the trailhead. An overlook offers the best views of Terry Peak from Big Hill. This trail is not groomed in the winter for skiing, and therefore is less used than the other trails. For mountain bike riders, Loop B is also much more challenging. The loop is hillier, and much of it is single track.

At 5.7 miles around and a total of 6.9 miles from the trailhead, *Loop C* is the longest loop. A short relocation on C, near the junction with C1, was made to bypass a steep hill which was followed by a sharp turn. This relocation may make the start of C1 difficult to find in winter. *Trail C1* is a 1.5 mile side trip to an overlook at the rim of Spearfish Canyon. You can't see very far down into the canyon, but the view extends north to the prairie, and east to Spearfish Peak and Ragged Top. When snow conditions are poor, an exposed ridge on the northern part of C may be bare of snow.

Loop D is 4.5 miles around and a total trip of 7.1 miles from the trailhead. Despite some grueling experiences on this loop while cross-country ski racing, it remains one of my favorite ski trails. The snow is usually good, and there is good balance in the length and difficulty of the hills. The meadow around Cabin Springs is a welcome break from the forest on the rest of the trails. About half way around on loop D, BHNF Road 222-F leads 0.6 mile south to the *Iron Creek Route.*

Big Hill is a popular site for cross-country ski racing. Throughout the winter the Northern Hills Cross Country Ski Club sponsors citizens races about every other weekend. Both classic and open technique races are offered. Big Hill is also the site of the Spearfish Challenge, the highlight of the Black Hills racing calendar.

Skiers should note that all Big Hill trails start downhill, and that the climb out of Eleven Hour Gulch back to the trailhead is deceptively long. No water is available along the trail or at the trailhead. There is a latrine in the parking area.

Big Hill is rapidly becoming popular among mountain bikers. With the exception of Loop B, all the trails are relatively smooth two-track dirt roads. The roads are little travelled and closed to motor vehicles year round. On the down side, cattle graze at Big Hill in the summer.

Big Hill trails are well marked, maintained and easy to follow. All trail junctions are well marked with carsonite posts.

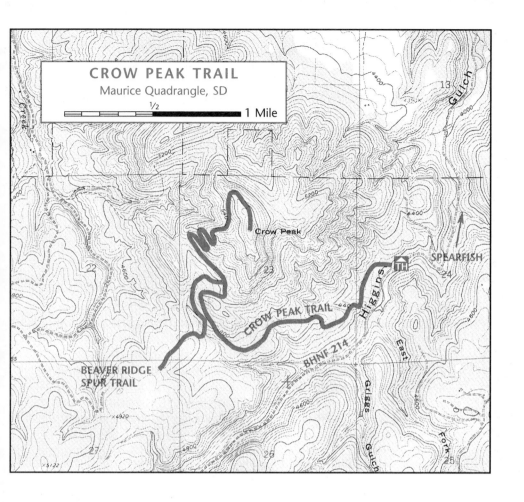

Crow Peak Trail

SPEARFISH RANGER DISTRICT,
BLACK HILLS NATIONAL FOREST

Description: A day hike to the top of Crow Peak along a well maintained trail.

General Location: Four miles southwest of Spearfish, South Dakota.

Highlight: Tremendous summit views of the northern Black Hills.

Access: The Crow Peak Trailhead is located four miles south of Spearfish on the Higgins Gulch Road (BHNF Road 214). There is a large parking area with a trail sign and register box on the west side of the road.

Distance: 7.0 miles round trip.

Maps: Black Hills National Forest Crow Peak Trail Map and page 137.

Dominating the skyline west of Spearfish is the distinctive double-humped profile of Crow Peak. One of the Black Hills National Forest's most popular hiking trails, it leads to the top of the peak that so captures your eye from Interstate 90.

From Higgins Gulch, the Crow Peak Trail winds west across the lower slopes of the mountain through mixed stands of ponderosa pine, aspen, and birch. The *Beaver Ridge Trail* leaves the Crow Peak Trail about halfway up Crow Peak and leads 0.5 mile southwest to an old logging road. Reaching the west side of the mountain, the Crow Peak Trail climbs up a series of switchbacks across loose talus slopes to reach the north ridge. The last section of trail stays on the ridge and follows gentler grades south to the summit.

Crow Peak is a popular hike and justifiably so. The views from the top are fantastic. Terry Peak, Spearfish Peak, Bear Butte, and Cement Ridge are the most prominent summits. More intriguing perhaps, are the Bearlodge Mountains and the Wyoming portion of the Black Hills to the west. Crow Peak may be the best vantage point for scouting Sundance Mountain and other outlying peaks, and is certainly a great spot for photographing them. On clear days, 75 miles away across the northern Great Plains, the Slim Buttes and Short Pine Hills are visible.

An ascent of Crow Peak offers an illustration of the effects of different rock types on soils and topography. The lower part of the mountain is composed of Minnelusa formation shales and sandstones that are easily eroded to form distinctive red soils and relatively gentle slopes. Farther up the mountain are the lighter-colored and more resistant rocks of the Paha Sapa limestone and the Deadwood sandstone which weather to form lighter soils and steeper slopes. The upper core of Crow Peak is quartz latite porphyry, a type of intrusive igneous rock. The porphyry weathers into the coarse plates that compose talus slopes below the summit. The quartz latite is very hard and resistant to erosion, consequently the steepest hiking on Crow Peak is at the end of the climb.

Sixteen hundred feet of elevation gain and numerous switchbacks across talus slopes combine to make this hike moderately strenuous. The hike should take about four to four-and-one-half hours round-trip. No water or other facilities are available along the trail or at the trailhead.

Hikers should be particularly careful to avoid afternoon thunderstorms on high exposed summits such as Crow Peak. Many hikers have had the dubious pleasure of being pelted with hail and gusts of wind during lightning storms on their retreat from the summit. The best strategy to avoid storms is to start your hike early in the day, and take cover or retreat if a storm does arise.

Burno Gulch Route

Description: A moderate mountain bike loop trip over jeep trails and gravel roads.
General Location: Four miles northwest of Lead, South Dakota.
Highlight: The historic mining town of Maitland.
Access: From Lead drive 2.1 miles north on U.S. 14A to the Maitland Road, which is BHNF Road 195. Drive 8.1 miles north on the Maitland Road to the junction of Burno Gulch and False Bottom Creek. Three roads intersect here, the route starts on the middle fork.
Distance: A 12.2-mile loop with a 1,400 foot climb.
Maps: USGS Spearfish, South Dakota 7.5-minute quadrangle and page 140.

The small town of Maitland is the starting point for some of the best mountain bike rides in the northern Black Hills. One favorite loop connects Burno Gulch with False Bottom Creek. To get all your climbing done at the beginning of the loop, and save the downhill ride for the end, start this trip where Burno Gulch joins False Bottom Creek.

From the confluence of Burno Gulch and False Bottom Creek take the middle of the three roads which intersect the Maitland Road. The road passes north of the gulch and south of some houses, but does not cross any locked gates or roads posted "No Trespassing." Follow the dirt road for 0.6 mile on the northwest side of Burno Gulch to a powerline.

Enjoy a steady climb along a two-track dirt road that keeps to the northwest side of Burno Gulch. An unnamed tributary joins Burno Gulch beside a cabin at 2.4 miles. A red dirt road follows the tributary, but our route stays left on a jeep trail along the main stem on what a sign soon declares to be "Miller Drive."

The jeep trail follows the powerline to a road junction at the confluence with Chism Gulch at 3.8 miles. Continue to ascend the main fork of Burno Gulch, passing a road on the left at 4.4 miles and another road on the right 4.8 miles.

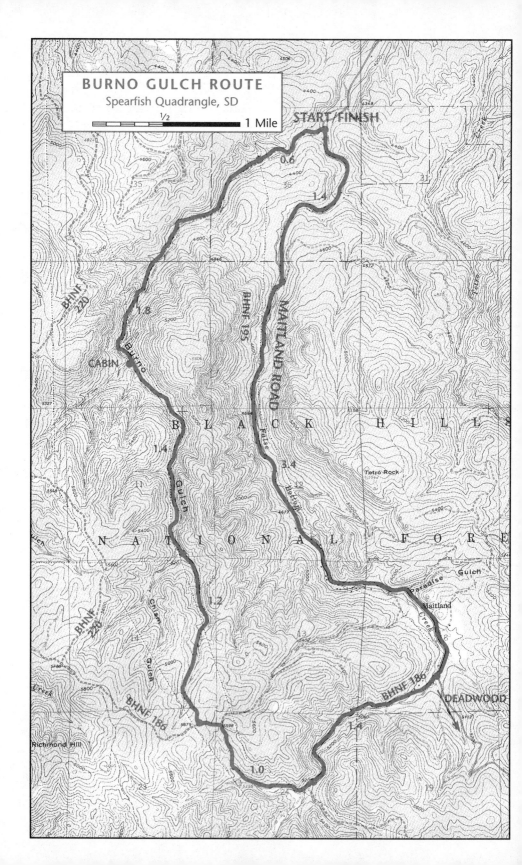

BURNO GULCH ROUTE
Spearfish Quadrangle, SD

½   1 Mile

START/FINISH

0.6

1.4

1.8

BHNF 220

CABIN

Burno

BHNF 195

MAITLAND ROAD

B L A C K   H I L L S

1.4

Gulch

1.1

3.4

False

Bottom

Tetro Rock

N A T I O N A L   F O R E

1.2

Paradise   Gulch

Maitland

BHNF 270

Chism

Gulch

1.4

1.3

Creek

.8

Creek

BHNF 186

BHNF 186

DEADWOOD

Richmond Hill

1.4

1.0

The route turns southeast to leave Burno Gulch at 5.0 miles, then climbs to 5.2 miles and a well-maintained dirt road on the Burno/False Bottom divide at 5,679 feet. Take a well-deserved break at the end of this relentless climb, for the rest of the ride will be downhill.

Turn east and follow the divide a short distance, passing a road on the left leading north. Drop into the headwaters of False Bottom Creek passing a small pond and dam at 5.5 miles. After crossing the familiar powerline, turn left onto BHNF Road 186, at 6.0 miles. Follow Road 186 to 7.4 miles and the junction with gravel BHNF Road 195 in the town of Maitland. Once in Maitland, turn left onto Road 195 and ride north for 4.8 miles back to the mouth of Burno Gulch at 12.2 miles.

The now quiet town of Maitland was once the site of a roaring gold mining camp. Gold was mined sporadically from 1876 until the mines were shut down by the U.S. government during World War II. The mines produced 100,000 ounces of gold primarily during the boom times from 1902 to 1915 and during the 1930s. Production came from several thousand feet of drifts linked by shafts that reached to 620 feet deep.

North Hanna Route

Description: An easy cross-country ski or mountain bike trip mostly on abandoned forest roads.

General Location: Six miles southwest of Lead, South Dakota.

Highlight: Isolated rides above Icebox Gulch.

Access: From the junction of U.S. 14A and 85 in Lead, drive 5.3 miles southwest on U.S. 14A and 85. Park where the Terry Peak Summit Road (BHNF Road 194) intersects the highways. The route starts a few hundred yards downhill and across the road where Snowmobile Trail 5 enters BHNF Road 549.

Distance: The long loop is 5.6 miles around.

Maps: USGS Lead, South Dakota 7.5-minute quadrangle and page 142.

North Hanna is an area of deep snow, gentle terrain and spectacular vistas that is perfect for cross-country skiing. The proximity to Lead, and the relatively small size of the area, make it ideal for evening or short weekend trips. The numerous open, west-facing ridges are ideal for watching the sun set before returning back home, guided by the lights on top of Terry Peak.

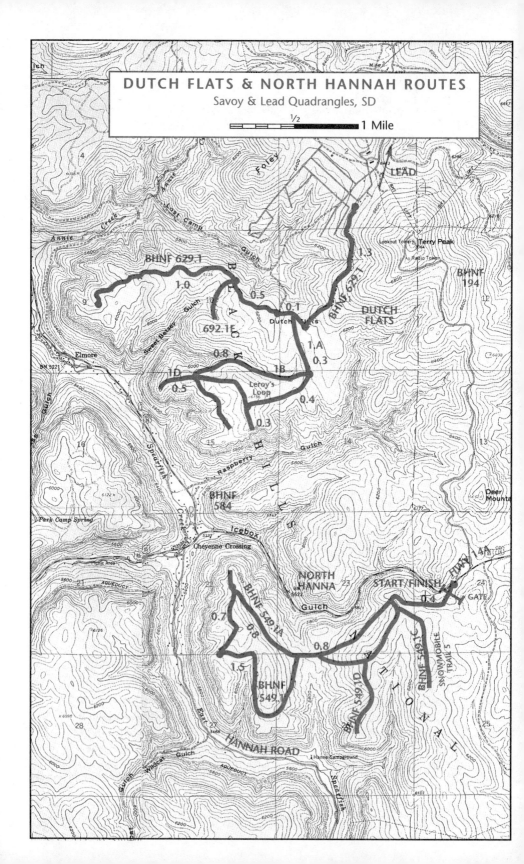

DUTCH FLATS & NORTH HANNAH ROUTES

Savoy & Lead Quadrangles, SD

½   1 Mile

From the start of BHNF Road 549, ski for 0.4 mile on Snowmobile Trail 5 to a road intersection on a ridge. From the ridge, Snowmobile Trail 5 follows BHNF Road 549-1C south to Road 627-1A. Our route descends southwest through open timber on Road 549, which is unmarked at this intersection. Follow Road 549 for 0.8 mile along this north facing slope to the west end of a small saddle and the junction of BHNF Roads 549.1 and 549.1A. This saddle is marked by a sign for 549.1A.

From the saddle, stay right in an open area and follow BHNF Road 549.1A northwest. Road 549.1A ends after 0.8 miles at a turnaround on a ridge. Skiers can follow this ridge due north to its end on a heavily wooded rim just above Cheyenne Crossing. To continue on the loop, ski south from the turnaround along the ridge crest for 0.7 mile to reach another turnaround that marks the end of BHNF Road 549.1. Mountain bike riders will probably have to push their bikes along this ridge crest due to the rough terrain. Ski Road 549.1 in a gentle "U" to return to the sign at the 549.1/549.1A junction after 1.5 miles.

To return to the start, either retrace the route from this point, or head due east to climb the next ridge. This climb is a steep cross-country route that should only be attempted by experienced skiers or mountain bikers. BHNF Road 549.1D follows this ridge north back to an intersection with Snowmobile Trail 5. The ridge route is more difficult, but offers superior views of Terry Peak and Icebox Gulch to the north. Along with the views, skiers will note the plentiful deer tracks along the ridge.

The North Hanna area is bounded by Icebox Gulch to the north, the Hanna Road to the south and west and Snowmobile Trail 5 to the east. Snowmobile Trail 5 and BHNF Road 549 provide access into the area. In the summer, the gate across Road 549 at U.S. 85 is closed, and motorized vehicles are prohibited in the area. During the snowmobile season, Trail 5 provides motorized access to the area. In any season the area is lightly used and there does not appear to be many skier/ snowmobile conflicts.

The route passes through a forest dominated by ponderosa pine. The area was once logged, but is now recovering. Deer and coyotes are common. Numerous standing dead trees provide homes for cavity nesting birds and small animals.

Due to summer road closures, this is an excellent area to explore on a mountain bike. Bikers should not attempt to ride the ridge south of Road 549.1, which is recommended as a return route for skiers. In addition to the route described here, there are a number of other abandoned roads in the area worthy of exploration.

Like many of the other areas in the Black Hills that are good for skiing, North Hanna is part of the Limestone Plateau. Soils developed on
the bedrock of Paha Sapa Limestone are rich in clay and break down
into thick, sticky gumbo when wet. To avoid the gumbo, try another
ride closer to Lead-Deadwood in wet weather.

Dutch Flats Route

Description: An easy mountain bike ride or cross-country ski trip with
many side trips to overlooks above Spearfish Canyon.
General Location: Six miles west of Lead, South Dakota.
Highlight: Spearfish Canyon overlooks.
Access: From Lead, drive one mile west on U.S. 85 to the Terry Peak
Road. Drive west on the Terry Peak Road to the end of the pavement,
then turn left onto a gravel road. Drive 0.6 mile on the gravel road
past the Terry Peak Ski Area to Deep Snow Trail. Park at a locked gate
across BHNF Road 629.
Distance: 6.8 miles round-trip to the overlook above Elmore or 4.7
miles for Leroy's Loop.
Maps: USGS Lead and Savoy, South Dakota 7.5-minute quadrangles
and page 142.

Dutch Flats is a high, isolated plateau located between Spearfish
Canyon, Icebox Gulch, Terry Peak and Wharf's Annie Creek Mine.
BHNF Road 629 and its subsidiary roads are closed to motor vehicles,
but offer access to superb overlooks for hikers, mountain bike riders
and cross-country skiers.

A locked gate across BHNF Road 629 marks the start of the trip.
Begin with a 1.3 mile descent to Dutch Flats and a major T-junction
located just past Dutch Flats Spring. From the T-junction two different
trips are possible.

The right fork follows a ridge to an overlook above Elmore. Continue on the ridge 0.1 mile beyond the T-junction where a grassy road
leads north into Lost Camp Gulch. After another 0.5 mile, pass BHNF
Road 629.1E that leads south from the head of Sweet Betsy Gulch.
Continue west along the ridge for another 1.4 miles to the end of the
road. For a great view down into Spearfish Canyon and the old town
of Elmore, climb the ridge to the west.

From the T-junction near Dutch Flats Spring, the left fork leads 0.3 mile on BHNF Road 629.1A to Leroy's Loop, which begins at the 1A/1B intersection. To complete the loop clockwise, head south 0.4 mile on rapidly deteriorating Road 629.1A to the west end of ridge 6,196. From the crest of the ridge, a side trail leads south 0.3 mile to an overlook above heavily forested Raspberry Gulch. Continue north on the ridge 0.3 mile, passing a turkey guzzler, to a four-way junction.

From the four-way junction BHNF Road 629.1D leads west 0.5 mile to an overlook above Spearfish Canyon. Road 629.1C leads left 0.5 mile southeast to a dead end. To continue on Leroy's Loop, turn right (east) at the four-way junction and follow 629.1C for 0.6 mile to a junction with Road 629.1B. Continue straight at the 1B/1C junction and turn left at the end of the loop to return to the T-junction.

Dutch Flats is equally interesting on a mountain bike or cross-country skis. The main road to Dutch Flats Spring is intermittently graveled, but otherwise the roads are relatively smooth, overgrown two-track dirt roads ideal for bikes. Not all the roads have signs, so carry a map for navigation. There has been no grazing at Dutch Flats since 1990, so the meadow around Dutch Flats Spring is surprisingly lush. Expect to see plenty of deer here in the summer.

The elevation at Dutch Flats ranges from 5,900 to 6,400 feet so the area receives deep snow. The tree cover is dense enough to shade the trails, but open enough so that the tree canopy doesn't intercept all the snow. Skiers should note that snowmobiles also use Dutch Flats.

There is only one drawback to a trip to Dutch Flats. The climb from Dutch Flats Spring to the gate at the start is long and unrelenting. Don't expend so much energy exploring all the side trails and overlooks and save a little for the trip out.

~

Pillar Peak Route

Description: A moderate cross-country ski or mountain bike trip from Galena which finishes with a short hike to the top of Pillar Peak.

General Location: Five miles east of Deadwood, South Dakota.

Highlight: Summit views from Pillar Peak.

Access: To reach Galena, drive south from Lead for 5.2 miles and turn off U.S. 385 onto BHNF Road 534. Drive 4.0 miles northeast to a bridge across Bear Butte Creek. Park on the roadside by the bridge.

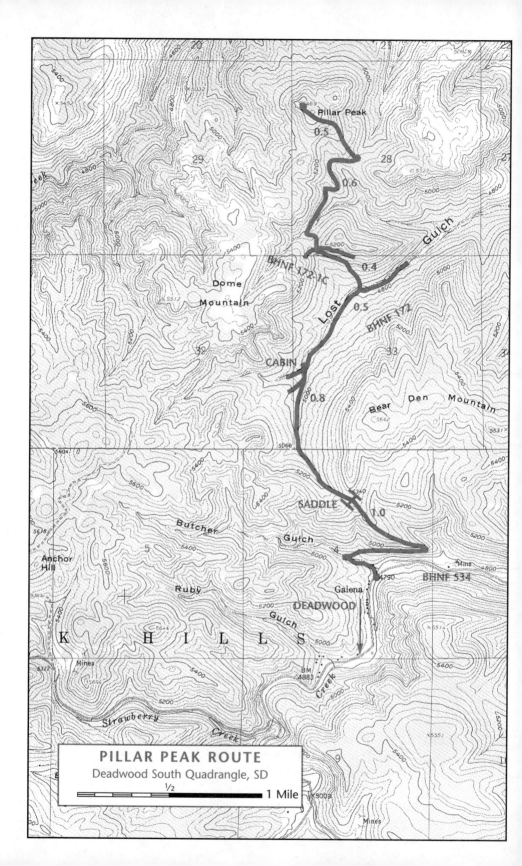

PILLAR PEAK ROUTE
Deadwood South Quadrangle, SD

½   1 Mile

Distance: 3.3 miles one way by bike or ski, and 0.5 mile of hiking to Pillar Peak.

Maps: USGS Deadwood South, South Dakota 7.5-minute quadrangle and page 146.

The town of Galena is a convenient starting point for exploring the northeast corner of the Black Hills, an area of rugged canyons and relatively low summits. Pillar Peak, one of the most interesting of these summits, can be reached via a four-mile trip through an area seldom travelled.

From the bridge over Bear Butte Creek, head northwest up Butcher Gulch for one-quarter mile. Leave Butcher Gulch at a sharp switchback to the right, and climb steadily to the nose of a prominent ridge overlooking Galena from the north. Beyond Butcher Gulch, the route is entirely on Black Hills National Forest Land. Follow the ridge northwest to a saddle on the southwest shoulder of Bear Den Mountain which is 1.0 mile from Galena.

Descend from the saddle to reach BHNF Road 172 in the valley of Lost Gulch. Pass the remains of an old cabin at 1.8 miles, then turn northwest onto BHNF Road 172-1C at 2.3 miles. Climb steadily along brush-covered road 172-1C to reach another saddle after 2.7 miles. Then follow the road along contour to a third saddle located on the southeast shoulder of Pillar Peak at 3.3 miles.

The last half-mile to the top of Pillar Peak is steep, rocky and without a trail. Both bikers and skiers should leave their equipment behind here and bushwhack to the summit.

Pillar Peak may have the best views in the northeast corner of the Black Hills; if not, at least you can see all the likely contenders from there. To the northeast is Bear Butte and to the north Whitewood Peak and Crook Mountain are particularly prominent. Mount Theodore Roosevelt, Terry Peak, Deer Mountain and Custer Peak surround the Lead-Deadwood area. Those unfamiliar with this part of the hills are struck by the deep rugged canyons draining the northern flank. Once you've planned a few more trips from this scenic spot, it is time to return to Galena by retracing your route.

The first discovery of silver in the northeast Black Hills occurred in March, 1876. By January, 1877, a town of 75 buildings housed 400 miners. The town was named Galena for the silver-bearing lead sulfide mineral that contained most of the ore in the district. Large-scale mining began in the area in 1878 with the opening of the Florence Mine by J. H. Davy, initiating the first of many boom and bust cycles typical of mining camps.

The reopening of the Branch Mint Mine by J. D. Hardin signalled a second burst of mining which lasted from 1904 to 1912. The most recent attempt at profitable silver mining at Galena was at the Double Rainbow Mine operated by Homestake Mining Company. The Double Rainbow headframe is just downstream of the bridge over Bear Butte Creek on the right side of the road.

The recent gold mining boom in the Black Hills has also touched Galena. Just up Strawberry Creek from Bear Butte Creek is the Gilt Edge Gold Mine. After nearly twenty years of intermittent exploration, the Gilt Edge Mine opened in 1987 as an open pit/heap leach operation.

BHNF Road 172 is open, but not maintained, in the winter. When snow conditions permit, the route is an excellent introduction to the potential for cross-country ski climbs of Black Hills summits. Snowmobiles, and some vehicles, may travel partway up the road along Lost Gulch. However, the area is lightly travelled except during hunting season, and skiers can expect to be alone and to break trail.

Several other possible routes exist in the Galena area including trips up Bear Den Mountain or Anchor Hill, and a loop that connects Butcher Gulch with the unnamed gulch that starts at the abandoned cabin.

~

Other Black Hills National Forest Trails

The *Mount Roosevelt Trail*, located north of Deadwood, leads 0.5 mile from BHNF Road 133 to a lookout tower. Regrowth of the forest around the tower has obscured the view.

The *Dutchman Loop Trail* is a 1.25-mile circuit from the campground on Deerfield Lake.

The *Pioneer Discovery Trail* is a 0.2-mile wheelchair accessible trail that starts from the entrance of the Sheridan Lake Campground.

The *Veterans Point Trail* is a 1.0-mile accessible trail that begins at the north end of Pactola Dam.

The *Aspen Leaf Trail* is a 0.2-mile interpretive route at the Pactola Visitors Center.

The *Lakeview Trail* is a 2.2-mile route along Pactola Reservoir that leaves from Pactola Campground.

Wyoming

Beaver Creek Cross-Country Ski Trails

CUSTER RANGER DISTRICT,
BLACK HILLS NATIONAL FOREST

Description: A moderate cross-country ski or mountain bike trip.
General Location: Four miles east of Four Corners, Wyoming.
Highlight: Scenic trails in a little-used recreation area.
Access: From Lead, South Dakota, drive 34 miles southwest on U.S. 85 to Four Corners, Wyoming. Drive 4.7 miles east on the Mallo Road (BHNF Road 810) to the junction with BHNF Road 111 at a parking area. There is a trail sign at the top of the hill. If road conditions permit, drive 0.6 mile down a steep hill to Mallo Camp and park in a turnout adjacent to the trail register.
Distance: The Highland Trail loop is 7.3 miles around. There are 15.9 miles of trails in the area.
Maps: Black Hills National Forest Beaver Creek Ski Trails and page 150.

Tucked far off the beaten track of Black Hills skiing is the Beaver Creek Ski Area. If you are tired of seeing the same terrain at popular areas such as Eagle Cliff or Big Hill, Beaver Creek offers a chance for solitude without compromising snow conditions or trail quality.

Beaver Creek is located on the western flank of the Black Hills along the South Dakota–Wyoming border. The area is high enough to receive, and hold, deep snowfalls. The topography and elevation make snow conditions at Beaver Creek similar to those at Eagle Cliff.

Beaver Creek trails are easy to follow. The trails are marked by blue plastic diamonds on trees, and trail junctions are lettered and marked with brown carsonite posts. Since the area is little-used, you can expect to break trail, so bring some friends along to help share the work and the fun.

The trail system is designed so that most skiers travel one of three loops. The trail over Highland Ridge is the most interesting and most used. To ski the Highland Loop, proceed north from Mallo Camp

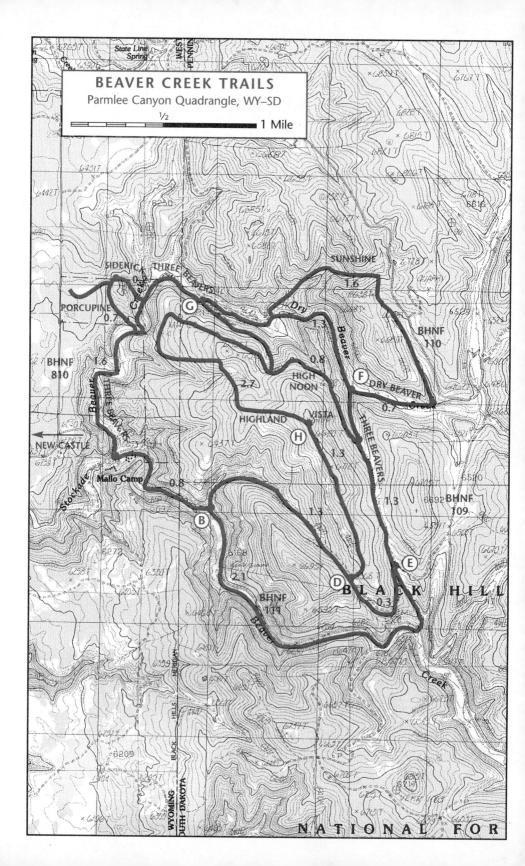

BEAVER CREEK TRAILS

Parmlee Canyon Quadrangle, WY–SD

½ 1 Mile

through open meadows along Dry Beaver Creek past the Porcupine and Sidekick trails. The trail crosses private land on the Wyoming side of the border, so be careful not to leave any signs of your passage. At 1.6 miles reach point "G" and the junction with BHNF Road 712, turn southeast up a small side drainage. Look for a switchback where the trail leaves this draw. Then, wrap around the northeast end of Highland Ridge, just skirting the Wyoming line, and then climb east to the open meadow and vista near the top of Highland Ridge.

At Highland Ridge, stop for lunch and enjoy the views of the little-travelled western flank of the Black Hills. When you become more cold than hungry, it is time to enjoy the rewards of your morning climb with a gradual ridgeline descent toward Beaver Creek. At point "D" turn northeast to follow a side draw to point "B" and BHNF Road 111 at 6.5 miles. Follow Road 111 back to Mallo Camp at 7.3 miles. BHNF Road 111 is also the route of Wyoming Snowmobile Trail 11.

The shorter and gentler Three Beavers route continues east from point "G" to "E" and "F" before rejoining the loop at "D." This outer circuit is 7.0 miles around.

From Mallo Camp to the Beaver Creek Campground, skiers share the trail with snowmobiles. If you ski this section, be especially careful and step to the side of the trail to allow snowmobiles to pass. Unfortunately, some of the other ski trails are also used illegally by snowmobiles. Copies of the trail map may be stored in the register box.

Sand Creek Route

Description: A moderately difficult off-trail hike through steep canyons in the northwestern corner of the Black Hills.

General Location: Eight miles south of Beulah, Wyoming.

Highlight: One of the Black Hills' most botanically diverse areas.

Access: From Interstate 90, take Exit 205 and follow the signs south to the Ranch A Fish Hatchery. Pass Ranch A 7.3 miles beyond I-90 and the BHNF boundary after 9.0 miles. Once in the Black Hills National Forest, the road becomes number 863. At 13.9 miles reach Bridge 302 over Sand Creek and a small turnout on the right side suitable for parking.

Distance: The short loop is approximately four miles long.

Maps: USGS Tinton and Red Canyon Creek, Wyoming–South Dakota 7.5-minute quadrangles and page 152.

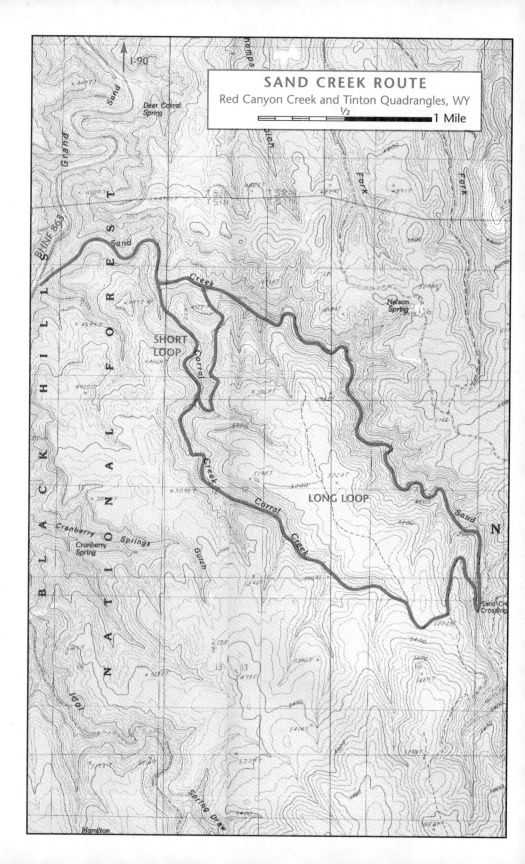

SAND CREEK ROUTE

Red Canyon Creek and Tinton Quadrangles, WY

½   1 Mile

SHORT LOOP

LONG LOOP

BLACK HILLS NATIONAL FOREST

I-90

Deer Corral Spring

Sand

Creek

Nelson Spring

Cranberry Springs

Cranberry Spring

Gulch

Corral

Creek

Corral Creek

Fork

Fork

Sand

Sand Creek Crossing

BHNF 863

Grand

Hamilton

Spring Draw

N

Sand Creek is perhaps the most botanically diverse part of the Black Hills. The area is wild, rugged and little-travelled. No maintained trails exist, and the only roads are abandoned, overgrown relics of early mining and logging operations. Creek bottoms and the abandoned roadways are the best routes of travel through Sand Creek. The creek bottoms are usually dry and reasonably clear of vegetation.

From the bridge over Sand Creek on BHNF Road 863, hike one mile up the cobble-strewn creek bottom to the confluence with Corral Creek. A now-collapsed cabin once stood here on a small bench above the creeks. To hike the *short loop*, continue to follow Sand Creek upstream to the east for a short distance until a narrow, overgrown tract begins to climb the south wall of the canyon.

About half-way up the canyon wall the tract fades away. Bushwack up the slope to a flat ridge that divides Sand and Corral creeks. At an elevation of about 4,800 feet on this ridge are the remains of an old roadway, which offers easy walking along contour. Follow the roadway for about .75 mile along the top of a resistant, cliff-forming bed of limestone. Just before reaching a major west-flowing tributary of Corral Creek, scramble down the cliffs and through the woods to Corral Creek. Once in the bed of Corral Creek, continue downstream for about a mile back to the confluence with Sand Creek. From the confluence, retrace your route back along Sand Creek to the bridge and BHNF Road 863.

Sand Creek is one of the largest roadless areas remaining in the Black Hills. Because of its large size, a very long day hike, or overnight backpack trip is possible. To make the *long loop*, continue along Sand Creek four miles beyond the confluence with Corral Creek to Sand Creek Crossing. From the crossing, hike west over a small ridge into the headwaters of Corral Creek. Depending on where you enter Corral Creek, it is about four miles back along the creek bottom to the crossing.

Even to the amateur, the diversity of the boreal (northern) forest of Sand Creek is a striking contrast to the ponderosa pine–dominated forest typical of the Black Hills. Cool, moist conditions allow this northern forest to prosper on the north-facing slopes. Paper birch and hazelnut are key indicator species found here, but quaking aspen, spruce and bur oak are also common.

The boreal forests are a remnant of the northern forests that advanced south during the last ice age. The remaining pockets of this forest, such as Sand Creek, contain a variety of rare plants. Sword fern, club moss, moschatel, and mite wort are a few of the isolated species found along Sand Creek.

Springtime brings an explosion of wildflowers to the creek bottoms and slopes of the canyons. Buttercups, larkspur, blue flax, geraniums, violets, and even the lowly hound's tongue brighten the valleys. The Nature Conservancy, a non-profit organization dedicated to preserving rare and endangered ecosystems, recognized that Sand Creek is the most important area in the Black Hills for rare plants. The Conservancy is pursuing a Special Botanical Area designation for parts of the drainage.

Carson Draw Cross-Country Ski Trails

BEARLODGE RANGER DISTRICT,
BLACK HILLS NATIONAL FOREST

Description: A moderate cross-country ski trip on groomed trails that are suitable for mountain bikes in summer.

General Location: Three miles northwest of Sundance, Wyoming.

Highlight: Groomed ski trails and summer solitude.

Access: To reach the trailhead from Interstate 90, take Exit 185 west of Sundance, and drive west on U.S. 14 for one mile. Turn north on BHNF Road 838 (the Warren Peak Road). Drive 2.5 miles to the parking area at the end of the plowed road. The trail starts 0.2 mile up the paved main road, which is used as a snowmobile trail. The Black Hills National Forest plans to construct new trailhead parking near Reuter Campground.

Distance: The short loop is 5.0 miles around. There are 6.9 miles of trails at Carson Draw.

Maps: Black Hills National Forest Bearlodge Trails and pages 158 and 159.

North of Sundance, near Reuter Campground, lies a network of groomed ski trails centered around Carson Draw. Beautiful trails, a variety of terrain and views stretching across the Bearlodge Mountains to Sundance and Inyan Kara mountains make this trail system one of the undiscovered gems of Black Hills cross-country skiing. The trail system consists of one main loop and a series of spur trails radiating away from the loop.

For an introduction to Bearlodge skiing, try a loop around Carson Draw. From the parking area, ski up the Warren Peak Road to post 1, which is located just before the first curve. Beyond this point snowmobiles are not allowed on the ski trails. By veering south off the trail between posts 1 and 2, skiers are treated to impressive views south of Sundance and Inyan Kara mountains. Both peaks are part of a chain of eroded volcanic centers that cut across the northern Black Hills from Devils Tower to Bear Butte.

Follow a gentle trail north to post 3, where the loop begins. To ascend the steeper hills, and descend the more moderate grades, turn right and follow the loop counterclockwise. A steady ascent soon brings skiers to post 4. From post 4, the ski shelter at post 5 can be reached directly by an easy traverse. The first spur trail leads north from here.

After enjoying a rest and some lunch at the shelter, ski to the trail junction at post 5. To return to the trailhead, ski downhill to post 7, first through an open meadow, then in a tighter, steeper canyon. The second spur trail leads west from post 6. Be careful not to build up too much speed. The steep, shaded canyon between posts 6 and 7 is the most exciting skiing within the trail system, as well as one of the most scenic sections. From post 7 climb steeply back to post 3, then return to the trailhead via posts 2 and 1. Part of the return trail briefly crosses private land and may eventually be relocated to stay completely within Black Hills National Forest land.

Trails are groomed weekly, usually after each snowfall, as part of a cooperative agreement between the Black Hills National Forest and Wyoming Department of Parks and Recreation. Ski tracks are set. Trails are marked by blue diamond-shaped markers and trail intersections are marked by numbered posts.

The terrain within the system offers trails for beginners to advanced skiers. The difficulty ratings on the map issued by the Black Hills National Forest are accurate. Grooming ensures that downhill runs are fast, and some of the most difficult trails can be treacherous if icy. The center lane of most trails is groomed for skating, the terrain and sugary snow ensure that the trails are perfect for this technique.

Two trails connect the Carson Draw Trails to the southwest corner of the larger *Sundance Trails* system. From Reuter Campground, the *Reuter Springs Trail* crosses BHNF Road 838, then climbs north along the west fork of Reuter Canyon. The first two miles are single track leading to a spring house and a junction with the unsigned *Carson Cut-Across Trail*. The last mile of the trail follows dirt BHNF Road 884. Across BHNF Road 838 from point 9 in the Carson Draw Trails, the Carson Cut-Across Trail, a mountain bike route, leads 0.6 mile east to join the Reuter Springs Trail. Riding uphill from east to west, the trail could better be called the "Carson Push-up Trail."

There is no water along the trails, although hikers and mountain bike riders using the trails in the summer can get water in season at Reuter Campground, located near the trailhead.

Sundance Trails

BEARLODGE RANGER DISTRICT,
BLACK HILLS NATIONAL FOREST

Description: Rugged trails for hikers, mountain bikers and horses in the Bearlodge Mountains.

General Location: Three miles northeast of Sundance, Wyoming.

Highlights: Exciting rides, open vistas and solitude.

Access: From Interstate 90, take Exit 189 east of Sundance. Turn left onto U.S. 14A for 0.4 mile before turning north onto Government Valley Road. Follow Government Valley Road for 2.2 miles to the Sundance Campground and Trailhead, which are on the left. See Carson Draw Trails for directions to Reuter Trailhead.

Distance: The South Fork–Tent Canyon Ridge loop is 9.8 miles. The entire Sundance–Carson Draw trail system covers over 50 miles.

Maps: Black Hills National Forest Bearlodge Trails, and pages 158 and 159.

This is one of the Black Hills National Forest's newest and largest trail systems, covering the southern end of the Bearlodge Mountains. The 44-mile-long system attracts horsemen, mountain bikers and hikers to an area known as the Sundance Burn, named after a 1936 blaze that burned 8,200 acres. Riders come to the area for views stretching from the Black Hills to the Bearlodge and for spectacular riding over challenging terrain.

Much of the trail system boasts outstanding views south to the Black Hills and east over Government Valley. Observant visitors may still see wagon tracks left behind by Custer's expedition as it traversed from Inyan Kara through Government Valley on the way to the present site of Aladdin.

For an introduction to the Sundance Trails, try a loop around the *South Fork* and *Tent Canyon Ridge* trails from the Sundance Trailhead. Begin with a steady 1.2 mile ascent up the *Sundance Trail*. Watch for views east to Crow Peak and north to Sheepnose Mountain. At 1.2 miles reach a junction with the *East Fork Quarry*, *Sand Pit*, and *Tent Canyon* trails. Take the right fork to Tent Canyon and follow it through aspen and oak groves to a T-junction on Ogden Creek at 1.9 miles. Go left at this junction for a few minutes on Tent Canyon Ridge Trail before reaching another junction at 2.0 miles where cattle may graze.

At the 2.0 junction, go left on the South Fork Trail on a route not recommended for horses. The path up the canyon is a narrow, twisted and brushy single-track. Look for aspen, oak and boxelder in the narrow riparian zone below the shallow cliffs. At 4.5 miles reach the west junction with the Tent Canyon Ridge Trail. Climb to the ridge top as the trail follows BHNF Road 899-1B. After a steep descent from the ridge on a recently refurbished trail, return to the 2.0 mile junction at 7.8 miles. Retrace your path to arrive at the Sundance Trailhead at 9.8 miles.

The Sundance Trails have nearly unlimited potential for mountain bike loops both on and off the established trails. The Black Hills National Forest rates the steepness of the trails for horses and mountain bikers from easy to difficult. The Carson Cut-Across, Edge, South Fork and North Fork trails are recommended for mountain bikes, but not horses. The trails are among the least-used in the Black Hills National Forest.

The *Sand Pit Trail* (4.9 miles) connects BHNF Road 838 on the west with the Sundance Trailhead. Most of the trail follows dirt BHNF Roads 899 and 904. East of Box Spring it is mostly a two-track road.

The *Edge Trail* is a 0.8-mile mountain bike route that makes a short loop with the Sand Pit Trail.

The *West Fork Quarry* (0.6 mile) and *East Fork Quarry* (1.4 miles) trails lead south from the Sand Pit Trail to the Black Hills National Forest boundary. With permission to ride on private land, a loop between the two forks is possible.

The *Whitetail Trail* (0.8 mile) leaves the East Fork Quarry Trail to dead-end at the Black Hills National Forest boundary.

The *Reuter Springs Trail* (2.9 miles) connects Reuter Campground with the Sand Pit and Upper Ogden Trailhead farther north on BHNF Road 838. After following the west branch of Reuter Draw, it turns east, drops into Reuter Canyon and follows BHNF Road 884.

The *Carson Cut-Across* (0.7 mile) connects the Reuter Springs Trail to the Carson Draw Trails.

The *Upper Ogden Trail* (1.3 miles) is a very scenic route that connects the Sand Pit Trail and BHNF Road 838 to the Ogden Creek Trail and BHNF Road 839.

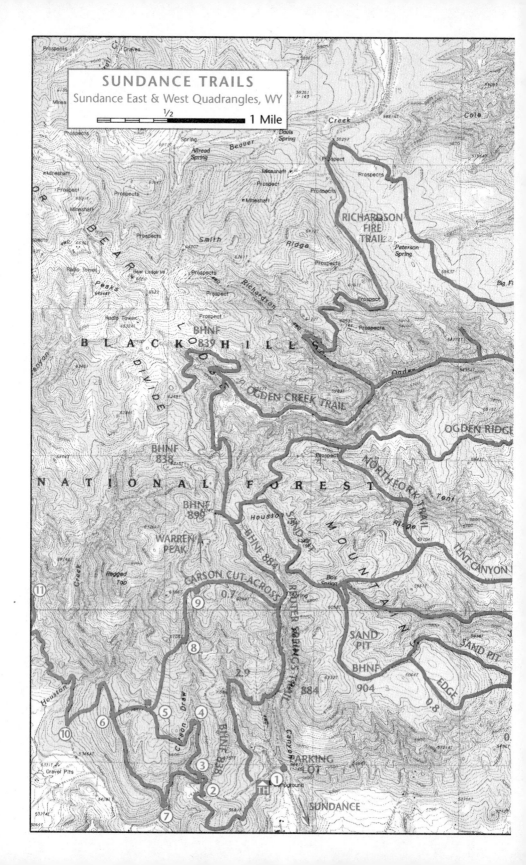

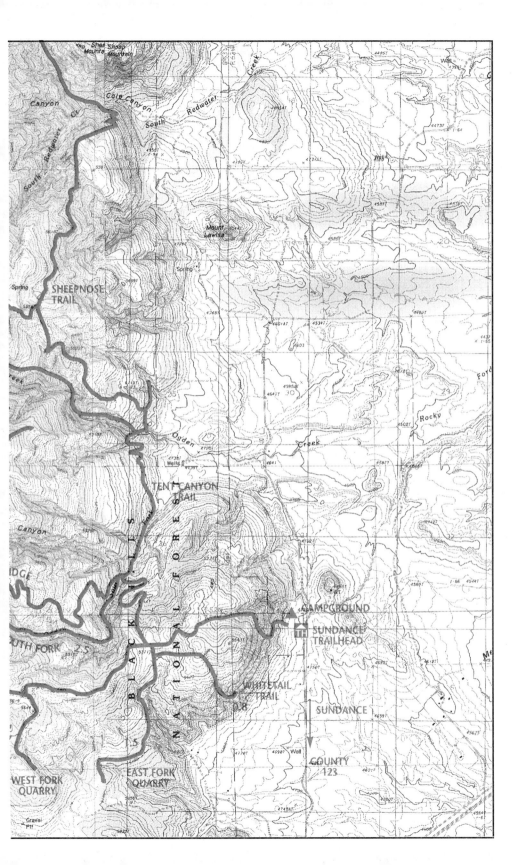

The *Ogden Ridge Trail* (2.8+ miles) leads from the Sand Pit Trail east along a ridge top blessed with many vistas, then down to Tent Canyon on a recently built extension. It follows BHNF Road 839.1A past many small prospect pits remaining from early exploration for gold.

The *North Fork Trail* (1.3 miles) connects Tent Canyon Ridge and Ogden Ridge.

The *Richardson Fire Trail* (5.4 miles) connects the *Sheepnose Trail* to the Ogden Creek Trail.

The *Ogden Creek Trail* (3.6+ miles) leads from BHNF Road 839 east to a junction with the Sheepnose and Tent Canyon Trails. From BHNF Road 839 to the junction with Richardson Fire Trail it follows Road 839. Bearlodge Ranger District trails specialist Jerry Hagen considers the Ogden Creek–Tent Canyon Ridge loop to be the area's most scenic ride.

The *Sheepnose Trail* (6.7 miles) is another of the Bearlodge's finest. It extends from BHNF Road 831 south to the Ogden Creek Trail and includes a side trip to scenic Sheepnose Mountain.

The *Tent Canyon Trail* (4.1 miles) connects the Sand Pit Trail to the Ogden Ridge Trail.

The Black Hills National Forest plans a multiyear timber sale in the area of the Bearlodge Trails beginning in 1999. The timber harvest could close up to 25 percent of the trail system at any one time.

Cross-country skiers can connect Sundance Trails with those at Carson Draw. However, the Reuter Springs Trail is part of Wyoming Bear Lodge Snowmobile Trail D. Snowmobile Trail B follows part of Ogden Creek Trail along BHNF Road 839 east to the northern limit of the Richardson Fire Trail.

~

Cliff Swallow and Cook Lake Trails
BEARLODGE RANGER DISTRICT,
BLACK HILLS NATIONAL FOREST

Description: Two easy loop trails through the northern Bearlodge Mountains.

General Location: Twenty miles north of Sundance, Wyoming.

Highlight: Wildlife and bird watching.

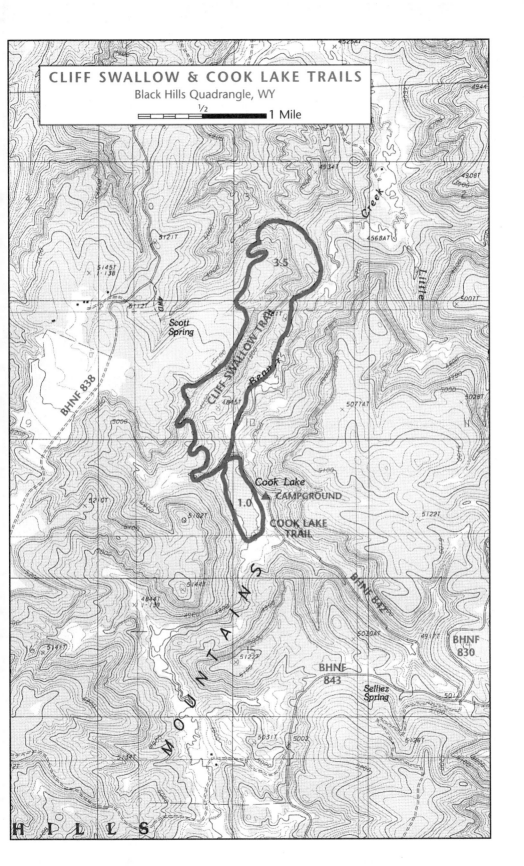

CLIFF SWALLOW & COOK LAKE TRAILS

Black Hills Quadrangle, WY

½   1 Mile

CLIFF SWALLOW TRAIL

3.5

Scott
Spring

BHNF 838

1.0

Cook Lake
CAMPGROUND

COOK LAKE
TRAIL

MOUNTAINS

BHNF 842

BHNF
843

BHNF
830

Selliez
Spring

HILLS

Access: From Interstate 90, take Exit 199 and drive north on Wyoming
111 for 4.2 miles. Turn west onto gravel BHNF Road 843 and drive
10.5 miles to gravel BHNF Road 842. Follow Road 842 northwest for
1.2 miles to Cook Lake Recreation Area and continue for 0.5 mile toward Campground Loop B to a hikers' parking area. The trails start
100 yards up the road and across from the restrooms.
Distance: Cliff Swallow is a 3.5-mile loop. Cook Lake is a 1.0-mile loop.
Maps: Black Hills National Forest Cliff Swallow Trail and Cook Lake Trail
map and page 161.

In contrast to the Black Hills, Wyoming's Bearlodge Mountains are
lightly used by hikers. Two trails at the popular Recreation Area at
Cook Lake, in the heart of the Bearlodge, may help hikers to discover
this area. The Cliff Swallow Trail was completed in 1991 and offers
hikers and mountain bike riders an excellent chance to explore the
Bearlodge off-road.

From the trailhead, climb on switchbacks to Campground Loop B.
The Cliff Swallow Trail follows the campground road a short distance,
then enters the woods near site 28, where there is a large trail sign and
map. Cross through a gate in a fence and traverse uphill along the side
of a steep ridge. After another set of switchbacks, the trail crosses
bluffs of brown sandstone and crests the ridge.

The Cliff Swallow Trail follows the ridge northeast for almost a mile
before descending again on switchbacks to a saddle that is crossed by
numerous cattle tracks. Be careful to stay on the hiking trail as it turns
southeast and crosses a gate in a fence just before reaching the valley of
lower Beaver Creek. The trail follows Beaver Creek on a bluff on the
northwest side back to the campground road. Near the Cook Lake
Dam are several large beaver dams, which seemingly threaten to flood
the end of the trail. The trail intersects the campground road about 100
feet from the parking area adjacent to another large trail sign and map.

The Cliff Swallow Trail is an excellent place to study the effects of
topography on forest composition. The Bearlodge forests contain a
mix of western climax conifers and eastern deciduous trees. The eastern slope of the ridge is covered with a mixture of ponderosa pine and
bur oak. Pine dominates the canopy, while oak is most abundant in
the understory. On the ridge crest, where pine is interspersed with
stands of aspen, different birds are found here. To the north, the pine-
covered ridge has many snags (standing dead trees) and birds are
more abundant. The Black Hills National Forest has inventoried 23
bird and 10 mammal species that depend on snags, and the cavities in

them, for shelter. The cliff swallow is not one of these species. These birds nest in the sandstone bluffs just below the top of the ridge.

The Cliff Swallow Trail is marked by carsonite posts and a well-travelled footway. This is one of the few hiking trails in the Black Hills National Forest that was constructed for hiking and mountain biking and is not a converted roadway. Although water is plentiful in lower Beaver Creek, cattle graze in most of the watershed. Get your drinking water from the campground. Cook Lake offers fee camping and non-motorized boating.

On July 17, 1997, fishermen working the west side of Cook Lake got the surprise of their lives. Instead of finding action out on the water, it was the earth under their feet that began to move. The tree-covered hillside above them began to slide slowly downhill, snapping trees and opening fractures in the earth. The slide continued to move slowly over two months. The force of the slide pushed up the lake bottom onto the opposite shore and left a 10 foot by 12 foot dike halfway around the lake that eventually help to prevent further slip. The main scarp left by the slide was 40 feet deep and nearly one-quarter mile long, but because of the slow rate of movement, no one was injured.

The Cook Lake slide wasn't the product of a single event such as an earthquake or sudden heavy rainfall. Research into the soils around the lake had already identified the slope as an area with a "moderate potential for massive land failure." Several consecutive wet summers saturated the soil profile to a point where the slide began. The slide has closed the west side of the Cook Lake Loop indefinitely, but the campground and Cliff Swallow Trail still remain open.

Tower Trail
DEVILS TOWER NATIONAL MONUMENT

Description: A paved loop around the base of Devils Tower.
General Location: Twenty-two miles northwest of Sundance, Wyoming.
Highlights: A close encounter with America's most recognized national monument.
Access: From the west side of Sundance, Wyoming, exit Interstate 90 onto U.S. 14. Follow U.S. 14 north for 22 miles to Devils Tower Junction. At the junction turn north on Wyoming 24 to reach the Devils

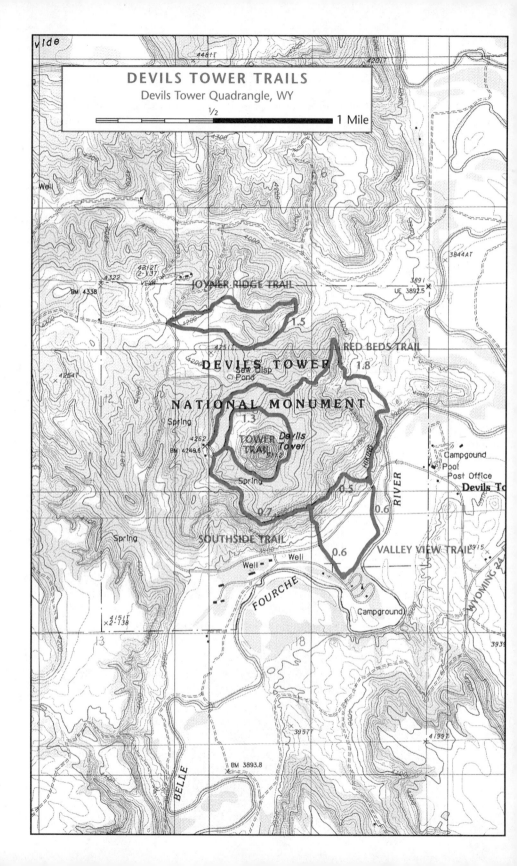

Tower National Monument Entrance Station. From the entrance, drive 2.8 miles to the visitors center.

Distance: A 1.3-mile loop.

Maps: Devils Tower National Monument Map, and page 164.

Few hiking trails are as awe-inspiring as the Tower Trail at Devils Tower. This paved interpretive loop circles the Tower at close range giving visitors a close-up view from all sides. The sheer number of visitors to the monument ensures that the Tower Trail is one of the most heavily used in the Black Hills region.

From the trail the individual columns that form Devils Tower are clearly visible. The Tower is an igneous intrusion formed as molten magma moved underground, pushing up through layers of softer sedimentary rocks. As the magma cooled underground, it contracted and broke into distinct hexagonal columns. Later the softer sedimentary rocks were eroded away by the action of the Belle Fourche River, exposing the Tower. The sharpest and most distinct columns are found halfway up and result from an especially rapid period of erosion.

Most park visitors are fascinated by both Devils Tower and by the climbers that scale it. The Tower's difficult rock climbs attract skilled climbers from all over the world. Nearly all the cracks that separate the Tower's columns have established climbing routes along them. Luckily for earthbound visitors, the Tower Trail is close enough to keep all these routes in view. The route names reflect the often irreverent nature of climbing. One can imagine a climber struggling to fit in the huge crack of "Good Holds for Godzilla," but what events led to "No Kiss for Dog Lips"?

Devils Tower, like its neighbors Bear Butte and Inyan Kara is considered a sacred place by many of the tribes of Plains Indians. A voluntary ban on rock climbing in the monument has been imposed for the month of June when the Sioux and other tribes gather for summer solstice dances and other sacred activities. Most, though not all, climbers have respected the ban, which does not effect hiking in the monument.

Joyner Ridge Trail
DEVILS TOWER NATIONAL MONUMENT

Description: An easy loop trail suitable for families with small children.
General Location: Twenty-two miles northwest of Sundance, Wyoming.
Highlight: Views of Devils Tower.
Access: From the west side of Sundance, Wyoming, exit Interstate 90 onto U.S. 14. Follow U.S. 14 north for 22 miles to Devils Tower Junction. At the junction, turn north on Wyoming 24 to reach the Devils Tower National Monument Entrance Station. Follow the park road for 2.3 miles to a paved, unmarked West Road leading north. The Joyner Ridge Trailhead is 0.3 mile farther north.
Distance: The loop is 1.5 miles around.
Maps: Devils Tower National Monument Map, and page 164.

Many visitors to Devils Tower are content to view the Tower from the park's roads, visitor center and Tower Trail. To escape the masses, and enjoy spectacular views of the Tower from the north, try a hike along the little-used Joyner Ridge Trail.

To hike the loop clockwise, start from the north side of the parking area. The trail traverses east along a ridge of Sundance formation sandstone through a forest of ponderosa pine, generally staying within view of Devils Tower. From the east end of the ridge, the trail descends on switchbacks to a juniper-filled ravine. The trail climbs gradually out of the ravine through a forest of bur oak and ash to reach the grasslands near the parking area.

The Joyner Ridge Trail has a well-defined footway, but no blazes. Four interpretive signs along the route highlight aspects of the monument's ecology. Since this trail is much less travelled than the Tower Trail, hikers have a better chance to see white tail deer or one of the 130 bird species which have been sighted within the monument.

No water is found along the trail. Bring a canteen, sun protection and your camera. In summer be prepared for sudden, often violent afternoon thunderstorms. Mountain bikes are not allowed on trails at Devils Tower.

The trail is named for former monument Superintendent Newell F. Joyner. Joyner's tenure at Devils Tower coincided with the opening of the Tower to rock climbing.

Red Beds Trail

DEVILS TOWER NATIONAL MONUMENT

Description: A beautiful loop trail that circles Devils Tower.
General Location: Twenty-two miles northwest of Sundance, Wyoming.
Highlight: Tower views and the red cliffs above the Belle Fourche River.
Access: From the west side of Sundance, exit Interstate 90 onto U.S. 14.
  Follow U.S. 14 north for 22 miles to Devils Tower Junction. At the
  junction turn north on Wyoming 24 to reach the Devils Tower Na-
  tional Monument Entrance Station. From the entrance, drive 2.8
  miles to the visitors center.
Distance: The loop is 3.0 miles long.
Maps: Devils Tower National Monument Map and page 164.

Devils Tower is one of the most recognizable landmarks in the United
States. The Tower has been made famous by countless photographs
and by the film "Close Encounters of the Third Kind." Devils Tower,
and the nearby Little Missouri Buttes, comprise the last gasp of the
Black Hills uplift as it fades westward into the prairie of the Thunder
Basin.

Hikers can explore the monument by following the Red Beds Trail
that circles the flanks of the Tower along the Belle Fourche River. The
Red Beds Trail starts at the south end of the visitors center parking
loop. The trail winds gradually downhill through ponderosa pine, bur
oak and juniper to a junction at 0.7 mile with the *Southside Trail*. From
the junction, the Southside Trail leads south 0.6 mile to Belle Fourche
Campground, and the Red Beds Trail continues the loop around the
Tower.

The Red Beds Trail skirts a bluff formed from brown sandstone of
the Hulett member of the Jurassic-age Sundance formation. Below the
rocks of the Sundance formation are the massive white gypsum beds
of the Gypsum Springs formation and the bright red sandstone and
siltstone of the Triassic-age Spearfish formation. At the bottom of the
bluffs, almost at the base of the Tower, is another junction at 1.2 miles
with the *Valley View Trail*, which leads south 0.6 mile to the Belle
Fourche Campground. From the intersection, the Red Beds Trail turns
north and passes through a sparsely vegetated badlands of easily
eroded Spearfish formation.

The Red Beds Trail next reaches grasslands and then traverses a
small northeast trending ridge that offers good views of Devils Tower.
Rounding the ridge, the trail heads south, then turns west onto an old

road bed. The loop ends at the Tower Trail about a hundred feet from the parking area.

Mato Tipila or "Bear Lodge" is an Indian name for the Tower. The scientific party of Col. Richard Dodge was the first white group to describe Devils Tower, and gave it the current name. Dodge's party was as awed by the Tower as any of the millions of later visitors. They described it as unclimbable.

The label "unclimbable" only serves as a challenge for some. In 1893 local ranchers William Rogers and Willard Ripley made the first ascent of Devils Tower using a ladder they had constructed by driving wooden pegs into a vertical crack between two of the columns. The last known climb using the ladder was made by Babe White (known as the "Human Fly"). The park service then removed the lower 100 feet of the ladder.

Modern rock climbing techniques were first successfully applied to Devils Tower by a three-man team led by the renown climber Fritz Weissner in 1937. The classic, and easiest, route to the top was pioneered the next year by Jack Durrance. The Durrance route begins at the "leaning column" and is clearly visible on the cover of "Geology of Devils Tower—The First National Monument," and is shown on an interpretive display on the Tower Trail. The history of rock climbing at the Tower has progressed steadily since the time of Weissner and Durrance, with 27,000 climbers reaching the top by 1990.

The top of Devils Tower supports a small prairie community. In 1992, researchers from the University of Wyoming identified twenty-one plant species including nine grasses, eight forbs and four shrubs on the summit. Mice, wood rats and chipmunks were also found.

Trails in the monument are well maintained with a gentle footway, but no blazes. Deer are often seen along the trails and the Red Beds Trail passes just north of the modest prairie dog town located between the campground and the park road.

North Dakota

White Butte Route

Description: An easy hike to the highest point in North Dakota.
General Location: Seven miles south of Amidon, North Dakota.
Highlight: Surprising views and prairie scenery.
Access: From Amidon, North Dakota, drive east two miles on U.S. 85. Then turn south and drive 6.5 miles on a gravel road to the Buzalsky Ranch. Stop at the ranch and get permission to make the climb. White Butte is directly west.
Distance: About 3.0 miles round trip.
Maps: USGS Amidon, North Dakota 7.5-minute quadrangle and page 170.

The highest point in North Dakota lies in the Chalky Buttes in the southwest part of the state. The buttes form a major divide between the Little Missouri River on the west, and Cedar Creek and the Cannonball River, which drain east into the Missouri River. White Butte is close to U.S. 85, the road that connects the Black Hills to Theodore Roosevelt National Park, and can be easily climbed in half a day. The trip is especially popular with "highpointers," those who aspire to climb the high points of all fifty states.

The Chalky Buttes are exceptionally pretty. To the south of White Butte, at the head of Sand Creek, are badlands that equal some of those found in Theodore Roosevelt National Park, or the Sage Creek Wilderness in Badlands National Park. To the west, across U.S. 85, is the Little Missouri National Grasslands and the Black Buttes.

There are no trails or established routes up White Butte. Though White Butte is on private land, the owners have been gracious in allowing public access to the highpoint. Hike west about 0.5 mile across a field from the gravel road. From the field, the route to the summit is straightforward. Either climb due west to the top, or swing south and climb up the southeast ridge. There is a USGS marker and a register on top.

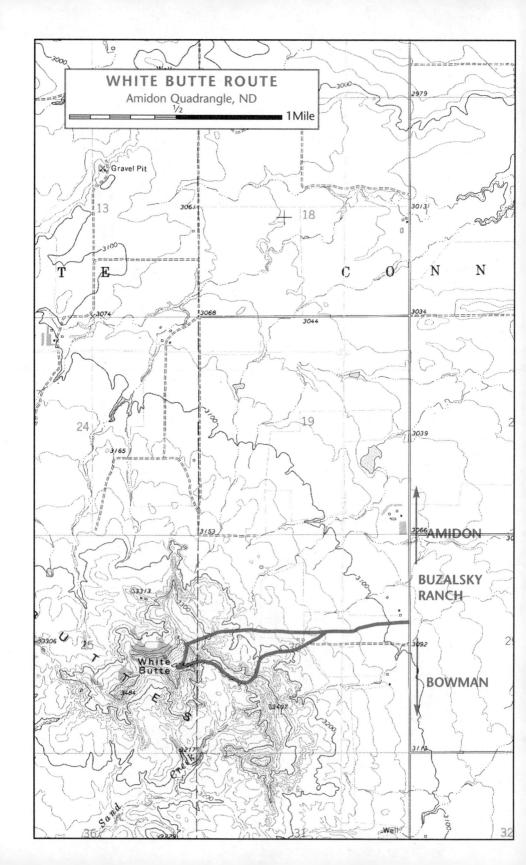

White Butte lies on the southwest side of the Williston Basin, a major oil-producing region. In the center of the Williston Basin the bedrock is mostly Paleocene-age Sentinel Butte Formation. The Chalky Buttes are a relict island of younger Oligocene-age White River Group sediment rocks standing above the prairie. The tops of White Butte, Radio Tower Butte and Black Butte are capped by even younger Tertiary sedimentary rocks.

For many years a sign on U.S. 85 caused confusion about the location of White Butte. The sign seemed to point to a Butte and radio tower only a mile east of the highway. At 3,472 feet, the Radio Tower Butte is still one of the highest points in the state, but not the highest. The sign has been moved to a point east of Amidon so that it points to the correct butte. This confusion has caused several "highpointers," and a few North Dakota natives, to return to the Chalky Buttes to reach the correct summit.

White Butte and the surrounding land are on property owned by the Buzalsky family. Please respect their private property and ask at the ranch for permission to cross their land. If no one is at the ranch, permission to cross is not mandatory. The Buzalsky's report that fossil hunters also frequent White Butte. For more information about White Butte, see "Highpoints of the United States" by Don W. Holmes or call the Buzalsky Ranch at (701) 879-6370.

~~

Jones–Lower Paddock Creek Trails Loop
THEODORE ROOSEVELT NATIONAL PARK, SOUTH UNIT

Description: A rugged circuit through the center of the South Unit for hikers or horses.

General Location: Three miles north of Medora, North Dakota.

Highlight: The wildlife watching includes bison and prairie dogs.

Access: From the visitor center at Medora, drive north on the paved Scenic Loop Drive for 8.4 miles to the parking area at the Jones Creek Trailhead. If your group has more than one vehicle, leave one at the Halliday Well Trailhead to avoid 1.5 miles of hiking along park roads.

Distance: The loop is 11.4 miles around.

Maps: Theodore Roosevelt National Park Backcountry Guide, USGS Theodore Roosevelt National Park South Unit 1:24,000 special topographic map and page 172.

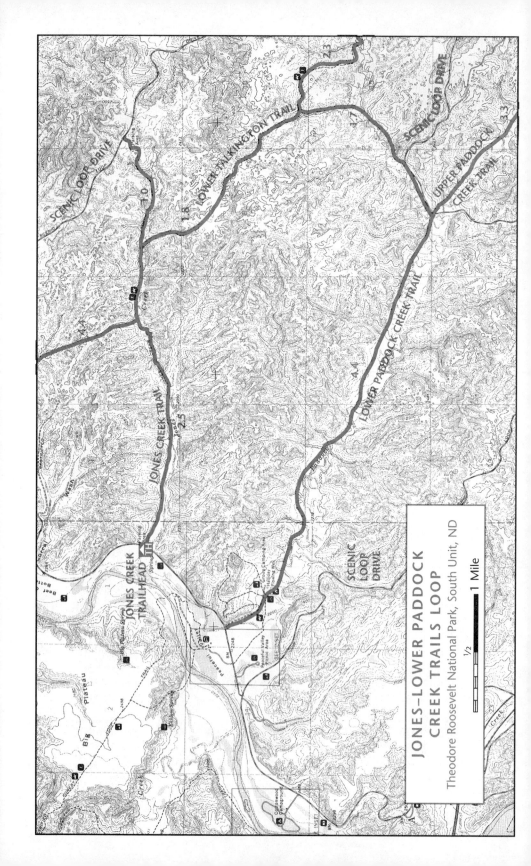

JONES–LOWER PADDOCK
CREEK TRAILS LOOP

Theodore Roosevelt National Park, South Unit, ND

½   1 Mile

One of the most popular trips in Theodore Roosevelt National Park is a loop that connects the trails along Jones and Paddock Creeks. This loop can be hiked in one long day, or combined with the Upper Paddock Creek and Talkington trails to make an overnight trip. The lower loop follows quiet creek bottoms through country much rougher than other trails in the South Unit.

Begin by hiking east on the *Jones Creek Trail,* crossing the main fork of Jones Creek twice. As the trail winds along the creek bottom through green ash and grasses, notice how clusters of juniper are found only on the shaded and moister north-facing slopes.

Near 2.0 miles a new horse trail leads left about 4.5 miles to the Roundup Group Horse Camp. At the next junction at 2.5 miles, a side trail continues left to the Scenic Loop Drive in 1.0 mile. Our route turns south to follow the *Lower Talkington Trail* over a butte that marks the divide between Jones and Paddock creeks to reach another junction at 4.3 miles. From here we leave the Lower Talkington Trail, which will reach the Scenic Loop Drive in 2.3 miles, and follow a connector trail which branches south from the Talkington Trail.

Follow the connector trail south down a tributary of Paddock Creek. The last one-half mile of the connector trail is adjacent to the park loop road. Along the way, pass areas where erosion of sandstone in the Bullion Creek formation has produced steep sand dunes. Reach Paddock Creek, and a small turnout from the road that marks the *Lower Paddock Creek Trail* at 6.0 miles.

Follow the *Lower Paddock Creek Trail* downstream and west to reach the Halliday Well Trailhead at 10.4 miles, keeping in the main valley. Along the way, notice how the meanders in Paddock Creek are tighter and more closely spaced than those in the Little Missouri River. The rate of water flow in a stream, the gradient of the stream and other properties of a watershed are related to the size of the stream. Streams cut meanders as a means of dissipating the potential energy of water. Subsidiary streams, such as Paddock Creek, have high potential energy that is spent on cutting more frequent meanders, while main streams, such as the Little Missouri River, have less potential energy and therefore more gentle meanders. The high level of erosion in subsidiary streams means that the bed of the stream bed is rougher and the flow turbulent. Despite appearances, water in a turbulent, subsidiary stream flows at a slower rate than water in a larger, smooth flowing river.

The Lower Paddock Creek Trail passes through a remarkably large prairie dog town. Bison often graze near the head of the dog town. The town fills the entire valley floor as you approach the Scenic Loop

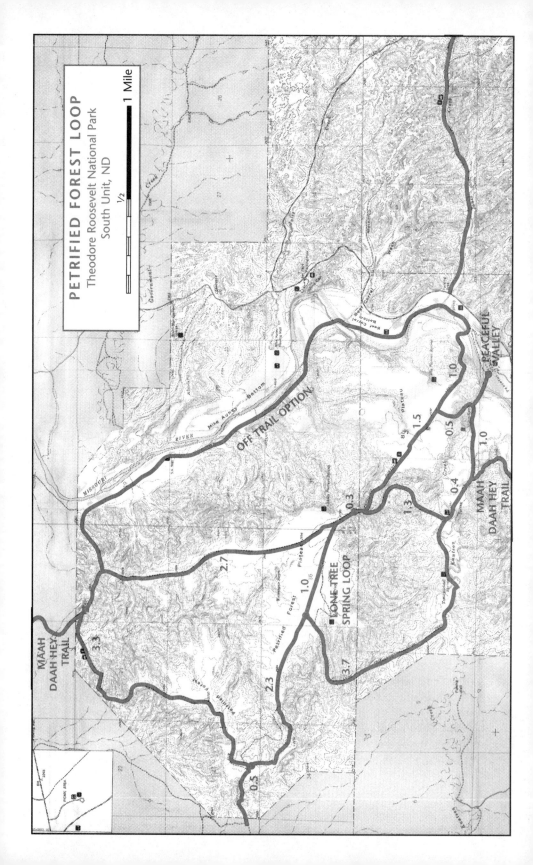

Road. If you were unable to leave a car at the Halliday Well Trailhead, you must walk 0.5 mile northwest along a dirt road, then 1.0 mile north along the Scenic Loop Road to the Jones Creek Trailhead. You may walk along the road, or follow a maze of trails created by the park's horse concessionaire on the west side of the road. Experienced hikers can also take a short cut north from the prairie dog town and head cross-country back to the Jones Creek Trailhead.

The Paddock Creek Trail is not shown on older park topographic maps, so stop by the visitor centers if your map is not current.

Petrified Forest Loop
THEODORE ROOSEVELT NATIONAL PARK, SOUTH UNIT

Description: An overnight hike into the South Unit that includes an off-trail hike along the Little Missouri River.

General Location: Three miles north of Medora, North Dakota.

Highlight: Petrified trees and wildlife watching in a wilderness setting.

Access: Exit Interstate 94 at Medora and proceed to the park visitor center in Medora. From the visitor center follow the paved Scenic Loop Drive for 6.8 miles north to Peaceful Valley Ranch. Parking is available at the saddle horse concession. If the Little Missouri River is too high to ford, try the 0.5-mile long feeder trail from the park's west boundary. Ask for a copy of the map and directions to the trailhead from the South Unit visitor center.

Distance: The off-trail loop is about 12.0 miles long. The Petrified Forest Loop Trail is a 14.5-mile loop.

Maps: Theodore Roosevelt National Park Backcountry Guide, USGS Theodore Roosevelt National Park South Unit special 1:24,000 topographic map and page 174.

Backcountry hiking is the best way to see Theodore Roosevelt National Park and the Little Missouri badlands. The park has a beautiful, well-developed trail system that is perfect for easy weekend backpack trips. A partially off-trail loop on the west side of the South Unit combines two areas of special interest, the Petrified Forest Plateau and the bottom lands along the Little Missouri River.

From Peaceful Valley, negotiate a maze of paths leading down to the Little Missouri River. In high water, crossing the river may be the most difficult part of the trip. Check current conditions before attempting a crossing. Once across, follow the Petrified Forest Loop Trail 0.8 mile up the riverside bluffs onto Big Plateau.

Big Plateau is covered by a large prairie dog town that also attracts mule deer, coyotes and bison. Beyond Big Plateau, climb another bluff onto Petrified Forest Plateau. Along the base of this short climb, the trail crosses a distinct geologic horizon that contains many of the fossil trees that give name to the plateau. Several weathered fossil stumps are visible from the trail. Remember that the National Park Service prohibits collecting fossil wood in the park in order to preserve the specimens that remain. At the top of the climb, reach a junction with the *Lone Tree Springs Loop* and the *Maah Daah Hey Trail* at 2.3 miles. The two trails are together until a split is reached at 2.6 miles.

Stay right at the split on the Petrified Forest Trail where the Maah Daah Hey Trail also goes right. At 3.1 miles a new horse trail leads right about 3.0 miles to the Roundup Group Horse Camp. Enjoy another mile of almost perfectly level walking before the plateau narrows to form a gentle ridge that extends toward the north boundary of the park. If you want to stay on trails from this point, continue along a narrow ridge to the north boundary of the park at 5.3 miles. Here the Maah Daah Hey Trail branches right to leave the park and enter the rugged Wannagan Creek Badlands. The Petrified Forest Loop crosses another stretch of badlands before reaching the west side of Petrified Forest Plateau. Descend to reach another impressive "grove" of petrified wood before reaching a junction with the west entrance spur trail at 8.6 miles. In about another mile visit the last display of petrified wood during a brief descent off the plateau. Intersect the Lone Tree Spring Trail Loop at 10.9 miles and close the loop at 11.9 miles.

If you want to complete an off-trail loop via the Little Missouri River, leave the Petrified Forest Trail near the north boundary and hike northeast down a series of bluffs to the river bottom. A fine cluster of fossilized stumps sits nearby on a small bench just below the level of the trail. An easy descent route follows an abandoned jeep track along the nose of a small ridge before dropping into a small dry draw. Two groves of cottonwoods between the north boundary and VA well offer plenty of campsites.

A riverside camp has the advantage of water, otherwise unavailable in the backcountry. The wells found scattered throughout the park are water sources for wildlife and do not produce potable water so treatment is necessary. An added bonus is that the river, which seemed so cold when you waded across in the morning, may be warm enough for swimming by afternoon. The bluffs on either side of the river are perfect for wildlife watching or photography.

On the second day, follow the river down stream for five miles back to Peaceful Valley crossing the new horse trail that connects the Petrified Forest Loop to Roundup Group Horse Camp. Bluffs along the river can be climbed or bypassed by wading in the river. Pass through another huge prairie dog town at Beef Corral Bottom. Beyond the dog town, cross the river once more to avoid bushwhacking along the narrow strip between the river and the paved park road. End your hike at the parking area at Peaceful Valley.

The rocks in Theodore Roosevelt National Park were originally deposited as sediments during the Paleocene epoch. Rocks of the Bullion Creek (also called Tongue River) and Sentinel Butte formations, which are both part of the Fort Union Group, are found here. These sediments were deposited by the rivers and streams that drained the ancestral Rocky Mountains to the west. At this distance from the mountains the streams carried clay, silt and sand, which are now the soft siltstone and sandstone beds of the Fort Union Group. As the ancestral Rocky Mountains began to rise, a chain of volcanoes became active in what is now Montana and Wyoming. Huge eruptions of these volcanoes sent ash as far east as the Dakotas. These ash deposits are found in the park as beds of the clay mineral bentonite, commonly called gumbo when wet. Bentonite has the remarkable ability to absorb five times its weight in water. Even more remarkable is how difficult bentonite is to walk on, or drive over, when wet. Gumbo is extremely sticky and slippery at the same time. There is no cure, only prevention; it is best to stay out of the badlands after a recent rain.

Recent paleontological excavations by the North Dakota Geological Survey in the Sentinel Butte and Bullion Creek formations have discovered fossils of a 55-million-year-old crocodile-like reptile called champosaurus. To learn more about the dig and the park's rich fossil history, visit the new paleontology exhibit at the Medora Visitor Center.

Petrified wood is common throughout Theodore Roosevelt National Park. The rapid rate of Paleocene sedimentation accounts for the formation of fossil wood. In the Paleocene climate much of the landscape was covered by thick forests and swamps. After rapid changes in stream channels, or volcanic eruptions, many trees were buried before they decayed. Following further burial, groundwater began to circulate through the sediments. Silica dissolved from the ash beds was redeposited in the wood as ground water saturated the buried trees. Eventually silica replaced and coated much of the woody

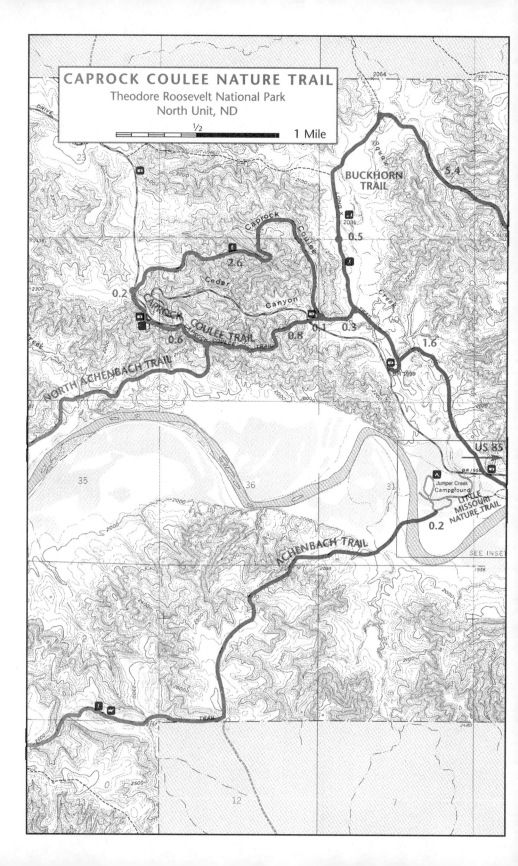

CAPROCK COULEE NATURE TRAIL
Theodore Roosevelt National Park
North Unit, ND

½   1 Mile

2064

BUCKHORN
TRAIL

5.4

Caprock

Coulee

0.5

2.6

Cedar

0.2

Canyon

CAPROCK COULEE TRAIL

0.6   0.8   0.1   0.3   1.6

NORTH ACHENBACH TRAIL

BM 1999

US 85

BR 1956

35   36   31

Juniper Creek
Campground

LITTLE
MISSOURI
NATURE TRAIL

0.2

ACHENBACH TRAIL

SEE INSET

1956

TRAIL

11   12

plant tissues to create petrified wood. In better preserved specimens growth rings and other features are still visible. The most common type of petrified wood in the park is preserved tree stumps.

Spring and fall are the best times to visit the Little Missouri Badlands. The change in seasons moderates the temperature extremes characteristic of the northern plains. Trails are well-marked and easy to follow. The huge posts that mark the trails across the prairie are testaments both to the longing of bison for good scratching posts and the perseverance of park rangers in marking trails.

At any time of year, carry plenty of water since none is found along the trails. No open fires are allowed in the backcountry, and mountain bikes are also prohibited. Most of the South Unit west of the Little Missouri River is designated wilderness. Overnight trips require a free backcountry permit that may be obtained at either visitor center between 8:00 and 4:30. There are no established backcountry campsites.

Caprock Coulee Nature Trail
THEODORE ROOSEVELT NATIONAL PARK, NORTH UNIT

Description: The first .75 mile of this loop is a self-guiding nature trail.
General Location: Thirteen miles south of Watford City, North Dakota.
Highlight: Spectacular geology and sweeping vistas.
Access: From U.S. 85, drive 6.5 miles west on the paved Scenic Drive to a parking area on the north side of the road.
Distance: The loop is 4.2 miles.
Maps: Theodore Roosevelt National Park Backcountry Guide, USGS Theodore Roosevelt National Park North Unit 1:24,000 special topographic map and page 178.

If you have time for only one hike in the North Unit of Theodore Roosevelt National Park, it should be the Caprock Coulee Nature Trail. The first .75 mile of this trail is a self-guiding introduction to the geology and botany of the badlands and prairie. Beyond the self-guiding portion lies some of the best ridge line walking found in the park. This trail is closed to horses.

Follow the numbered posts north from the trailhead along Caprock Coulee. At the end of the self-guided trail, turn west, then south, to climb through a grove of juniper and green ash. Western wheatgrass is the dominant grass in these groves. The trail turns west again at the top of a narrow ridge. Follow the ridge west as it widens into open prairie before reaching the paved Scenic Drive at 2.6 miles.

Follow the Scenic Drive south to Riverbend Overlook at 2.8 miles, where a side trail leads south to a stone shelter. The trail stays on the roadside and crosses the heads of two small coulees. Then turn right off of the road onto the crest of a ridge leading east. Reach a junction with the *North Achenbach Trail* at 3.4 miles and continue east. Cross two small saddles offering spectacular views over the Little Missouri River, before turning north off of the ridge. Descend steadily to the trailhead at 4.2 miles.

The diversity of the Caprock Coulee Nature Trail makes it an ideal introduction to Theodore Roosevelt National Park. The trail crosses most of the park's major habitats: narrow coulees, juniper groves, narrow badlands ridges and open prairie. The views are superb, particularly on the south side where the trail overlooks the Little Missouri River. Coyotes, mule deer and rabbits find the trail easy going, and you may also see tracks from one of the park's rare bobcats.

The display of geologic features along the trail is impressive. On the self-guided portion, you'll learn how water cuts the soft bedrock and creates badlands. You will see examples of lignite seams, beds of bentonite, landslides, slump blocks and caprocks.

Theodore Roosevelt National Park personnel, along with assistance from the North Dakota Fish and Game Department, and research from Montana State University, began an effort to introduce bighorn sheep into the North Unit in 1996. Native Audubon bighorns became extinct in the early 1900s from hunting pressure and loss of habitat. An effort by the North Dakota Fish and Game Department to transplant California bighorn sheep into the Little Missouri badlands began outside of the park in 1956 and eventually included the South Unit. The earlier effort resulted in a stable herd of around 250 sheep. However, the historic sheep range in the North Unit of Theodore Roosevelt was unoccupied until nineteen California bighorns were released into the park in 1996.

Eight lambs were born the first year and seven were born in 1997. The current band numbers around twenty-four and mingles with other groups living outside the park. But for the most part, the newcomers are remaining in the park near the areas that researchers expected. Theodore Roosevelt National Park has a long history of successful wildlife reintroductions, which includes bison in 1956 and elk in 1985.

There is no water on the Caprock Coulee Trail, and you'll probably need a lot after being exposed to North Dakota's special combination of sun and wind. The Scenic Drive is open as far as the Caprock Coulee Trailhead in winter. Juniper Campground is open in winter, but there is no water. Winter is a good time to study the abundant animal tracks in the snow.

Achenbach Trail Loop
THEODORE ROOSEVELT NATIONAL PARK, NORTH UNIT

Description: A multiday wilderness loop for hikers and horses.
General Location: Fourteen miles south of Watford City, North Dakota.
Highlight: Wilderness solitude along the Little Missouri River.
Access: From U.S. 85, drive 4.9 miles west on the paved Scenic Drive. Turn south onto the road to Juniper Campground. The Achenbach Trail starts across the river from the campground.
Distance: Use parts of the Caprock Coulee and Buckhorn trails to form a 17.6-mile loop.
Maps: Theodore Roosevelt National Park Backcountry Guide, USGS Theodore Roosevelt National Park North Unit 1:24,000 special topographic map and page 182.

The Achenbach Trail explores some of the roughest terrain found in Theodore Roosevelt National Park. In the park's North Unit, relief is greater and the terrain more rugged than in the South Unit. Except for a narrow corridor around the park scenic drive, most of the North Unit is designated wilderness. Through the heart of this country is a loop that is long enough for a two- or three-day trip.

From Juniper Campground, hike 0.2 mile southwest to the Little Missouri River. Check with the park staff on current conditions before attempting to cross. Ford the river, and then cross the floodplain, before climbing through a mixture of badlands and juniper groves. Once onto the prairie above the river, follow the trail west and then south to a point near the park boundary. Continue west on a north-facing slope to reach a junction with an old two-track road that leads southeast to the park boundary. Then enter the Achenbach Hills and reach a junction with a faint trail leading north to Achenbach Spring at 4.7 miles.

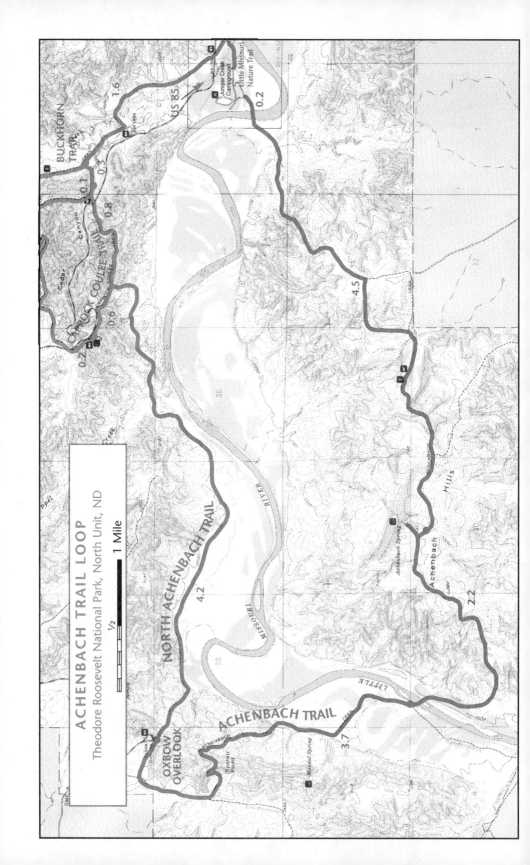

ACHENBACH TRAIL LOOP
Theodore Roosevelt National Park, North Unit, ND

1 Mile

½

BUCKHORN TRAIL

Juniper Creek Campground

Little Missouri Nature Trail

0.2

1.6

US 85

0.3

0.1

0.8

SHEEP COULEE TRAIL

Cedar Canyon

0.6

0.2

Creek

NORTH ACHENBACH TRAIL

4.2

MISSOURI RIVER

4.5

Achenbach Spring

Achenbach Hills

2.2

LITTLE

OXBOW OVERLOOK

ACHENBACH TRAIL

Sperati Point

Sawdust Spring

3.7

Continue across the Achenbach Hills through open prairie. Descend gradually to reach the Little Missouri River at 6.9 miles. Take special care to follow the trail along the river bottom and across the river. Hike about one mile north along the west side of the river before climbing steadily up to Sperati Point. Once out of the valley, and onto the prairie, continue north to a junction with an old dirt road. Then hike north through the prairie for 0.5 mile before turning east to reach Oxbow Overlook at 10.6 miles.

From the overlook, descend steadily back down to the river bottom. The *North Achenbach Trail* follows the north edge of the river bottom to the crossing of Appel Creek. From Appel Creek climb gradually east, then steadily north to reach a junction with the *Caprock Coulee Nature Trail* at 14.8 miles.

To return to Juniper Campground, follow the Caprock Coulee Nature Trail south of the road to 15.6 miles and a junction with the Scenic Drive and the trailhead for both the Caprock Coulee and Prairie Dog trails. Then follow the *Prairie Dog Trail* for 0.3 mile east to the *Buckhorn Trail*. Follow the Buckhorn Trail back to the campground at 17.6 miles.

In hot weather, access to the river is a luxury for most travellers. Neither river crossing is normally difficult, however, the river can be hazardous or impossible to cross. The water is usually less than knee deep, although it can be much higher. The warm, silty water isn't ideal for a midday swim, but you can cool off by wallowing in some of the deeper pools. Channel catfish, goldeye shiners and flathead chub live in the river within the park.

As with any hike in the badlands, you may confuse your trail with those made by bison. Carry a compass and topographic map, and know how to use them. This is a good area to watch wildlife, particularly wild turkeys, but you may also encounter ticks, prairie rattlesnakes and poison ivy. There is no drinking water along this loop, so carry your own. If you must drink from the silty Little Missouri River, filter the water with a unit designed to remove giardia bacteria. To save wear on your filter and pump, prefilter with a double layer coffee filter, or let the water settle overnight.

Backcountry regulations are the same as in the South Unit. Horse groups and hikers planning to camp overnight must obtain a free backcountry use permit in person. Open fires are prohibited and you must practice no trace camping.

Theodore Roosevelt arrived in the Dakotas in 1883, when western North Dakota was becoming known for ranching and hunting. Few bison remained when TR arrived for a hunt; he soon turned his attention to ranching. This was the era of open range, when cattle grazed without fences. Roosevelt's Maltese Cross Ranch was located south of Medora, but he preferred life on his isolated Elkhorn Ranch. Unfortunately for ranchers, the cattle boom was short lived. The harsh winter of 1886–87 killed large numbers of stock and the subsequent summers were much drier.

This short period profoundly influenced Theodore Roosevelt. His writings are filled with an appreciation for the quiet simplicity of ranch life and the beauty of the natural world. He saw the near extinction of bison, and he emerged from this experience as a powerful force in American conservation. The solitude and beauty found today in the North Unit is a fitting tribute to the president who most strongly shaped our park system and conservation ethic.

~

Other Theodore Roosevelt National Park Trails

The *Coal Vein Nature Trail* (0.8 mile, South Unit) is an interpretive loop that explores an area where a seam of lignite coal burned underground from 1951 through 1977. If you ever wondered about the source of the red "scoria" used on so many of North Dakota's gravel roads, this is the place to find the answer.

The *Skyline Vista Trail* (0.2 mile, South Unit) is a short walk from the Scenic Loop Drive to an overlook above I-94 and the Little Missouri River.

The *Ridgeline Nature Trail* (0.6 mile, South Unit) explores a prairie environment, focusing on plant life and the effects of fire.

The *Wind Canyon Nature Trail* (0.5 mile, South Unit) leads from the Scenic Loop Drive to an overlook above the Little Missouri River.

The *CCC Trail* (1.0 mile, South Unit) connects the Jones Creek Trailhead parking area with the start of the Petrified Forest Loop Trail across the Little Missouri River.

The *Painted Canyon Nature Trail* (0.9 mile, South Unit) leaves from the picnic area near the Painted Canyon Visitor Center near Interstate 94. The trail descends through badlands, passes through a juniper grove, then winds along a grassland before climbing back to the start. The views of the South Unit from Painted Canyon are among the park's finest.

The *Painted Canyon Horse Trail* (2.0 miles, South Unit) starts from the end of a gravel road leading east from the Painted Canyon Visitor Center. It initially heads east along the rim above Paddock Creek, then descends through several rock layers containing petrified wood. The trail ends near the mid-point of the *Upper Paddock Creek Trail*.

The *Lone Tree Spring Loop Trail* (11.7 mile round trip, South Unit) starts near the park boundary at Interstate 94. The first 2.8 miles is a feeder trail that stays within the floodplain of the Little Missouri River. At 3.2 miles, the 6.3-mile loop begins. The 3.2-mile feeder and the first 1.6 miles of the eastern side of the loop are part of the *Maah Daah Hey Trail*. Highlights along the way include examples of petrified wood and prairie dog towns.

The *Roundup Horse Trails* (3.0 miles West Trail and 4.4 miles East Trail, South Unit) were opened in 1997 to provide trail access from the new Roundup Group Horse Camp. The west trail leads from the Roundup Group Horse Camp across the Little Missouri River to the *Petrified Forest Loop Trail* at a point about one-half mile north of the junction with the *Lone Tree Springs Loop Trail*. The east trail extends from the start of the side road to the horse camp east across the Scenic Loop Drive to join the *Jones Creek Trail* about one-half mile west of the junction of the Jones Creek and Lower Talkington Trails.

The *Upper Talkington* and *Upper Paddock Creek* trails (15.4-mile loop, South Unit) visit some of the park's remotest areas. Here's a chance to see the park's hundred head of feral horses. By parking at Buck Hill and hiking south cross-country to the Upper Paddock Creek Trail, hikers can shorten the loop to around 10.5 miles.

The *East Boundary Horse Trail* (about 3 miles, South Unit) which was opened in 1997, begins at a horse camp at the park's east boundary.

The *Little Missouri Nature Trail* (1.0 mile, North Unit) interprets the geology, flora and fauna of the badlands along the river. It begins at the Juniper Creek Campground.

The *Buckhorn Trail* (11.4-mile loop, North Unit) visits a wilderness area and two prairie dog towns. The west side of the loop is also called the *Prairie Dog Town Trail*. The loop passes through two large dog towns then returns through bottom lands along the Little Missouri River.

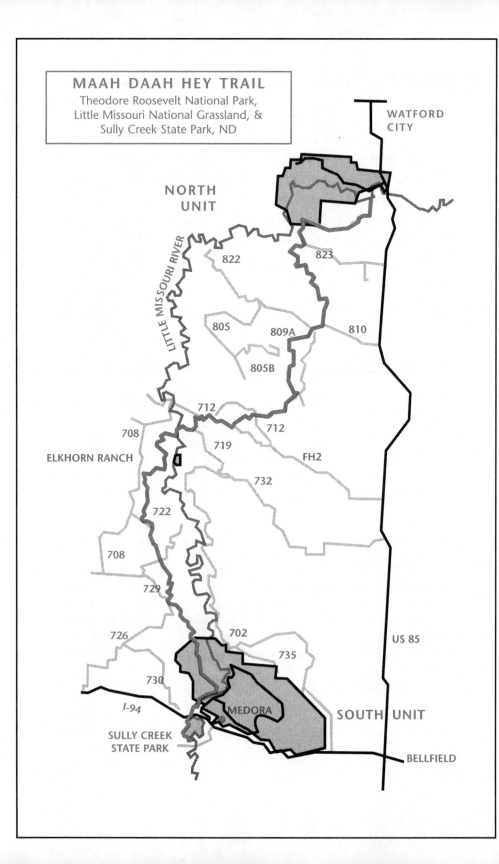

Maah Daah Hey Trail
MEDORA RANGER DISTRICT

Description: A 100-mile trail for hikers and horses across the Little Missouri badlands linking the South and North units of Theodore Roosevelt National Park. Mountain bikes are allowed on the trail in the Little Missouri National Grassland, but not in the national park.

General Location: From Medora, North Dakota, to the North Unit of Theodore Roosevelt National Park.

Highlight: A unique long trail through badlands and short grass prairie.

Access: To reach Sully Creek State Park from Medora, turn south from Pacific Avenue, onto East River Road South. After 0.5 mile, the road turns to gravel. At 1.9 miles turn right onto 36th Street at a sign for the park. There is parking at 2.8 miles at the beginning of the campground loop. The Maah Daah Hey Trail begins across the river from the north end of the campground. The Maah Daah Hey Trail in Theodore Roosevelt National Park can also be reached from the north end of the Exit 24 interchange from I-94. Look for a crawl hole next to a locked gate in the bison fence. To reach the *Forest Service CCC Campground* and the north end of the trail, turn west off U.S. 85 south of the Little Missouri River about 0.5 mile south of the boundary of the North Unit of Theodore Roosevelt National Park.

Distance: Approximately 100 miles.

Maps: The Forest Service Maah Daah Hey Trail map (can be ordered from the Medora Ranger District) and page 186.

North Dakota's Maah Daah Hey Trail is an exciting addition to the region's recreational trails. From the start at Sully Creek State Park the trail winds north to connect the South and North units of Theodore Roosevelt National Park by a route mostly through the Little Missouri National Grassland. The project was originally conceived by horse riders seeking a long, challenging route across the plains, but the trail is also open to hikers. Mountain bikers can ride the trail except in Theodore Roosevelt National Park, where the trail crosses two designated wilderness areas.

The Maah Daah Hey Trail begins in Sully Creek State Park with an immediate ford of the Little Missouri River. After one-quarter mile on private land, the trail heads west, then north through Little Missouri National Grassland property, mostly on new trail. The Maah Daah Hey Trail enters the South Unit of Theodore Roosevelt National Park under Interstate 94 at the interchange west of Medora. Once in the

South Unit, the trail follows the Lone Tree Spring Loop Trail north along the Little Missouri. After climbing to Petrified Forest Plateau, the route joins the Petrified Forest Loop Trail to its northern limit, then exits the park.

In the Little Missouri National Grassland, the trail follows some informal trails, newly constructed trails and a variety of little-used dirt roads across the grasslands. The Maah Daah Hey Trail follows a long abandoned two-track dirt road for a short distance through the North Unit of Theodore Roosevelt National Park before reentering the grassland and ending at the Forest Service's CCC Campground which is currently under construction.

The Little Missouri badlands have a scenic beauty all their own. The landscape is a mix of short grass prairie and seemingly barren badlands. It is a terrain that combines sweeping vistas with often overlooked wildflowers, rock formations and wildlife among the sculpted coulees and grassy tablelands. The grassland is a chaotic patchwork of public and private land. Thus it cannot support the diversity of wildlife seen in Theodore Roosevelt National Park, but mule deer, pronghorn, coyotes, and prairie dogs are common, and lucky visitors might spy rare elk or bighorn sheep.

The Maah Daah Hey Trail should prove a worthy challenge to hikers and mountain bikers. The first of these challenges will be finding water. The trail fords the Little Missouri River at Sully Creek and near the Theodore Roosevelt National Park Elkhorn Ranch site. Otherwise travelers are dependent on non-potable stockwater wells or eight artesian wells or springs adjacent to the trail. There will be no water sources at the six campsites or trailheads along the route, but non-potable water will be located within one-quarter mile of the overnight sites.

Severe wind and cold during winter and the hot, dry heat of summer will likely ensure that the trail receives more use in the spring and fall. At any time of year be prepared for extremes of temperature, sun and wind. Bikers should note that wet spring weather or a summer thunderstorm could turn parts of the trail into a sticky quagmire.

Though the Maah Daah Hey Trail crosses mostly park or forest service land, it does cross both state and private land. Travelers must stay on the trail where it crosses state or private land. The western Dakotas are one of the country's least populated regions. Keep in mind that you're on your own in these badlands.

As of late 1998 trail marking was finished, but construction of the trail was not complete between the North Unit and the McKenzie/Billings county line near LMNG Road 808. Look for 4×6 posts bearing the emblem of a turtle. The Forest Service also plans to install mile markers across the entire route. Six campsites with vault toilets will be built by the Forest Service in 2000. Mountain bikers can bypass the South Unit of TRNP on gravel roads to the west of the park, but a by-pass route around the North Unit has not yet been determined.

Maah Daah Hey Trail Mileage Table

Mileages between LMNG 808 and TRNP North Unit are estimated

Site	Mileage between Sites	Total Mileage
Sully Creek State Park	0.0	0.0
TRNP South Unit	5.1	5.1
Lone Tree Spring Loop Trail	3.2	8.3
Petrified Forest Loop Trail	1.6	9.9
Leave TRNP South Unit	3.3	13.2
Cross LMNG Road 726, campsite	2.8	16.0
Cross LMNG Road 725	6.5	22.5
Cross LMNG Road 722, campsite	3.5	27.0
Cross Road FH 2	8.5	35.5
TRNP Elkhorn Ranch Site is 0.1 mile east		
Cross LMNG Road 708	3.5	39.0
Ford Little Missouri River	5.2	44.2
Campsite	1.0	45.2
Cross LMNG Road 712	2.8	48.0
Leave LMNG Road 711	5.5	53.5
Cross LMNG Road 712, campsite	3.0	56.5
Near LMNG Road 808	7.0	63.5
Join LMNG 809, campsite	9.5	73.0
Join LMNG Road 810	0.5	73.5
Join LMNG 823, campsite	13.5	87.0
Enter TRNP North Unit	3.5	90.5
Leave TRNP North Unit	1.8	92.3
Cross LMNG Road 825	2.5	94.8
LMNG CCC Campground	5.0	99.8

APPENDIX A

High Points of the Black Hills

For many people their ideal hike ends on a tall, scenic mountaintop. Unfortunately, for a number of reasons it is hard to achieve this ideal in the Black Hills. There are only a handful of accessible distinctive peaks, and few of these are among the tallest ones. Years of road building have established road access to many of these, but some still only have trail access, while others have no roads or trails. Once these few summits have been reached, finding other Black Hills peaks to climb on foot can be challenging.

Finding an interesting climb in the Black Hills requires substantial searching through USGS and BHNF maps to find a peak, a route and public access to both. The few good climbs that result from this search (Sylvan Peak, Silver Peak, Spearfish Peak and Pillar Peak), compensate for some of the poor routes.

The list developed below required making, and bending, a few rules. First, the list is not strictly by elevation. Many points on the Limestone Plateau between Bear Mountain and Crook's Tower rise over 7,000 feet above sea level, but the plateau offers few summits worthy of ascent. Secondly, the peak must be a point of interest geologically, historically or otherwise. Finally, there must be a reasonable nonmotorized route to the summit.

At just half the elevation of the giants in nearby Colorado, the 7,000 foot summits of the Black Hills form an even more select group. With the exception of Harney and Sylvan Peaks, all the 7,000-footers have access roads that can be driven or easily ridden on a mountain bike.

Black Hills National Forest fire lookouts are another group of peaks with interesting views. These summits will all have currently maintained access roads, though alternative routes to many can be found. Abandoned and dismantled fire lookouts can be found by searching USGS quadrangles and previous editions of the BHNF map. Without the added advantage of the tower, some, such as Cicero Peak, have no view at all. Still, the access roads to the abandoned towers are usually fun rides on a mountain bike.

In addition to Harney Peak, a few other interesting peaks have access only by trail. These few routes are all described in this guide.

The final group of summits is a wish list. Inyan Kara Mountain, Sundance Mountain and the Missouri Buttes are all on private land, or access to them is completely restricted by private land. Through careful research, and a tactful approach, some may be climbed by obtaining permission of the landowners involved. Unfortunately, all three are still off limits to the public.

The list developed below is subjective and reflects personal experience much more than elevation. Technical climbs, such as Devils Tower or the Cathedral Spires are beyond the scope of this guide. Emphasis has been placed on trips at least a half-day long or with at least 1,000 feet of vertical climb. The major geologic divisions of the Black Hills are represented: Terry Peak in the Tertiary intrusive igneous rocks in the north, Battle Mountain in the Dakota Hogback, Crook's Tower on the Limestone Plateau, Harney Peak in the Harney Peak Granite, Scruton Mountain in the Precambrian metasedimentary rocks, and Bear Mountain in the Archean granite-gneiss terrain.

Whether or not the Black Hills needs its own equivalent of the Colorado's "fourteeners" or the Adirondack "forty-six," these summits should provide enough goals for those who need or want them. Many of the mountains listed are not described further in this guide. For those peaks, section, township and range data are listed. The Black Hills National Forest map shows all the peaks listed except Mount Warner and Missouri Buttes.

High Points of the Black Hills

ELEV.	NAME (Tower), USGS Quad, (section, township, range)
7,242	Harney Peak (Tower), Custer, SD
7,200	Odakota Mountain, Ditch Creek, SD
7,166	Bear Mountain (Tower), Berne, SD
7,164	Green Mountain, Ditch Creek, SD, (S21, T1S, R2E)
7,137	Crooks Tower, Crooks Tower, SD (S6, T2N, R2E)
7,064	Terry Peak (Tower), Lead, SD (S11, T4N, R2E)
7,048	Crows Nest Peak (tower removed), Crows Nest Peak, SD (S11, T1N, R1E)
7,000	Sylvan Peak, Custer, SD
6,937	Flag Mountain (tower removed), Deerfield, SD (S1, T1N, R2E)
6,890	Little Devils Tower, Custer, SD
6,804	Custer Peak (Tower), Minnesota Ridge, SD
6,650	Warren Peak (Tower), Sundance West, WY (S20, T52N, R63W)
6,623	Cement Ridge (Tower), Old Baldy Mountain, WY-SD (S5, R60W, T50N)
6,483	Signal Hill (tower removed), Signal Hill, SD (S2, R2E, T3S)
6,468	St. Elmo Peak, Custer, SD (S13, T2S, R4E)

6,368	Inyan Kara Mountain, Inyan Kara Mountain, WY (S19, T49N, R62W)
6,358	Castle Peak, Rochford, SD (S35, T2N, R3E)
6,166	Cicero Peak (tower removed), Cicero Peak, SD (S29, T4S, R5E)
6,096	Old Baldy Mountain, Old Baldy Mountain WY-SD
6,096	Summit Ridge (Tower), Fanny Peak, WY-SD (S19, T2S, R1E)
6,023	Mount Coolidge (Tower), Mount Coolidge, SD (S35, T3S, R5E)
5,922	Scruton Mountain (Tower), Silver City, SD (S16, T1N, R5E)
5,889	Mount Warner, Mount Rushmore, SD
5,824	Sundance Mountain (Tower), Sundance West, WY (S24, T51N, R63W)
5,810	Silver Peak, Silver City, SD
5,800	Spearfish Peak, Spearfish, SD (S34, T6N, R2E)
5,760	Crow Peak, Maurice, SD
5,676	Mount Theodore Roosevelt (Tower), Spearfish, SD (S16, T5N, R3E)
5,662	Elk Mountain (Tower), Clifton, WY-SD (S7, R1E, T4S)
5,469	Pillar Peak, Deadwood South, SD
5,374	Missouri Buttes, Missouri Buttes, WY (S33, T45N, R66W)
5,333	Veterans Peak (Tower), Deadwood Mountain, SD (S5, R5E, T4N)
5,331	Boulder Hill (Tower), Mount Rushmore, SD
5,112	Devils Tower, Devils Tower, WY
5,013	Rankin Ridge (Tower), Mount Coolidge, SD
4,848	Parker Peak (tower removed), Minnekahta, SD (S31, T7S, R4E)
4,788	Pilger Mountain (tower removed), Jewel Cave SW, SD (S29, T6S, R2E)
4,434	Battle Mountain (Tower), Hot Springs, SD (S18, T7S, R6E)
4,426	Bear Butte, Fort Meade, SD

Trail Running in the Black Hills

The sport of trail running is a hybrid of hiking and distance running. An excellent aerobic workout, trail running also provides the solitude and escape normally associated with a leisurely hiking trip. In the Black Hills, runners can use maintained hiking trails, little-used dirt roads or the access roads to fire towers and lookouts for trail runs.

Trail running builds strength, endurance and aerobic capacity. These workouts do little to improve speed or quickness, although running on steep hills or rocky trails can improve agility. Trail runs are more difficult than ordinary distance runs. This is not a sport for someone beginning an exercise program, as a solid running base is required. The sport is best suited to distance runners, or hikers and backpackers who want to improve their fitness. Trail runs are also excellent training for local races such as Mystic Mountain.

Done correctly, trail running provides the opportunity for midweek explorations that can free your weekends for more ambitious projects. Most of the hiking trails in the Black Hills are designed for day hikes, and most can be done as afternoon runs. My preference is to seek out routes that end on mountain tops, preferably those with good views. Fire towers, lookouts, and summits with hiking trails generally make the best routes.

Trail running requires more preparation than normal running. Carry water and food in a fanny pack with a water bottle holder. If unfamiliar with an area, it is a good idea to carry a copy of the map of the area in a ziplock bag. In spring, beware of afternoon electrical storms and be prepared to retreat from exposed areas if a storm strikes. Plan on a slow, steady pace. Most of the runs described below can be done without walking, so unless you're training for a race that combines running and walking try to maintain your run. It is not unusual to go slower than a ten minute mile pace on long or steep hills, and you'll be able to make up the time on the descent.

Bear Butte: 3.5 miles round trip and 975 feet of ascent. Bear Butte State Park is located 2.5 miles north of Sturgis on South Dakota 79. This is the shortest of the mountain runs, and the best for beginners. Follow the Summit Trail, which is also the last 1.75 miles of the Centennial Trail, unrelentingly to the top. To make a loop on the way down, follow the Ceremonial Trail back to the parking area. This is a very scenic course; if you don't like this route you probably won't enjoy trail running.

Mount Theodore Roosevelt: 7.0 miles round trip and 1,080 feet of ascent. This is a standard hill workout for runners in the Lead-Deadwood area. Start at the junction of Main and Denver streets in Deadwood, or as close as you can park. Denver Street soon becomes a gravel BHNF road. Follow the gravel road to a picnic area then follow a short hiking trail to the tower on top. The last mile of the course is relatively flat, but the climb is a killer.

Crow Peak: My personal favorite. The trail climbs 1,600 feet in 3.5 grueling miles. The Crow Peak Trail starts 4 miles south of Spearfish on the Higgins Gulch Road. The trail becomes increasingly steeper and rockier toward the top. Your reward for the climb is a beautiful view of Spearfish and the northern Black Hills.

Old Baldy Mountain: The trailhead is located 1.2 miles north of BHNF Road 222 on BHNF Road 134. This 6.5-mile loop actually loses elevation between the trailhead and the summit of Old Baldy. This is a great run over rolling terrain with good views. Only the last 0.5 mile of the climb up the cone of Old Baldy is steep.

Terry Peak: There are two sane routes for this peak. The Terry Peak Summit Road leads 3.3 miles and 880 feet from U.S. 85 to the lookout tower. A short, steep option is to follow a maintenance road from the base of the Blue Chairlift, 1,100 lung-searing feet to the top.

Custer Peak: Another peak with multiple routes. The simplest is to start at the junction of U.S. 385 and BHNF Road 216 and follow Road 216 to the junction with the summit road, which is located on the saddle at the west shoulder of Custer Peak. The summit road spirals around the cone of Custer Peak to the top. This is a ten-mile round trip and includes 1,300 feet of ascent.

Veteran's Peak: 4.0 miles round trip and 870 feet vertical. From the junction of BHNF Roads 170 and 135, follow Road 135 south to a dirt road heading east that leads to the radio towers on top. Veteran's offers good views of the ski runs on Terry Peak and Deer Mountain.

Scruton Mountain (Seth Bullock Lookout): From the junction of U.S. 385 and BHNF Road 251 follow Road 251 to BHNF Road 156. Turn right onto Road 156, cross a gate barring vehicle traffic and grunt up a series of switchbacks to the lookout tower on top: 920 feet of climbing are packed into this six-mile round trip.

Harney Peak: If you want to avoid the crowds on the route from Sylvan Lake, try the north side. From the Willow Creek Trailhead, it is five miles and 2,200 feet to the top, plenty of time to learn more than you'll ever want to know about controlling your pace.

Cement Ridge: A five-mile round trip with 400 feet of climbing. Drive west of Savoy to the north junction of BHNF roads 134 and 222.

Follow Road 222 for 3.0 miles to a junction with BHNF Road 103 and Snowmobile Trail 3. Run up Road 103, which becomes BHNF Road 867 in Wyoming. Follow Road 867 up the southeast ridge to the tower on top of Cement Ridge. This is a great fall run when the aspen leaves have colored the Limestone Plateau.

Many other peaks in the Black Hills are used for trail runs or have good potential. Battle Mountain near Hot Springs, Warren Peak near Sundance, Bear Mountain, Crook's Tower, Pillar Peak and Whitetail Peak near Rochford are just a few. Other trails that are fun to run include the Centennial Trail, the Lake Loop, and the trail systems around Harney Peak and in Wind Cave National Park.

APPENDIX C

Selected Bibliography

Conn, Herb and Jan. *The Jewel Cave Adventure,* Cave Books, 1977.

Dewitt, Ed, J. A. Redden, Anna Burack Wilson, David Buscher and John S. Dersch. "Mineral Resource Potential and Geology of the Black Hills National Forest, South Dakota and Wyoming." USGS Bulletin 1580, 1986.

Fielder, Mildred. *A Guide to Black Hills Ghost Mines,* North Plains Press, 1972.

Froiland, Sven G. *Natural History of the Black Hills and Badlands,* The Center for Western Studies, 1990.

Gardiner, S. and D. Gulimette. *Devils Tower National Monument: A Climber's Guide,* The Mountaineers Books, 1986.

Hauk, Joy Keve. *Badlands, Its Life and Landscape,* Badlands Natural History Association, 1969.

Horning, D. and H. Marriot. *A Mountain Bikers Guide to the Black Hills, South Dakota and Wyoming,* Poorperson's Guidebooks, 1987.

McGee, D. and the Last Pioneer Woman. *Black Hills Needles—Selected Free Climbs,* Poorperson's Guidebooks, 1981.

McGee, D., and the Last Pioneer Woman. "Free Climbs of Devils Tower," 1990.

Melius, Michael. *True,* Tensleep Publications, 1991.

Parker, W. *Gold in the Black Hills,* University of Nebraska Press, 1966.

Patterson, C. J. and A. L. Lisenbee, editors. "Metallogeny of Gold in the Black Hills, South Dakota," Society of Economic Geologists Guidebook Series, Volume 7, 1990.

Piana, Paul. *Touch the Sky,* The American Alpine Club, 1983.

Raventon, Edward. *Island in the Plains,* Johnson Books, 1994.

Raventon, E. and P. Horsted. *A Piece of Paradise: A Story of Custer State Park,* Falcon Publishing Co., 1996.

Raymond, W. H. and R. U. King. Geologic Map of the Badlands National Monument and Vicinity, West-Central South Dakota, USGS MI Map I-934, 1978.

Robinson, C. S. *Geology of Devils Tower National Monument, Wyoming,* Devils Tower Natural History Association, 1985.

Rosga, K. *Jewel Cave National Monument: The Story Behind the Scenery.* K.C. Publications, 1998.

Scoch, H. and B. Kaye. *Theodore Roosevelt: The Story Behind the Scenery.* K.C. Publications, 1993.

Terry, R. *Wind Cave National Park: The Story Behind the Scenery.* K.C. Publications, 1998.

Information Sources

Badlands National Park, P.O. Box 6, Interior, SD 57750, (605) 433-5361 or 433-5362. www.nps.gov/badl

Bear Butte State Park, Box 688, Sturgis, SD 57785, (605) 347-5240.

Bearlodge Ranger District, P.O. Box 680 Highway 14 West, Sundance, WY 82729, (307) 283-1361.

Black Hills National Forest-Supervisors Office, RR2, Box 200, Custer, SD 57730, (605) 673-2251. www.fs.fed.us/bhnf

Black Hills Parks and Forests Association, RR 1, Box 190, Hot Springs, SD 57747, (605) 745-7020.

Black Hills Trail Office, South Dakota Department of Game, Fish and Parks, HC 37, Box 604, Lead, SD 57754-9801, (605) 584-3896.

Custer Ranger District, 330 Mt. Rushmore Road, Custer, SD 57730, (605) 673-4853.

Custer State Park, HC 83 Box 70, Custer, SD 57730, (605) 255-4515 or 255-4464 for the Peter Norbeck Visitor Center in summer. Call for camping reservations at (800) 710-2267.

Devils Tower National Monument, P.O. Box 10, Devils Tower, WY 82714, (307) 467-5283. www.nps.gov/deto

Elk Mountain Ranger District, 1225 Washington Blvd., Newcastle, WY 82701, (307) 746-2783.

Fort Meade Recreation Area, Bureau of Land Management–South Dakota Resource Area, 310 Roundup, Belle Fourche, SD 57717, (605) 892-2526.

Friends of the Mickelson Trail, 615 Washington Street, Custer, SD 57730.

Harney Ranger District, 23939 Highway 385, Hill City, SD 57745, (605) 574-2534.

Jewel Cave National Monument, RR1 Box 60 AA, Custer, SD 57730, (605) 676-2288. www.nps.gov/jeca

McKenzie Ranger District, HC02, Box 8, Watford City, ND 58854, (701) 842-2393.

Medora Ranger District, 161 21st St. W., Dickinson, ND 58601, (701) 225-5151.

Mount Rushmore National Memorial, Box 268, Keystone, SD 57751, (605) 574-2523. www.nps.gov/moru

Nemo Ranger District, US 14A East, Box 407, Deadwood, SD 57732, (605) 578-2744.

North Dakota Parks and Tourism Department, 604 E. Boulevard, Bismark, ND 58505. (800) 437-2077.

Pactola Ranger District, 803 Soo San Dr., Rapid City, SD 57702, (605) 343-1567.

South Dakota Department of Game, Fish and Parks 523 E. Capitol, Pierre, SD 57501 (605) 773-3391. www.state.sd.us/sdparks

South Dakota Department of Tourism, 711 E. Wells Ave., Pierre, SD 57501-3369, (800) 732-5682.

Spearfish Ranger District, 2014 N. Main, Spearfish, SD 57783, (605) 642-4622.

Sully Creek State Park, North Dakota Parks and Recreation Department, 1835 Bismark Expressway, Bismark, ND 58504, (701) 328-5357.

Theodore Roosevelt National Park, P.O. Box 7, Medora, ND 58645, (701) 623-4466. www.nps.gov/thro. The North Unit can be reached at (701) 842-2333.

Trails Illustrated, P.O. Box 4357, Evergreen, Colorado 80437-4357, (800) 962-1643. www.trailsillustrated.com

Wind Cave National Park, Rt. 1 Box 190, Hot Springs, SD 57747, (605) 745-4600. www.nps.gov/wica

Wyoming Division of Tourism, I-25 at College Drive, Cheyenne, WY 82002, (800) 225-5996.

Index

Other Guidebooks from Johnson Books

Arizona's Mountains: A Hiking Guide to the Grand Canyon State
Bob and Dotty Martin

Colorado Mountain Club Pocket Guide to the Colorado 14ers
Edited by Ania Savage

Colorado Scenic Guides: Northern Region and Southern Region
Lee Gregory

Colorado's High Thirteeners: A Climbing and Hiking Guide
Mike Garratt and Bob Martin

From Grassland to Glacier:
The Natural History of Colorado and the Surrounding Region
Cornelia Fleischer Mutel and John C. Emerick

Guide to the Colorado Mountains
Colorado Mountain Club with Robert M. Ormes

Island in the Plains: A Black Hills Natural History
Edward Raventon

Land Above the Trees: A Guide to American Alpine Tundra
Ann Zwinger and Beatrice E. Willard

Mexico's Copper Canyon Country: A Hiking and Backpacking Guide
M. John Fayhee

Roadside History of Colorado
James McTighe

Rocky Mountain National Park Dayhiker's Guide:
A Scenic Guide to 33 Favorite Hikes Including Longs Peak
Jerome Malitz

State Parks of the South: America's Historic Paradise
Vici DeHaan